Thomas Banks Strong

Christian ethics. Eight lectures preached before the University of Oxford in the year 1895 on the foundation of the late Rev. John Bampton

Thomas Banks Strong

Christian ethics. Eight lectures preached before the University of Oxford in the year 1895 on the foundation of the late Rev. John Bampton

ISBN/EAN: 9783337263294

Printed in Europe, USA, Canada, Australia, Japan

Cover: Foto ©Lupo / pixelio.de

More available books at **www.hansebooks.com**

CHRISTIAN ETHICS

EIGHT LECTURES

PREACHED BEFORE THE UNIVERSITY OF OXFORD
IN THE YEAR 1895

ON THE FOUNDATION OF THE LATE REV. JOHN BAMPTON, M.A.
CANON OF SALISBURY

BY

THOMAS B. STRONG, M.A.

STUDENT OF CHRIST CHURCH

EXAMINING CHAPLAIN TO THE LORD BISHOP OF DURHAM

LONGMANS, GREEN, AND CO
LONDON, NEW YORK, AND BOMBAY
1896

MATRI SUAE

GRATIAS PIETATEM AMOREM

TESTIFICATURUS

HUNC LIBRUM DICATUM VOLUIT

AUCTOR

EXTRACT

FROM THE LAST WILL AND TESTAMENT

OF THE LATE

REV. JOHN BAMPTON,

CANON OF SALISBURY.

—— " I give and bequeath my Lands and Estates to the
" Chancellor, Masters, and Scholars of the University of
" Oxford for ever, to have and to hold all and singular the
" said Lands or Estates upon trust, and to the intents and
" purposes hereinafter mentioned; that is to say, I will and
" appoint that the Vice-Chancellor of the University of Ox-
" ford for the time being shall take and receive all the rents,
" issues, and profits thereof, and (after all taxes, reparations,
" and necessary deductions made) that he pay all the
" remainder to the endowment of eight Divinity Lecture
" Sermons, to be established for ever in the said University,
" and to be performed in the manner following:

" I direct and appoint, that, upon the first Tuesday in
" Easter Term, a Lecturer be yearly chosen by the Heads
" of Colleges only, and by no others, in the room adjoining
" to the Printing-House, between the hours of ten in the

Extract from Canon Bampton's Will.

" morning and two in the afternoon, to preach eight Divinity
" Lecture Sermons, the year following, at St. Mary's in
" Oxford, between the commencement of the last month in
" Lent Term, and the end of the third week in Act Term.

" Also I direct and appoint, that the eight Divinity Lecture
" Sermons shall be preached upon either of the following
" Subjects—to confirm and establish the Christian Faith, and
" to confute all heretics and schismatics—upon the divine
" authority of the holy Scriptures—upon the authority of
" the writings of the primitive Fathers, as to the faith and
" practice of the primitive Church—upon the Divinity of our
" Lord and Saviour Jesus Christ—upon the Divinity of the
" Holy Ghost—upon the Articles of the Christian Faith, as
" comprehended in the Apostles' and Nicene Creeds.

" Also I direct, that thirty copies of the eight Divinity Lec-
" ture Sermons shall be always printed, within two months
" after they are preached; and one copy shall be given to the
" Chancellor of the University, and one copy to the Head of
" every College, and one copy to the Mayor of the city of
" Oxford, and one copy to be put into the Bodleian Library;
" and the expense of printing them shall be paid out of the
" revenue of the Lands or Estates given for establishing the
" Divinity Lecture Sermons; and the Preacher shall not be
" paid, nor be entitled to the revenue, before they are printed.

" Also I direct and appoint, that no person shall be quali-
" fied to preach the Divinity Lecture Sermons, unless he
" hath taken the Degree of Master of Arts at least, in one
" of the two Universities of Oxford or Cambridge; and that
" the same person shall never preach the Divinity Lecture
" Sermons twice."

PREFACE

THE will of the late Reverend John Bampton in respect of one of its provisions, has not, of late years, been fulfilled to the letter. It has rarely happened that the Lecturers have produced their Lectures in printed form 'within two months after they have been preached.' But though many of my predecessors have postponed publication for a short time beyond that indicated in the will, I feel that I owe the University a fuller apology for my much greater delay. The reason is that I found myself called upon to undertake the office of Censor of Moral Philosophy shortly after my appointment as Bampton Lecturer, and have in consequence found my time in the Vacations largely occupied by College business. Those who know the conditions of modern Oxford will understand how greatly the possibility of continuous work depends on free Vacations.

Perhaps I may be permitted to cherish the hope

that the separation of the delivery and publication of these Lectures by one year may relieve the world from the full shock of a year without Bampton Lectures.

The conditions under which the Bampton Lecturer finds himself are somewhat difficult. A subject which is of sufficient importance to occupy eight University Sermons will almost necessarily require some considerable amount of illustration, and a Lecturer will therefore have two courses open to him. He may either write eight considerable chapters, embodying all his arguments and illustrations, and read to the University as much of each as he can get through in an hour; or he may write and preach eight sermons and reserve his illustrations for the notes. I have chosen the latter course, which seemed to me, on the whole, more nearly in accordance with the provisions of the will. It has, however, this disadvantage—as I have found increasingly during the preparation of the book for publication—that it is extremely difficult to get the matter into the right order and the right place. I have aimed at placing in the Lectures discussions arising out of the New Testament, and those bearing on the general theory of Ethics; while the notes consist of illustrations from conspicuous writers of the theory presented in the Lectures. But I am aware that I have not avoided repetitions. Statements made summarily in the Lectures are occasionally repeated more at large in notes. I doubt whether, under the conditions, this could have been wholly avoided.

It may be well to summarize here the position maintained in the Lectures. It is briefly this: that the Christian theory of moral life is not merely a new formulation of the old experience; nor is it merely a restatement of the old truths with certain new virtues added; but it is a view of life based upon a radically different experience of facts. The reconciliation of the finite and Infinite—of man and God—which the Incarnation achieved, was at most a dream of the most enlightened Greek philosophers, and a hope to the most enlightened Jews. When it happened, man was admitted, in proportion to the certainty of his faith in it, into a clear and decisive knowledge of the spiritual Divine order. The appearance of the Word of God in human flesh did not indeed explain itself fully in philosophical language, but it declared finally the fact that man's nature, however frail and limited it may be, is the scene of a spiritual history and is explicable only in spiritual terms. The Christian Ethic is the detailed presentation of this fact, in relation to the end of life and human nature[1], the theory of virtue[2], the idea of evil[3], and the general order of the universe as a whole[4].

It may probably seem that there is little here that is new or that requires saying in the present day. The connexion of the Christian doctrine of the Incarnation with the Christian view of life may seem to be

---

[1] Lect. III.   [2] Lect. IV.   [3] Lect. V.   [4] Lect. VI.

a commonplace. There is doubtless a strong conviction that in some sense the facts of Christian history are to be effective in Christian life, but there is also a marked failure to keep the two together. It is constantly affirmed that the Christian type of life depends upon the Christian doctrines, but little is done to show the closeness of this union. And the result is that, however fully the general truth as to the nature of Christian morality is set out, it has become almost a paradox to assert that the separation of Christian life from the deposit of Christian truth is simply a relapse upon Paganism.

I have endeavoured to show that this result proceeds in part from an inadequate estimate of Christian thought before the Reformation. However profoundly we are indebted to this movement, it remains true, that the ethical thought which extends over the previous centuries is distinctively Christian; and false, that the Christian ethical spirit obtained its due expression for the first time in the sixteenth century. The moral principles which prevailed in those ancient days were, no doubt, sadly restricted in range. But they really represented an effort to translate into practical precepts the truths of the Christian Faith.

Though not very novel, it seems that this view may still be worth asserting. It is often said that there is no real moral progress in life, and that evil always remains more or less at the same level. There is an element of truth in this. It is true that the growth of civilization does not relieve any individual from his own conflict with sin. In every age under all conditions this warfare is incessant. It may be worth while, then, to urge that as the warfare is the same, the weapons for waging it are not grown old or obsolete: that the victory may still be won in the strength of the Spirit of the Incarnate Son of God.

I have referred in the footnotes to various books which I have used in preparing the present work, and I have endeavoured to make the list complete. The book from which I have learnt most is Neander's *Geschichte der christlichen Ethik*. I have also consulted occasionally Dorner's *System of Christian Ethics* (in the English translation); Luthardt's *Geschichte der christlichen Ethik*, and Gass's work under the same title. In the passages relating to the Schoolmen I have used Baur's *Lehre der Dreieinigkeit*, Bd. II; Bobba, *Storia della Filosofia rispetto alla Conoscenza di Dio*; and, with less profit, Hauréau, *Histoire de la Philosophie Scolastique*.

I am also greatly indebted to Mr. W. O. Burrows, Principal of Leeds Clergy School, for reading a large portion of the proofs, and for many valuable suggestions.

ANALYSIS

LECTURE I.

PRELIMINARY: GREEK AND JEW.

The air of disappointment and failure which marks the ancient world in its attitude towards life requires some explanation. . . pp. 1–3.

I. Among the Greeks it seems to have been due to two special causes.

1. A disposition to treat ethical science merely on the analogy of other sciences, i.e. as a formulation of ethical facts. . . pp. 4–7.

2. The tendency of the ethical systems to express themselves in the shape of ideal figures—necessarily external to the will. . . pp. 7–8.

This was the case with Plato and Aristotle, also with the Stoics and Neoplatonists. . . . . pp. 8–11.

These ideals, though valuable in ethical history, failed as guides to life. . . . . pp. 11–12.

II. The Jews reach a similar result from a different cause.

The ruling idea of Jewish religion and polity was the Covenant idea which expressed itself in various forms—in the hands of prophets, psalmists, lawgivers. Of these the most familiar was the Law, which, in the best minds and in its latest forms, combined in itself the various strains of earlier thought. . . . . pp. 12–18.

The Jewish mind, therefore, being under Law, was not perplexed by philosophical questions like those of the Greeks; but, owing to the condition of the human will, it failed to achieve its ideal. . pp. 18–20.

III. The Sermon on the Mount belongs to a transitional state of things. It comes with a new authority and offers a new hope of perfection, but it is still a law, commanding from without. . . . . pp. 20–22.

Thus the Greek ethical systems, the Jewish Law, and the Sermon have one thing in common; they command from without—the Greeks, by means of philosophical ideals, the Jews and the Sermon, by positive command. . . . . pp. 22-24.

Besides this the Jew regarded human nature as fallen, and was saved from the despair, which such a belief might have produced, by the hope of a Deliverer. . . . . pp. 24-25.

NOTE 1.

RULING PRINCIPLES OF LIFE IN CLASSICAL DAYS.

The difficulty of estimating a bygone period of life is only partially overcome by a study of its literature. The descriptions of satirists are apt to exaggerate the evil; and, on the other hand, great literary skill may lead to a onesided view in the opposite direction. . . pp. 26-28.

The true ground for estimating the views of another age would be found in the ruling principles (if we could reach them) which governed their whole judgement of life. . . . . pp. 28-29.

In the case of Greece there are two lines of thought in which the general attitude of the people towards life was expressed.

I. The idea of divine $\phi\theta\acute{o}\nu o\varsigma$, and that of inexorable necessity ruling alike the lives of gods and men imply a belief that life is ultimately irrational. . . . . pp. 29-31.

II. The strong sense of the unmanageable character of passion points in the same direction: passion was not so much to be controlled as extinguished: it was never fully brought into a theory of life. pp. 31-33.

NOTE 2.

JUDAISM AND THE LAW.

I. The essential difference between Judaism and all other religions lies in the doctrine of God. The means of approach to God—prayer and sacrifice—were the same in all nations alike, as several of the Fathers pointed out, but the Jews derived a different result from their religion. Any disabilities which belonged to the sacrificial method as such, belonged also to the Jews. . . . . pp. 35-37.

II. The prophets continually denounce formalism (frequently connecting it with the practice of sacrifice), and dwell upon the need of spiritual religion. This does not imply what is now called 'a purely spiritual religion.' For (1) such a notion is out of harmony with the ideas of the age; (2) the prophetic language is not inconsistent with the prevalence of a complicated sacrificial system. . . . . . . pp. 37-40.

III. The worship of Jehovah after the Captivity is continuous both with the prophetic preaching and the previous practice. The fact of the special right to approach God, and the peculiar need for holiness in the Covenant people are expressed in the Law. Thus the Jews are under command both moral and ceremonial, and it is this which St. Paul identifies with the unfulfilled position of the Law. . . . pp. 40-44.

The glory of Judaism was that it led directly to the new order: its fault was that the new order had not come. In the Sermon on the Mount is the moment of transition. . . . . . pp. 45, 46.

LECTURE II.

CHRIST AND THE APOSTLES.

We must now pass to the consideration of ethics under the influence of Christianity, and inquire how far Christianity succeeded where previous efforts had failed. . . . . p. 47.

In the Gospels we find a totally different atmosphere to that of ethical philosophy. The Gospels are historic—even the discourses rise out of the history. They aim at describing a life—which is at the same time a moral ideal. . . . . pp. 48-51.

The historic character of this ideal is not its finally distinctive character. This is to be found in the relation of Jesus Christ to the Father, which also explains the difference between the moral tone of the Gospels and, for instance, that of the Psalms. . . . . pp. 51-55.

Even this only describes Christ's personal life, without explaining how His example is to be made good for others. But the promises in the last discourses clearly show that a new order is to date from His life and work, and we are thus referred to the history of the Church. . pp. 55-58.

I. As Christ had continually pointed to His union with the Father for the explanation of His action, so the Apostles in their preaching proclaim Jesus as Lord—basing their statements on their personal experience of Him, and especially on the Resurrection. . . . . pp. 58-62.

II. Closely connected with this comes the assertion of the reconciliation of man to God—the breakdown of the old Jewish sense of separation.
pp. 62, 63.

III. These truths are brought to bear on the conditions of human life. They completely change the position of man; they do not justify sin; they make it possible to avoid it. . . . . . pp. 63-65.

IV. Through these facts man is admitted into a new moral environment; his social being is seen in the light of a spiritual order. pp. 65-67.

Thus all definitely Christian ethical theory is erected on this basis—of a new spiritual life given through the Holy Spirit. . . . pp. 67-70.

It is true that this theory labours under various difficulties, of which the greatest is the prevalence of sin in the world. But this may be met by the actual present power of the Faith to destroy sin—a power which any one may experience for himself. . . . . . pp. 71-73.

LECTURE III.

THE THEOLOGICAL VIRTUES.

The first form in which men became conscious of the new life was in direct experience, which, at first, seemed likely to lead to antinomianism. The Apostles condemn this tendency, and are led by circumstances to deal with various ethical problems. . . . . . . pp. 74-79.

Their treatment of such questions is mostly incidental, but certain predominant ideas come into view, notably, Faith, Hope, and Love. pp. 79, 80.

These terms are somewhat ambiguous, especially $\pi i\sigma\tau\iota s$, and all are unfamiliar in the technical language of philosophy. . . pp. 80-82.

They get their primary meaning from their relation to the facts on which the Creed rests, concentrating in themselves the attitude of man towards the new truth. . . . . pp. 82-84.

And they have also a philosophical meaning: (1) they throw a new light upon the old problem of the end of human life. The end of man is seen to be union with God in love—not mere mystical absorption into the Divine Being, but a conscious intercourse with the Father. And this view of the end affects practical life by means of the trustful certainty which comes of faith—the unwavering hope in the promises of God—the loving and free obedience to His will. . . . . . . pp. 84-94.

(2) These virtues also affect the nature of man especially by his intellect and passions. Faith is the virtue of the intellect. Hope and Love are rooted in the emotional nature, and give it a new dignity. Thus a new unity was given to the nature of man, and it was related to a new end. . . . . pp. 94-100.

NOTE 1.

ON SOME USES OF THE WORD VIRTUE.

NOTE 2.

ON VARIOUS MEANINGS OF $\pi i\sigma\tau\iota s$.

LECTURE IV.

THE CARDINAL VIRTUES.

We must proceed to consider the effect of Christianity upon those moral ideas which were already prevalent, especially the cardinal virtues. pp. 114, 115.

These four were the typical virtues of Greek life, as is shown by their history in Plato, Aristotle and others. . . . . pp. 116, 117.

The life regulated by them was a high and beautiful one, in which various conflicting interests would be harmoniously adjusted, and a certain amount of self-sacrifice required from the individuals composing the society. . . . . pp. 117–120.

In strong contrast with this stands the Christian ideal, with its severe renunciation of the world, combined with the warm brotherly intercourse between the members of the Body, and modified by the responsibility of aiming at the conversion of the whole world. . . . pp. 120–125.

This view of the Church expresses itself conspicuously in the social virtue of humility of which St. Paul has so much to say. pp. 125–129.

But the contrast between the two moral ideals rests upon a deep inward difference—the difference in the estimate of human personality. p. 129.

Every human life is, as such, of infinite value. This explains both the truceless war with the world and the principle of universal love—the desire that all men should be saved. . . . . pp. 129–134.

To adjust this view of personal right and wrong to the predominantly civic conceptions of Greek ethics, was a serious problem for the Church. In the course of its history, the Church took up and moulded the social idea with its four virtues in relation to the new spiritual environment, and the virtues appear as modes of the love which is the life of the new society. . . . . pp. 134–142.

NOTE TO LECTURES III AND IV.

The growth of moral theory in the Church was slow, and was due to special circumstances. But it was distinctive throughout. It did more than combine Judaism and Hellenism. There was an added element besides these, which was its own. The present note aims at illustrating this position. . . . . pp. 143, 144.

The first name of importance in this connexion is that of Philo. For Philo attempted to combine the two previous strains of thought, but lacked the mediating idea. . . . . . . pp. 144, 145.

Analysis.

There are some serious difficulties attaching to the study of Philo, yet it seems possible to get at a general view of his position. In three points he is fairly constant : (1) he treats God always as transcendent even in regard to the creation of the world; (2) he thinks of the world as a great πολίτεια or state under one law, hence his treatment of ethics tends to be physical; (3) he rests with great confidence upon the Mosaic law, but almost always allegorizes its provisions. . . . . pp. 145–153.

With these positions in view we can approach Philo's treatment of the virtues. The keynote of his ethical theory is separation. The soul is buried in the body and hindered by it from its highest aims. It learns separation by a gradual process of education, of which the chief end is knowledge. His account of the cardinal virtues is closely parallel to the ordinary Greek view; on more religious ground he is more original, especially in regard to the *rewards* bestowed by God on certain patriarchs. He also speaks of political virtue. . . pp. 153–162.

The whole theory is affected by the doctrine of ascetic separation, which was due to metaphysical considerations, and really left practical life very much alone. . . . . pp. 162–164.

Those Church-writers who stood nearest to Philo were the great Alexandrines, Clement and Origen. It will be seen that the strictly philosophical interest was modified by Christian doctrine.

The *Paedagogus*, in which Clement describes the outward semblance of the true Christian life, applies directly the standard of Christ's life. The precepts and example of Christ take effect in simplicity of life. In his more elaborate work, he develops a contrast between two aspects of Christian life—the lower, the life of faith, and the higher, the life of knowledge. . . . . pp. 164–172.

The view of Origen, though in places he shows the influence of specially philosophical ideas, is deeper and more theological than that of Clement. He emphasizes against Celsus the need for complete reformation of life, and maintains the possibility of this through Christ alone. The doctrine of a higher and lower life reappears in Origen.

pp. 172–178.

In the Western Church the most important name for our purpose is that of Augustine, born in the African Church, converted in Italy, and then called back to Africa for the work of a bishop.

The African Church was marked by an extreme rigour which the Church as a whole has not followed. But its circumstances led to the declaration of certain principles which appear in the ethical language of the Church. The writings of Tertullian and Cyprian assert in the strongest way the separateness of the Church from the world, the close unity among Christians, and the moral importance of the whole scheme of Christianity. Thus they also seek for the explanation of life in the Incarnation. pp. 179–185.

Analysis.

With Ambrose, the spiritual father of Augustine, we reach the stage at which the Church had begun to systematize its moral theory. His *De Officiis*, though closely allied with Stoic doctrine and modelled on Cicero's work, is definitely Christian in character. . . . pp. 186–188.

Augustine admits the presence of the Spirit of God among the Gentiles, and sees in Platonism (though he is more critical of it than the Alexandrines) a striking instance of it. But he notes their failure to accept the doctrine of the Incarnation, which is to him the pivot on which the whole system of things turns. . . . . pp. 189–192.

He emphasizes the truth of the Fall and the freedom of the will, and connects the possibility of restoration with the Sacrifice of Christ.
pp. 192–194.

He bases a theory of morals on these doctrines, in which the older philosophy is transformed. He is more liberal to the philosophers than his African predecessors, and has much less fear of paganism. In fact, by his date paganism was vanquished. . . . . . pp. 194–199.

Few of his successors added much that was new to the doctrine of virtue. They drew largely on Augustine and gradually introduced more and more system into ethical theory. . . . . pp. 199–203.

The Greeks seem to have developed rather in the direction of canon law than in that of systematized moral theory. . . pp. 203–205.

Summary. . . . . pp. 205, 206.

LECTURE V.

THE ETHICAL MEANING OF SIN.

The fact of evil is one of the most obvious of all ethical facts: the treatment of it philosophically forms a distinguishing feature between various philosophies. . . . . pp. 207–208.

It may be regarded (1) as a necessary effect of finite existence; or (2) as an abnormality, which even finiteness of being cannot justify.
p. 209.

I. The first of these theories is characteristic of ethical systems of which the predominant interest is metaphysical. Assuming that evil is the result of one or other of the necessary conditions of human life, they are compelled to regard it externally and in its effects in the first place, and only deal secondarily with the motives and movement of the will.
pp. 209–212.

II. From the other point of view all evil is ultimately rebellion. This, which has prevailed in many ages and in various parts of the world, has come to Christianity through Judaism and has been developed to the highest point in the Church. We are concerned chiefly with this form of it. . . . . pp. 212-213.

Three fundamental principles govern this conception of evil.

1. The combination of confidence and fear which marks Jewish religion is explained in the belief that God is holy and that man's true life consists in the imitation of God. The continual reflexion upon the nature of God accounts for the passionate hatred of sin. pp. 213-217.

2. That man is free to depart from his ideal. This doctrine in Christian thought results in the extension and definition of the meaning of sin. . . . . pp. 217-222.

3. That men are so closely bound up together that the sin of one affects all. This falls in with the belief in Christ's death as a Sacrifice for sin, and governs the use of discipline in the Church. . pp. 222-226.

The Catholic Church has always resisted the temptation to anticipate the Divine order, and find the ideal sinless Church upon the earth. It has dealt seriously but without panic with sin as a fact—defining its varieties and ecclesiastical effects. This may be illustrated by the treatment of cowardice and sloth. . . . . . . pp. 226-232.

NOTE TO LECTURE V.

The doctrine of sin belongs more closely to the moral atmosphere of the Church than to that of philosophy; hence it will be chiefly necessary to illustrate the Christian doctrine. . . . . . . p. 233.

The normal attitude towards evil in the Greek schools treats it as a failure or inadequacy rather than a wrong; notably Philo and Plotinus. pp. 233-235.

The Christians inherited from the Jews the theory of sin as a rebellion on the part of a free will against the will of God. It is soon found that this apparently simple theory contains very serious problems. St. Paul's language makes it plain that the will stands in no very simple relation to the will and purpose of God. . . . . p. 236.

Hermas betrays a consciousness of difficulties of this kind. And the Alexandrines, in spite of their indebtedness to Greek philosophy, speak with clearness on the nature of sin. Clement insists on the need and the reality of salvation through Christ—on the reality of man's freedom; though he seriously complicates the question by maintaining that pain and punishment are always remedial. . . . . pp. 236-239.

Origen, like Clement, asserts man's freedom, but is perplexed by the language of St. Paul as to agency of God in connexion with evil. His theory of ante-natal experiences is a way of meeting this. pp. 239-241.

Analysis.

Among the Latins Tertullian and Cyprian deal with the question primarily from a practical point of view; they are emphatic on the reality of freedom where it is necessary for them to be so. The question of sin first became elaborate when the Pelagian discussion arose. This introduced two points to the notice of thinkers: (1) the true relation of man to his environment; (2) the need of adjusting old language about responsibility to the new conception of the individual. . . . pp. 241–243.

This involved a change from a political to a moral view of man's life; representing him as an individual placed in an environment which he did not choose and cannot control, and yet responsible for what he does quite apart from its political effect. . . . . . . pp. 243–245.

St. Augustine approached this question in the light of his own personal experience, and from the point of view of the psychological doctrine which he had evolved. . . . . pp. 245–251.

The final doctrine of the will came from the side of the theology of the Incarnation. . . . . p. 251.

As regards classifications of sins, there is very little precision in the N. T. Hermas shows that the ethical sense of the Church was gradually developing in accuracy, and the disciplinary distinction between pardonable and unpardonable sins is clear in Tertullian and Cyprian. . pp. 252–257.

St. Augustine, though his classifications vary, distinguishes clearly between various kinds and degrees of evil. . . . pp. 258–259.

The well-known classification of seven deadly sins seems to have been based indirectly on words of Origen, and to have come to the West through Cassian from the Egyptian ascetics. In the East it remains monastic in character, but in the West, owing largely to the influence of Gregory the Great, it affects the entire moral atmosphere of the Church. It expresses the regular Christian view of sin. . . . pp. 259–266.

LECTURE VI.

MORALITY AND REASON.

Christianity is always treated in the N. T. as forming a definite stage in the evolution of a purpose. This purpose is the expression upon the human field of the wisdom of God. . . . . . pp. 267–271.

The wisdom of God in the ancient Jewish view was practical rather than theoretic: i.e. it dealt not with abstract and universal ideas, but was conceived as the power which moved the process of history, and governed the circumstances of individual life. It was in this idea that a philosophical sanction was found for the moral life. . . . . pp. 271, 272.

This idea, though not directly applied to the moral life in the N. T., indicates the way to a solution of a somewhat seriously difficulty. p. 272.

The nature of God is set before men as in some way offering them their moral ideal: and this is translated into the practical command to love. But this, though it is rendered possible by the new life given, still retains the form of a command which compels the individual will, but of which the rational justification may still be asked. pp. 272-276.

The answer to this difficulty, for human faculties, lies in the idea of the Divine Wisdom: through which the whole course of things, including the lives of individuals, are brought under the control of the Providence of God. The moral law can no longer be regarded as an arbitrary command; it is the expression of the wisdom of God. . pp. 276-278.

This position is not affected by the progressive character of moral ideas. Nor is it open to the objection that it involves a separation of wisdom and love in the nature of God. . . . . . pp. 278-280.

Such a separation has occurred in the history of theology, and was brought to its climax in the scholastic discussions between the followers of Aquinas and those of Scotus and Ockam. It must always occur when the idea of speculative wisdom is allowed to overpower that of practical wisdom. . . . . pp. 280-286.

A similar separation is a theological danger at the present time, owing to the disposition to trust instincts, and acquiesce in the incapacity of reason. . . . . pp. 286-287.

The Incarnation is the typical expression of the Divine wisdom and love: in the light of it, man can partly see wisdom where some still see only foolishness—in the Cross. . . . . . pp. 288-291.

Note to Lecture VI.

Religion has two functions, philosophically speaking : to explain nature, and to explain moral life. The two aims are not necessarily incompatible ; but the former, if followed exclusively, ends in abstract metaphysic: the latter preserves always the notion of a Personal God. . . p. 292.

The Christian Church had to combine these two points of view : i.e. to determine the attributes of God. This question, which Gnosticism forced forward, was answered with no uncertainty. A particular character was ascribed to God, on the basis of Scripture, tradition, and Christian experience. . . . . pp. 293-295.

But the philosophical relation between the two points of view was long undetermined: in fact, it was left undecided till the Scholastic Age. p. 296.

Analysis.

The works of Dionysius the Areopagite brought into the Church a purely speculative theology, based on *a priori* considerations and tending strongly towards Pantheism. . . . . pp. 296-298.

The controversy between Nominalism and Realism offered the alternative between a philosophy tending towards Pantheism and pure Materialism. In the light of these various lines of speculation the question of the Divine attributes was approached. . . . . . . pp. 298, 299.

Aquinas, influenced by the Dionysian writings and accepting Realism, defines both the attributes of God and the relation between them. The will of God is inseparable from the reason. Hence, as the moral law is the true expression of the will of God it cannot change. pp. 299-301.

Scotus, on the other hand, with premisses somewhat similar, denies immutability to anything but the Divine nature itself. Everything created is contingent, and therefore dependent on the free choice of God —including even the moral law. . . . . . pp. 301, 302.

Ockam, denying universals in every form, denies all but arbitrary action to God. . . . . p. 303.

The questions are not futile. The Dionysian mystic agnosticism is attractive and seems to be necessary. Yet the question as to the nature of God is the theological way of asking whether we can trust the moral sense, or whether we must regard it as subject to an inherent irrationality. To assign supremacy to reason is simply to assert that reason is the fundamental presupposition of all life. . . . pp. 303-309.

LECTURE VII.

ETHICS AND THE REFORMATION.

The moral principles, described in previous lectures, supplied the forms of moral thought till the time of the Reformation, and were in large measure successful in practice. . . . . . pp. 310-312.

This is shown (1) by the prevalence of monasticism, (2) by the extant Penitential literature. These put in clear light the fact that the Church had really taken in hand the task of moralizing the world. pp. 312-318.

But since the Reformation—in spite of the moral earnestness out of which it arose—a division has arisen between Creed and Life. This result, so little answering to reasonable expectations, was largely due to various influences, chiefly secular, which were at work at the time of the Reformation. . . . . pp. 318-320.

1. The Church had suffered serious corruption, owing to its assumption of political power. Though it had been inevitable that it should do this, the time for its political activity was over. . . . pp. 320-322.

xxvi   *Analysis.*

2. As a consequence of this the moral tone of Churchmen had degenerated, and the poor were neglected. And this happened in spite of the protests of individuals, and of the great orders. . . pp. 322-324.

3. The speculative separation between faith and reason aided this degeneration, so that Humanism, in its most pagan form, easily made way. . . . . p. 325.

Under these conditions, when, moreover, national feeling had come into existence, and universal supremacy of Emperor or Pope was already an anachronism, change was to be anticipated. . . . . pp. 325-327.

The requirement of the age was *reformation*: restoration of a pure creed, of moral discipline in the Church, of personal religion. The presence of exaggerated and revolutionary elements seriously modified the result. . . . . pp. 327-329.

The assault upon unrighteous authority and the assertion of the rights of individuals ended in the separation of individual religion from the spiritual society, and established the State as the proper and sole environment for man's moral life. . . . . . . pp. 329-332.

The result was logically involved in the revolutionary exaggerations: it is often practically suspended in the case of individuals and churches.
pp. 332-336.

Various evils follow from this position, e.g. moral philosophy tends to revert to a pagan type—moral effort ceases to be systematic.
pp. 336-341.

LECTURE VIII.

CHURCH DISCIPLINE.

The claim of Christianity is supreme and covers the whole of life. This it does in virtue of its character as an inward guiding force quickening the will from within. . . . . p. 346.

This life is embodied in the Christian society, and requires for its complete manifestation that the whole body of Christian people should be guided in all regions of their activity by one set of principles, moral and dogmatic. . . . . pp. 346-349.

To the fuller attainment of this result in the present state of things two conditions are requisite: (1) The sense of Churchmanship must be quickened. The lack of this is an obvious cause of much failure and disappointment in the work of the Church in the world. pp. 349-352.

(2) The Church must resume its functions of discipline. This is probably an unpalatable suggestion and may seem to assail our reasonable feelings of independence. Also it is often supposed to lead

either to an immoral casuistry or a hard sacerdotalism. But these dangers do not necessarily arise from discipline. . . pp. 352-354.

The danger of casuistry consists in a certain moral temper, which appears whenever the intellect is allowed to paralyze the will—whether this results in positively immoral action or not . . pp. 354-356.

And the danger of sacerdotalism also consists in a moral temper, by which laity and priesthood are separated. This arises equally if the priesthood make exaggerated claims, or if the laity leave all the real work of the Church to the priesthood and seek only a lower ideal of Church membership. . . . . pp. 356-358.

The reappearance of discipline would counteract rather than encourage these evils. Discipline in the true sense means the assertion by common consent of the Christian principle in all departments of life. pp. 358-362.

This conflicts in no way with any principle except pure Individualism, nor does it involve undue interference with secular life. Discipline deals only with the moral aspects of things. . . . . pp. 362-367.

Nor again is it ineffective, although it operates indirectly. For it leads to concentration of purpose, and is an ascetic rule of life in the best sense: and both these characters are sources of strength. . pp. 367-372.

Conclusion. . . . . pp. 373-375.

INDEX . . . . pp. 377-380.

CHRISTIAN ETHICS

LECTURE I

'I delight in the law of God after the inward man: but I see a different law in my members, warring against the law of my mind, and bringing me into captivity under the law of sin which is in my members.'—ROM. vii. 22, 23 (R.V.).

IT is an old story that a note of disappointment and weariness sounds in the writings of the ancient world. Experience was apt to mean disillusionment, for the gods were envious, and old age crept on, and death was never far away. The hopes men had entertained in early life belied their expectations if they were realized, and left them with an unsatisfied longing if they were continually deferred. For there was a mystery in life: reason had not gripped it as a whole, and so the best calculations and the most carefully laid plans would not ensure a satisfactory issue; even prayer to heaven might involve considerable risk.

If this is true of the ordinary pursuits and desires of men, it is truer still on a higher level. All the eager and profitless searching in the world seems to be concentrated in systems of philosophy. For a system of philosophy aimed higher than at a mere temporary self-satisfaction. It attempted to grasp the whole problem of man's existence, to provide a theory of the facts of the world which should leave nothing out, and a theory of man's life and interests which should leave no occasion unforeseen or unprovided with resource, and so to rationalize the irrational search for satisfaction, and find a resting-place for the restless passion of desire.

To find such a solution for the problem of existence seemed easier, at first, in the natural world. Some one element, some one aspect of being, seemed to be easily traceable throughout the complex of things, and in the light of the application of this principle the chaotic and unintelligible variety of nature seemed to fall under the dominion of order and reason: the world, at any rate, seemed to be guided by a purpose: nature, at any rate, did nothing in vain. And therefore, if nature surrendered to reason, it seemed all the more intolerable that man's life should be void of rational significance. Man himself was conscious of purpose in his own individual actions, he was perfectly familiar with the relation of means to ends; and therefore looked, not unnaturally, to be able to satisfy his desire for philosophical completeness in regard of his own life, at least as well as he had done in regard of the world. The decision of right and wrong cannot be left to accident, thinks Plato, or the suggestion of circumstances, or the promiscuous impressions of one's neighbours. Desire cannot be empty and vain, Aristotle holds: there must be some guiding principle which will explain it all, and supply a proper rule for action. There must be some positive reality or some single end to justify the use of terms like 'right' and 'wrong,' upon which all agree, but which it is not so easy to define.

But here, as indeed in the philosophy of nature, the usual disappointment attended man's efforts. Definitions and theories were put forward, but the question remained still open to discussion. Seek for knowledge, said one, and care for nothing else; seek for pleasure, said another, for pleasure is the one thing that makes life tolerable; seek for virtue, for self-development in every way, said others. Some tried to live by these rules, and to help others so to live. But the philosophers always tended to become an eccentric clique: for the most part life went on apart from them: men bought and sold, and married and gave in marriage, were eager or listless, quarrelsome or calm, and no one could say why. And to the thoughtful this was just the most cruel part of their fate, that they were forced either to stand aside from the interests and pursuits which occupied other men, or to fall in with the general drift of life without knowing whether there was any sufficient reason for so doing[1].

It will be worth while to ask, as we look back over this history of anxious inquiry and very partial attainment, whether we can point to any reason that will throw light upon the want of success. Can we lay our finger on any common characteristic of all these

---

[1] Cf. Plat. *Rep.* 496 E; Justin Martyr, *Dial. c. Tryph.* ch. 2; Lucian, *Hermotimus*, esp. ch. 72 and following.

speculations which will explain their futility? Or must we say simply that it happened because man is doomed to aimless search, and his life is an insoluble enigma? For, if we consider how very largely the thinkers of ancient Greece have laid down the lines within which all subsequent speculation has moved in the spheres of Physics and Metaphysics, we may fairly expect that they would have been as successful in the field of Ethics, if they had had at their disposal the materials for success. Was there, then, any definable reason why such men, in spite of their keenness of moral perception, and their practice in the handling of problems, should have achieved so much less in the decision of the greatest problem of all?

It seems to me that there are two common characteristics presented by all ancient Greek systems which in part explain their failure. In the first place there was a confusion as to the exact method or place of an ethical system. Human life was treated too much on the analogy of other branches of scientific investigation. Moral life presents two strikingly different series of facts. On the one side there are the moral ideas—the general notions of right and wrong. These may and do vary with different individuals, different ages, and different societies. But wherever such notions exist, they form a sort of rough standard by which the particular actions of life are measured. Amidst all this variety there is, of course, some principle to be found. Moral facts, like facts of any other kind, cover with their variety an underlying identity. There are certain residual convictions which every man must hold in whom the moral sense is developed at all. Some of these are essential to the existence of society: some arise naturally as men emerge from barbarism: a minority of them consist of inexplicable local usages which run back upon a state of things long past and long forgotten. It is, comparatively speaking, a simple matter to introduce order into this region of discussion, and to arrive at some common standing-ground by the summation and co-ordination of facts. Such a process would be little more than a classification such as is performed constantly in connexion with the progress of science, and would result in a general and rough conception of the meaning of moral life for man.

And, supposing it done, the other class of facts would then rise into view. It would be found by evidence no less immediate and convincing than that of ordinary observation, that this quasi-scientific generalization would not have quite the same effect in morals as in other things. It would not affect action in quite the same way. A scientific generalization becomes a permanent property. Once proved, it becomes part of the regular stock of the human mind: it affects practice as well as theory. Even a philosophical construction of facts may turn the course of human thought and mark an epoch; such was the effect, for instance, of the dictum of Anaxagoras that reason was the power that brought order into the world. Even if it meets with violent opposition from those who cling to a more ancient point of view, yet all the increasing numbers who accepted it are dominated by it, and take it as their guide in the interpretation of the world. With morals it is different. Not only are the uneducated herd left outside the influence of the generalizations of philosophers, but the philosophers themselves, those who do profess and really mean to take these principles for their guidance, these are the people who fail to do so : fail so conspicuously as to become a byword[1]. This difficulty is not adequately provided for by the recognition that theory and practice are not the same. For that leaves out of sight the fact that the theory itself is incomplete : that the definition of virtue, even the conviction that a man knows how to obtain it, cannot provide against disastrous surprise and fall. In one word, we have here one reason which certainly operated to hinder the complete success of moral speculation. The life of man was treated too much as a branch of natural history. The inquirers set out by simply noting existing facts and theories about it, as they might have done in order to explain any ordinary natural phenomenon ; and the acquisition of a consistent and intelligible account of the moral facts examined seemed to lead at once to the enunciation of moral principles. And that led necessarily to disappointment. Men expected more than they had any right to expect from speculations of this character, and in the degree in which they did so they doomed themselves to failure.

Of course, I do not mean—no Oxford man could admit such a thing for a moment—that the work done by the ancient moralists was in all respects and in all

[1] Cf. Plat. *Rep.* 487 D.

relations a mere failure. They did for moral philosophy what pioneers have the special mission to do. They broke up the ground: they defined and distinguished: they noted the bearing of motives and the importance of the estimate of them: they deduced (with more or less clearness) the demand for virtue from the essential nature of man. In all these regards they did work of permanent value. But they were too great themselves not to aim at a higher result than this; they meant to supply an inspiration to their age, and strengthen the hold of moral ideas upon the wills of men: and this, except for a narrow following of disciples whom each gathered round him, they all largely failed to do. They stood aloof from human nature, and viewed it from the outside as an object of natural history. They described its actual movements as they saw them, and their speculations were strictly limited by what they had observed.

Such a confusion then as to the exact method and value of ethical speculation inevitably led to failure; but this is not the only cause of it. There is a second, which is, in part, a consequence of the first. As there was a disposition to treat human life from the point of view of the external observer, so, as a true artistic impulse rises out of accurate observation, it was inevitable that speculative ethics should express itself in the construction of ideal figures. Assuming man in relation to certain forces, it would seem to confirm and illustrate any definition of virtue or of the end of life that might be attained, if an ideal man in an ideal relation to these forces could be contrived by the imagination. Speculation would then seem to become intelligible. It would be possible to cite the behaviour at various junctures of the wise man, the σπουδαῖος, or whatever else he might be called, and to take his conduct as a model for one's own: and the crude process of speculation would seem to become more reasonable and approachable than could ever be while it remained in abstract terms or even took the form of moral precept. It was an artistic impulse, characteristic of the nation which developed sculpture to such supreme perfection, and it represented the endeavour to express abstract principles in concrete form.

But yet it was one chief cause of the failure of Greek ethics to be practically impressive. For the ideal figure always tended to pass beyond the range of ordinary conditions, and it was always hard to bring him back into the prosaic, inartistic region of practical human life. Plato knew men well, and read the causes of their failure with unique power and insight. But his philosopher-king was the creation of a state which no existing conditions were adequate to produce. In order to bring him on to the human stage, a clearance had to be effected of all that had in it associations with the evil past. That such a man should occur in the ordinary Greek state seemed beyond all hope. And so Plato's ideal figure disappears into the clouds— though his nature is defined by strict philosophical necessity, and every element in it is based upon observation and logic—because the stage upon which alone he can be active is not forthcoming.

So with Aristotle. He too has entered thoroughly

into the conditions of human life, and has endeavoured to imagine the way in which they might be ideally met and realized. He comes closer in some ways to the ordinary levels of human experience than Plato does even in the *Laws*. At all points in his inquiry we can recognize the facts which he describes: indeed the danger is that his remarks should seem too obvious and self-evident. But his ideal also seems to require an ideal society as its background. His society, as he describes it, involves perhaps less startling changes in the existing order than Plato demanded, but still the changes required are complete. It is a new society that is wanted, with peculiar conditions of number, place, and internal order, if the supremely balanced character is to be produced, which observation and reflexion prove to be the ideal possibility for man.

These were social ideals, conceived while the glories of the old Hellenic city-state still haunted the imagination. But there are others besides these, the product of the conviction that the world as a whole was beyond the hope of reformation, and that the less wide aspiration must content the philosopher—to keep himself independent of the sordid pursuits of the unenlightened, and to feast alone upon his philosophy. Such was the ideal of the Stoic. His conception of true manhood was the life according to reason and nature, which gave up the riddle of the world, and simply accepted with a dull passion of endurance whatever came. It was a logical structure, the strict outcome of principles which were laid down at the start, but there was little chance of its being ever fully realized. For the Stoics more than any one else, though their interest in the individual life led them further than their predecessors in the direction of casuistry, overshot the mark of actual reality. Their wise man was out of the question from the first, except as supplying a regulative principle for the life of an individual here and there. A state peopled with men fulfilling Stoic principles would be a monstrosity and a nightmare. No group of persons could conceivably have so separated themselves from all the desires and activities of ordinary human beings as to have attained it. And therefore there was always a second or lower ideal running somewhat in parallel lines with the first, and more in accordance than it with human experience.

And then, again, in later days there was the Neoplatonist. He too thought of the ideal life of man from the individual point of view. His ideal also rests upon despair. But he gave it a semblance of warmth and life by making its chief characteristic to be the passionate yearning for union with God—the supreme principle of Unity and Good, out of whose superabundant life, as Plotinus thought, the whole universe had been developed [1]. Porphyry tells us in his life of Plotinus [2] that during the time that he knew the master and studied with him, Plotinus had four times attained to moments of this ecstatic contemplation, in which the turbulence of sense and

---

[1] Plot. *Enn.* v. ii. 1 : πρώτη οἷον γέννησις αὕτη· ὂν γὰρ τέλειον τῷ μηδὲν ζητεῖν μηδὲ ἔχειν μηδὲ δεῖσθαι οἷον ὑπερερρύη καὶ τὸ ὑπερπλῆρες αὐτοῦ πεποίηκεν ἄλλο.
[2] *Vit. Plot.* c. 23.

intellect was stilled, and he simply feasted on the presence of the Divine. We rarely hear of a philosopher realizing so much of his ideal as this.

Again, I must guard against a possible misapprehension. I do not mean that these conceptions of the ideal man have been mere waste labour. On the contrary, they have all of them done work that is permanent in the history of ethics. Plato and Aristotle brought to light in a way in which no one had ever done before, the close relation between man as an individual and the society in which he dwells. They emphasized the truth, and it should never have been forgotten, that man alone is not sufficient to himself: that he is radically a social being. And the later history of ethics brings to light the real value of the careful analysis of moral states which the Stoics first attempted, and the mystic contemplation which was the goal of all the striving of the Neo-platonist.

But when all this has been said, it still remains that for the most part these ideals were remote, and insufficiently made effectual on the will. Though it might be true that man at his best might look to attain to something like them, the will remained untouched except so far as the ideal happened to exercise an attractive charm over it. And even if the ideal itself proved charming, there was still the inveterately irresolute and indecisive will to be strengthened to the point of persistent struggle with circumstances that made against all determined action on principle. There was lacking the mediating idea or force that would change the conceptions won by so much earnest thought from ideals to inspirations. And this was the other reason why, on the whole, the ancient philosophies ended in failure. They had great influence in their time, especially in the first three centuries of the Christian era: at least, the philosophical profession was held in high honour. Rich men kept philosophers in their houses, like private chaplains; and, in spite of the mischievous suggestions of Lucian, that they cared more for the rich man's table than for moralizing his life, we cannot but believe that their influence was in many cases for the good. But it remains that their philosophy, from the necessity of the case, was rather a rule of thumb than a system of effective principles. It rose out of experience, like the old proverbial philosophies which it had displaced, and it was limited only less narrowly than they. Its ideals were the utmost aspirations that the life of experience suggested; yet when they came to be applied it appeared sometimes that they were impracticable, sometimes that there was no motive strong enough to force the will to conform itself to a standard thus externally imposed, however fully its moral beauty might be allowed.

But I shall be met here with an objection. I shall be asked, Have you not forgotten the Jews? What of their Law? Did not that, at any rate, succeed in part? And these questions clearly require consideration.

Judaism of course stood in a peculiar position. It depended in the last resort upon the covenant-relation between God and the chosen people, and this determines all that was specially characteristic in it. There were, of course, historical elements of various kinds imbedded in the Jewish religion. Ancient conceptions running back upon the common Semitic heathendom; ancient practices depending for their explanation upon obsolete beliefs as to powers in nature: these are still traceable in Jewish ordinances, and enable us to explain many things which otherwise would seem arbitrary and obscure. But these are not the characteristic features of Judaism, and they are mythological rather than religious. The most characteristic feature of the Jewish religion is the strengthening of the old conception of a tribal god into the idea of a union so close between Jehovah and the children of Israel that it can be described in the terms of a marriage[1]. Moreover this, which was the most characteristic feature of Jewish religion, was also the ruling idea of the Jewish nation. Just in proportion as it regarded itself as being the special object of Jehovah's love and interest, its exclusive national feeling grew in intensity. In earlier days the people fell away, as we all know, with extraordinary frequency towards the gods of the neighbouring tribes: and it was only after the stern lesson of the Captivity that their religious allegiance and national exclusiveness became confirmed habits of mind. Still, when they reached, as a people, the conviction of their unique relation to Jehovah, they only attained what

---

[1] Cf. Gen. xii. 1-3, xvii. 1-14; Exod. vi. 2-9; Deut. iv. 7. 8, vi. 14. 15, vii. 6-11, xxxi. 16; 1 Sam. xii. 20-25; Hos. ii. 14-23; Jer. iii. 8; Isa. liv. 5, 6; Ezek. xvi; and other passages.

had all along been the guiding idea of all their greatest men—prophets, lawgivers, and psalmists—and therefore their morality was guided throughout by the one ruling principle, which their greatest men had developed and kept before the conscience of the people.

In the history of Judaism this one notion of the relation of God to man took various forms. The one which we are most accustomed to identify with the name of Judaism is the development of legislation. The Jewish Law assumed from the first that God was to be known by, and to accept, the worship and friendship of His chosen people. But His character of supreme holiness involved a certain risk in approaching Him. There was danger lest, by too suddenly intruding into His presence unprepared and unprotected, the rash intruder might come to harm. And therefore a complex system of ceremonial was devised, which, though it resembled in many ways the ceremonial systems of many other nations, and preserved many archaic conceptions long after they had really ceased to rule men's minds, yet differed from all these in that it rested finally on the notion of the holiness of God. It was this moral character pervading the Jewish ceremonial that preserved it from degradation in the direction of fetish-worship and prevented it from complete obsolescence as the mind of the people grew in power and range. For it is certainly a curious and unique fact that the palmy days of the law of ceremonial observance came, if criticism is right in its conclusions, in the last period of the history of Judaism. It is not as if the system of ceremonial

Preliminary: Greek and Jew

were exceptionally free from pre-historic ideas, or were exceptionally intelligible to minds which had passed beyond pre-historic associations with the notion of God: many of its regulations are only explicable in full by reference to the customs and beliefs of primitive races[1]. We cannot, then, account for the tenacious hold of such primitive practices and ideas upon the mind of a race which was already developing, except upon the supposition that this ceremonial order enshrined for the people many of their moral ideas. The careful regulations necessary for approaching God may, in some minds, have occupied the whole horizon. Their interest would exhaust itself in accuracy of detail, and the God who was thus surrounded with a barrier of ceremonial would be wholly forgotten. In such minds, religion would be already on the move towards fetichism. But in others, the elaborateness of the ceremonial order would emphasize the unapproachable holiness of God, and make men only the more anxious to fit themselves for His presence.

That this result was possible even upon the basis of the Law seems to be proved by the union in the latest developments of Judaism of the two other strains of thought which existed and grew separately in earlier days. The prophets from an early date had been engaged in vigorously denouncing mere formalism. They felt the need of some outlet for their more spiritual desires and yearnings, and the mere external routine of ceremonial—of sacrifices and feasts at special times—troubled and wearied them. It was this class

[1] Cf. p. 42.

of men who searched their own hearts most anxiously: and it is to them that we owe that deeper view of human nature, its temptations and capacities, which gives the Old Testament its peculiar value throughout all time. It was the prophets again who displayed most completely the working of moral laws in the field of politics. Similarly, later on, it was the psalmists who analyzed most elaborately the subtle inward movements of the individual human soul. They revealed the mysteries of penitence, they understood the pain of world-weariness and the awful desolation of spirit which comes when the righteous man seems to be forsaken even by his God. These and other such intuitions of comparatively remote and rare moral conditions point to a habit of introspection which is beyond the usual degree of intensity.

I have said that the Jews had little interest in philosophical questions, strictly so called. They accepted, apparently without difficulty, a simple theory of the being of the world, and their reliance upon revelation for their moral order made it unnecessary for them to raise any of the metaphysical discussions which lie round the moral ideas. At the same time their practical men arrived at a view of the right order of life, which we find in the Proverbs and other sapiential books. These practical philosophers developed the conception of the wise man and the fool: the man who made the most of his position, was careful, diligent, and religious, and the man who was at all points wilful, idle, and unsatisfactory. The wise man, in their view, was expected to be successful; and failure

Preliminary: Greek and Jew

in the pursuits of ordinary life was connected with folly and misdoing. Virtue is the wisest course, and should reap its due reward. Out of this somewhat utilitarian and, as it seems, uninspiring view of life, however, there arises one of the most profound of all human problems—the question of the relation of God's providence and foreknowledge to human activity. And again in this connexion we find the idea of Divine Wisdom, the mysterious plan or thought which is gradually expressed in the order of things, with which it is man's wisdom to correspond, to which, though he cannot fathom it, he must submit. It was this circle of ideas which satisfied the philosophical instincts of the Jews, and helped to make them ready in time to mingle with the stream of Hellenic thought[1].

I have been obliged to allude thus shortly to these very familiar facts, in order to bring out the special characteristics which marked the Jewish moral ideas. The Law, in spite of the repulsive appearance which it bears to our minds, was after all the centre of the combination of the various influences at work in Judaism. Later psalmists, such at the author of Ps. cxix, find their spiritual desires satisfied in the Law of God; the Temple services and the worship there are the delight of the author of Ps. lxxxiv; and throughout the Psalms, which seem to have been written for the Temple, there breathes a religious enthusiasm which we find very difficult to put in any connexion with hosts of slaughtered animals and steaming sacrifices.

[1] Cf. Driver, *Introduction to the Literature of the Old Testament*, pp. 369, 370.

So again the Law appeared to the Jewish philosopher as the great manifestation of the divine wisdom: it was the wisdom of God which brought man out of his first fall, and ordered the nations upon the earth, and chose the people of Israel for His own, and gave them this Law to guide them. It was the moral order, as expressed in the Law, which was the conspicuous instance of the supreme wisdom of God, for in regard of human life it was most mysterious and unfathomable. There were always mysteries remaining unsolved; but for man the fear of the Lord was the beginning of wisdom, and to depart from evil was understanding [1].

The Jewish moral system was, therefore, a lofty and elaborate one, and was attached by the closest associations to the legislative code which ruled the ceremonial observances of the people. However strange it may appear to us, though we may note with curious interest the comparative absence of moral delinquencies in the law of sacrifice, it was the law which moulded the minds of the people; and their predominant notion of a moral code was legal. By a process of synthesis, which we can only partly understand, the deepest spiritual yearning for communion with God was to be found in those who were careful of the external duties imposed by the law rather than amongst those who sat loosely to it. The Sadducee priesthood, who reduced their faith within the narrowest limits, were no more ready to meet Christ when He came than the Phari-

[1] Wisd. vi-ix.; Ecclus. xxiv., especially verse 23. Cheyne, *Job and Solomon*, pp. 161, 162.

sees. Their contempt for the casuistry and pettiness of the legalist party represented no high spiritual scorn for the mere external; it merely meant the most hopeless indifference to religion of any kind. The true spirit of Judaism was enshrined in the Law.

Thus the ethical system of Judaism escaped one danger which beset those of the Greeks. Judaism never lost itself in questions whether virtue was or was not knowledge, and the like, for it had no opportunity of raising such problems. The belief in the direct inspiration of Moses, and the position held by all the books which gradually formed the Canon, acted so as to prevent that sort of inquiry into the nature and the claims of the moral ideal. The moral law was, as it were, given already in the religious experience of every devout Jew and needed no explanation. The man who believed in Jehovah and His love for His chosen people believed, on the same evidence, in the same breath, as it were, in the moral code conveyed by the Law. There was no room for further discussion if this were once admitted.

But on the other ground, over which the Greek ethical systems also failed to realize all that was expected of them, the Jewish Law failed as signally as any. It stood outside and issued commands, as it were: and righteousness came not by means of it. Those who searched into the heart of man among the Jews plunged far more deeply even than Plato or the highest of the Stoics into the recesses of human nature. They had more to say about the causes of moral failure; they knew that there was more in it than a deficiency of knowledge, or than the mere existence of a blundering chaotic principle like matter. They sought the springs of moral evil in the will, and learned by experience many of the subtle ways in which the conscience persuaded itself to wrong-doing. But they believed that somehow the Law, which was their delight, was in some way to solve all the difficulties, though it was just this which as yet it had never done. It was external, like the Greek ideals. Acting on the specially prepared mind of the Jewish nation, it affected them more deeply, and reached further towards impressing and moulding their wills. But, like the Greek ideals again, it did its full work with those only whose spiritual nature was such as to understand its bearing. In these it produced the patient temper that waited for the hope of Israel, for it pointed constantly out of itself to a future where its failures would be redressed. In hard, narrow, unspiritual natures it produced the most unlovely character almost that has yet appeared in history: with less moral depth, and more stiff self-righteousness than has been developed under any other system of moral principles. When it failed, it failed grievously. When it succeeded, it declared itself incomplete.

In the Sermon on the Mount the climax of Judaism was reached, and in the same moment its death-knell was sounded. This Sermon as it stands in St. Matthew's Gospel gives, it is true, the law to the new kingdom; but it stands in close connexion with the language and ideas of the old. And it comes with authority—it asserts the new authority of a new teacher; but at the same time it is a teacher who interprets—who comes not to destroy, but to fulfil. Again, it lays stress throughout upon spiritual conditions, and throws them up in strong relief against an external observance from which the true spirit is lacking; but it still runs in the form of a law. It thus belongs to a transitional period, and, as it were, hangs between the old and the new order. In the sense that it directs attention to a new teacher, who claims a personal right to set His interpretation against the prevalent tradition, it belongs wholly to the new; but in its emphasis upon the spiritual as opposed to hollow externalism, though it goes deeper into things than the writers of old, it does but follow the best traditions of Hebrew religious thought. The golden rule itself is followed by the words, 'For this is the law and the prophets.'

There is yet another point in which the Sermon passes wholly beyond anything which occurred under the old covenant. There is a promise of perfection, based on a comparison with the Father: according to the true text, 'Ye therefore shall be perfect, even as your Father which is in heaven is perfect[1].' This was a hope for which the old fathers hardly dared to look: the Law hardly offered any such possibility. But though the Sermon makes this promise, it does not say any word as to the way of realizing the perfection which it preaches. And thus, even in view of this promise, it takes its place rather with the older dispensation than the new. It is still a law:

[1] St. Matt. v. 48.

still gives commands to the will, and sets before it an ideal. The will is left to find its own way to this perfect type: no guidance, no direct promise of guidance is given. So that the Sermon on the Mount kills, to use St. Paul's language, as relentlessly as the Law[1].

We look at it so often from the point of view of a complete Christianity that it has somewhat quaintly been taken to be the sum total of the Christian message. As if a law were made easier to keep by being made more difficult: as if the burden of compliance with an external rule were made lighter by applying the rule relentlessly to the shifting movements of the soul, which only the most careful watchfulness can keep in view. Whatever language may be held, and held rightly, as to the lofty spiritual character of the morality inculcated in the Sermon, it cannot be said to do more than place the ideal before the mind. Those to whom it appeals—and these will necessarily be many—will grope after it in the obscure ways of life. They will see in its light their own failures, and they will learn the endless variety of the causes of their falls. And if they try to face its full meaning without evasion or diminution of its force, they will find out how it constrains and presses upon the will at every turn—how it closes avenues of action, and opens a narrow and difficult path which few indeed will dare to tread.

The Greek ethical systems, the Jewish Law, the Sermon on the Mount, have all this one character in common, that they command from without. They

[1] Cf. Holland, *Creed and Character*, Sermon xvi. pp. 238, 239.

vary, of course, indefinitely in other respects; there is a long interval between the ideal of Epicurus or even of Plato and that of the Sermon on the Mount. They appeal differently also to the enlightened conscience of mankind; even from the point of view of mere attractiveness the ideal of the new kingdom has far the widest appeal. Indeed, the world is apt to think itself Christian, and profess as its ideal a slightly amended version of the Sermon on the Mount, condemning as narrow and self-pleasing even the grim seclusion of the Stoic philosopher. But the world is apt to exaggerate its own disposition to virtue, and to be contented with moderate attainments: and therefore it fails to see the wide interval which separates ordinary practice from the professed ideal. It is natural that this should happen. An ideal does not necessarily translate itself into action: it exists apart to be referred to at will. And in a society in which various ideas prevail it is additionally hard to put them into practice. If we imagine a man compelled to choose his own ideal of life, and then called upon to put it into practice in his own strength, amidst all the various voices in the world, which call him different ways, we shall not be surprised if in many cases no wide success or lofty attainment rewards his efforts. He will be almost inevitably bewildered; he will lose his head, and miss the connexion between his ideal and his life; he will become uncertain of his convictions, and will almost inevitably end by falling in with the type of action around him. It is the uniform characteristic of all this dispensation of Law to address a man from outside, and confront him with some rule or some ideal, and supply no force that will enable him to perform it. He sees what is right: he agrees with the law that it is good; but this bare knowledge is not strong enough to cope with the forces of society: righteousness comes not through the law. The presence of mere ideals, however lofty, is apt to end in a quiet surrender to fashion.

There is of course one broad distinction between the Greek and the Hebrew elements in this period to which I must again allude. The Greeks assumed practically that man was either in an unfallen state, or that his fall was irremediable, depending upon the inclusion of his soul in an alien matter, which subdues and impedes its action. The Jew started from the conception of a fallen human nature, but to his mind the fall was somehow to be reversed; it depended upon no ultimate impassable physical barrier, but upon the will. This is why the loftier and more elaborate moral conceptions of the Jews produced no such hopelessness as I have had occasion to notice among the Greeks. No Stoic withdrawal or Neo-platonist mysticism was indigenous among the Jews. It was the hope which dwelt in the Jewish heart that kept them from a deeper despair than any that could have beset other nations: the despair of men who knew more of the unmanageable character of the disease under which they laboured, and the fruitlessness of offering sacrifices to the God to whom all the beasts of the forest belonged, so long as the heart was not right with Him.

In this hope lies the suggestion of the cure for the

constant failure which we noted at the beginning of this lecture. It is not so much a new moral system that is required, as a new force to move the will. The various ethical systems failed, not because they led to wrong or false or even insufficient conclusions, but because they dealt inadequately with human nature itself. The moral philosopher can never be fully satisfied with barely abstract definitions; the end of that investigation is essentially not knowledge, but action. And to secure this end it is of comparatively slight avail simply to represent the ideal good, however well, as an ideal. For if the nature of man, from which the whole departure is made, is touched with incapacity, the moral system which does not meet this must inevitably display its inadequacy at some point. It may produce a theory of good that fails to correspond with the whole nature of man, or it may fail altogether to set the will in motion by ignoring the necessity of some direct operation upon it. In the succeeding lectures we shall have to inquire whether Christianity has supplied any such force, and whether we can trace any corresponding differences in its treatment of action and motive. The question is no light or academic one. It is more even than a question involving our lives and happiness. It is in the last resort the question whether God rules and has declared Himself to the world.

NOTES TO LECTURE I.

Note 1.

Ruling Principles of Life in Classical Days.

The statements made in the lecture as to the failure and the sense of inefficiency characteristic of ancient moral history require some comment. It is proverbially hard to estimate the character of another age, to appreciate the aspect it bore to those who lived in it, and to disabuse ourselves of those prejudices and prepossessions which imperceptibly lay hold of us in consequence of our own experience and our own moral ideals. It is this difficulty which largely accounts for the various estimates which prevail of life in the classical times. To some it seems as if that age were hopelessly remote from all that we know in our own experience; to others, as if it would be nearer and more intelligible to us than any of the ages lying between. The former judgement depends in great measure upon the satirists[1]; the latter, upon an aesthetic appreciation of the beauty of classical life as it survives in the best literature. For the satirists draw attention to the most startling features of the worst side of ancient life: and we, forgetting what a Juvenal might find to say of our own age, hug the thought that we have nothing such as this in modern times. And, on the other hand, we know most of the classical period, and it would be strange indeed if we did not find many ideas in common with it.

But both these views are probably one-sided. They lay emphasis on one single aspect of ancient society without allowing for the effects of abstraction, in giving an air of unreality to what was once solid, and living, and concrete. If, however, this danger can be avoided, it may be possible to

[1] But compare the aspect of life presented in the *Metamorphoses* of Apuleius.

Note 1 to Lecture I

indicate with some approach to truthfulness the real character of ancient life and morality, and to bring out without exaggerating the points of difference between ancient moral ideas and our own.

In order to do this, it will be necessary to define beforehand, as far as may be, the features of life and speculation which are most significant of the real tendency of the people in question. It does not follow that these, whatever they are, will be the most striking at first sight. Some aspects of life will be really secondary, though they may arrest the attention and seem to be decisive. It is possible even that upon these elements the interest and success of a satire may depend. The satirist is bound by the conditions of his work to produce an impressive picture. He lashes the vices of his age, shows up its inconsistencies, and lays his chief emphasis upon the more contemptible actions of men. And this he may do either from a real moral abhorrence of what is bad or from a cynical conviction of the impossibility of all real virtue. But it does not follow that his condemnation falls on the real spot of wrong. The actions condemned may be a genuine outcome of a low moral state, or they may spring from a class which is in no way typical of the general culture of the people. And however unreservedly we accept the satirist's view of the facts, it is not necessary that our condemnation and his should be really based upon the same principles. We may agree with him in condemning a certain practice, and yet find that were we to argue upon the subject there would be little enough upon which we could come to terms.

If this is true of the evidence provided by satirists, it is no less important in estimating the evidence provided by a literature like that of Greece. Even in modern times men are apt to look away from the evil side of a picture when their aesthetic feelings are satisfied by the picturesqueness of a custom or a mode of life. We regret, for instance, in a degree far beyond reason, the destruction of ancient buildings if they look attractive, even when the retention of them means discomfort and a backward style of life to those who dwell in the neighbourhood. And if we are capable of this when our impressions could so easily be corrected by our experience, there can be no doubt that we are liable to a similar error in dealing with an age of which we can never have any direct knowledge. We attain through a literature, such as that of Greece, for instance, a view of life as it appeared to the highest minds of the day. They express themselves in terms which we can partially understand, and give voice to judgements with which we find it easy to sympathize. But there is a real danger of imagining hastily that these thoughts ran in all respects in the same groove as our own, of reading our own fundamental modern associations into our estimate of what they say, and of ignoring, in our pleasure at the beauty of the picture, the shadows and distances which are necessary to make it solid and real.

It is not enough, therefore, to note the events which they criticize or to approve the criticisms which they pass. For in both these cases we may be dealing with details and accidents, and building imaginatively upon these. We condemn and admire in the terms of the ancient writers the acts or practices which they condemned and admired, and we infer hastily that the moral judgement is identical throughout. The inference is far from being necessary. An illustration will make the point clear. All moralists condemn an act of cowardice, and by consequence commend the virtue of courage. But it is obvious, without going back into ancient days, that moralists of different schools mean very different things by their judgements, in spite of the external appearance of complete agreement. The moralist who finds the evil of cowardice in selfishness as such—in the excessive assertion by the coward of his private right to live and be free from pain —means something very different by his condemnation to that of some rival of another school, who condemns the coward because he has miscalculated the balance of ultimate pleasure and pain. Both condemn the same acts, both lay down the same rules; but their principles are different.

Hence the decision of the question, whether the ancient

Note 1 to Lecture I

systems of morality are or are not in real agreement with our own, will depend upon our ability to trace in them the real principles which underlie their appearance of agreement or disagreement, and to say whether these have or have not been modified by succeeding history. It will not matter so much whether we find or fail to find anticipations of our own judgements in ancient writers; but it will be a matter of great importance if we can detect in them the working of principles by the aid of which we can explain both the agreement and the difference between our judgements and theirs.

I. There are two ideas, widely distributed among the Greeks, which moulded their view of life in its widest sense and coloured all their expectations. These are the well-known conceptions of φθόνος or envy, and the stern, inexorable necessity which was supreme even over the will and intentions of Zeus. The first of these comes before us, for the most part, in an anthropomorphic shape in connexion with Greek theology. The gods envy those whose prosperity rivals their own, and bring them to ruin out of sheer jealousy. Such a view as this, of course, gave place at length to a less childlike conception of God and the motives of his action. But while it lasted it was a simple and unreasoned way of emphasizing the finally inexplicable character of much that happens. It meant that man cannot altogether count upon the principles which are at work in the world. He may do his best, and may seem to be successful; but he is really at work in the dark. A principle for the emergence of which he can never be wholly prepared may suddenly enter and overthrow him. Sometimes overweening insolence, as in the case of Xerxes, brings about the mischief; the failure of the most elaborate preparations is there partially explained. But failure may quite easily be due to mere jealousy at success on the part of the gods, i.e. it may be finally inexplicable. A similar result follows from the conception of the inexorable necessity of fate. That this is a naïve and childlike way of expressing the inexplicable character of much of human experience is plain from the use of it in connexion with tragic irony. From this point of view a man or a family live in the power and at the mercy of some force stronger than they. At times they are aware that they are thus under constraint to fulfil a particular destiny; at other times it breaks out and is revealed suddenly and unexpectedly. In the hands of a writer like Sophocles, a moral interest is given to the puny efforts of the individual to resist the burden of his destiny and define the course of his own life. But these are the signs of a change in the conception of God: they betray a spirit of revolt against the naïve admission of irrationality which the ancient stories themselves make in regard of life as a whole. The passionate interest of the Oedipus Tyrannus is due to the genius of Sophocles; the story itself is a revolting legend, the existence of which can only be explained by reference to a course of ideas which was already disappearing.

The substitution of a more reasoned and reasonable belief in an inexorable destiny for the simpler conviction of envy in God made but little difference in the final drift of the religious idea. In whatever terms it may be expressed, it means that in the end there is nothing to be said about things except that they happen. Epictetus, or some other convinced Stoic, may feel that he has no cause to complain of the arrangement of the world[1]: that he is merely an individual, and has, therefore, only an individual interest in it and knowledge of it. But this grim acceptance of hard facts is a concealed way of asserting that they have no explanation. If it is obvious that, in a world containing many men, interests must conflict and every one cannot be comfortable, still it is not explained why the world, if made at all, was not made better[2].

These ideas, then, which cover between them a large area of Greek thought, are symptoms of an underlying sense of

---

[1] Cf. Epict. *Diss.* I. i. 11.

[2] The rejection of all order whatever, as by the Epicureans, and the ascription of all events to chance, differs rather in frankness than in philosophical cogency from fatalism. To deny all rational order in things is a candid assertion that the world is an insoluble enigma. And sheer

Note 1 to Lecture I

irrationality pervading the whole scheme of things. They explain the ring of genuineness which sounds in the ancient lamentations over the shortness of life and the ceaselessness of change. They show that the risk which was felt in praying for any definite object[1] sprang from a real and widespread uncertainty as to the meaning of life at all. Men felt themselves in the hands of a power greater than they, of which the movements could be registered as fact, but not explained.

II. Not only is life in its general character incapable of control or explanation, but there is to the Greek mind an element in it which is productive of surprise and painful disaster. This element is passion. Without being wholly and irretrievably evil, passion is still a dangerous and subversive force. It throws off rational control and hurries the man into action which he deplores in cooler moments. Closely connected with passion is pleasure; and this too is a mysterious factor in experience, which can be estimated only, according to Plato, in terms of more and less[2]. It is always an element in our calculations, always present in our estimate of things. And it leads men into mischief or charms them away from virtue, even when their minds are set towards the right. Against all such things it was necessary to be on guard. And yet so predominant was the influence of pleasure in life that some made it actually the test of right and wrong, defining it variously. It was manifestly a thing of which it was necessary to take account; a life from which it was wholly ejected would be impoverished and deformed; but it was always just in connexion with passion and pleasure that the practical ordering of life was hardest. There is generally a sense of anxiety in the discussions of the philosophers when

---

fatalism offers no real answer to the riddle. It affirms the close interconnexion of all mundane events: but it has nothing more to say of them.
'I heard one voice from all the three
We know not, for we spin the lives of men
And not of gods, and know not why we spin.'
(Tennyson, *Demeter*, p. 19.)

[1] Cf. Plato, *Laws*, p. 687; Juv. *Sat.* x. 346 and following.
[2] Plat. *Phil.* p. 24 B, 27 E.

they reach this point. It is essentially the unmanageable element in life.

There are signs in various regions that the temptation to excess in passion was a very real and pressing one to the Greeks. Perhaps the most conspicuous is to be found in the history and influence of the principle μηδὲν ἄγαν in Greek moral thought. Its first and most obvious application connects it with passion and indulgence in pleasure. It is an exhortation to moderation and reserve belonging to the proverbial stage of moral thought. As such it would guide ordinary men of the world in their desires and enjoyments. But its significance does not stop here. The idea, or rather the ideal, of moderation or reserve affects the whole of Greek moral and intellectual life. It was one eminently suited to the genius of an artistic people, and is perhaps one cause of the charm of their art. But when it is taken in connexion with the uncertainties and mystery of life, it gives rise to a most startling attitude to life as a whole. The danger of excess in all regards is strongly impressed upon the minds of men; but it is not easy always, in the darkness which overhangs the region of moral activity, to say what is and what is not the due measure. Hence, in view of the strange calamities which befall men in life, we find so sober and religious a poet as Sophocles condemning the folly of wishing to live long, and declaring that the best of all lots is never to be born at all [1]. Nor is this a mere isolated expression required by the dramatic situation; it recurs in various forms, and is clearly characteristic of the thought of the writer. The almost despairing resignation of all attempts to solve the problem appears most strikingly in Stoicism. The brutal savagery of the Cynic, as represented in Diogenes, belongs to a paradoxical and eccentric type of mind which we need not regard as conveying much instruction. But the Stoic who adapted cynical principles to something like a human life is under the same sense of uncertainty and confusion that has been noticed in Sophocles. He is aware of the danger and ruinous results of excess in passion—of giving way to the

[1] *O. C.* 1210 seqq.

Note 1 to Lecture I

impulses which lead to the satisfaction of desire. But he has no criterion by which he can decide the right measure in such matters. He has no ideal of life, to fall short of which is to display a maimed and imperfect humanity; he is blindly and perforce contented with what is. He does not forbid enjoyment, but in view of the extreme improbability of satisfaction and the risk of all experiments, he strongly recommends his followers to dispense with all that is 'indifferent.'

It will not be worth while to heap up instances of so very familiar a Stoic doctrine, but for the present purpose it may be well to recall the treatment by Seneca of the passion of anger—that is, the treatment of anger by a philosopher who, though he was not a Greek, was imbued with thoroughly Greek ideas. In his treatise on the subject Seneca displays an entire incapacity to deal with the problems raised by anger. He does not really distinguish between the true and the false occasions for it, and ends by condemning it altogether from sheer inability to decide when and how it should be manifested. He says many beautiful things: if it be not irreverent to say so, the book is a mine of respectable quotations, but the real moral duty of anger has escaped his notice; he is afraid to encourage a passion of which the excess is so unfortunate. Against so forcible and incalculable a power as passion, nothing but total abstinence will prevail.

The Stoics represent in all probability the high-water mark of Greek moral speculation. And their views on points such as this are fairly typical. The Epicureans, as is well known, differed from the Stoics far more in the philosophical account they gave of things than in their practical precepts, and on this head these later sects preserved the traditional attitude. Plato applies his principle ϵἰς ἓν πράττει to the exclusion of everything from the ideal state but the barest necessities; and Aristotle, who does his best to defend the existence of the ordinary man of the world, is driven by his logic to the point of saying that this civil life is second to the ideal life of contemplation from which all that belongs to passion—all that depends upon the composite nature—has been excluded.

It would be possible to work out these few hints in much greater detail than has been done here. But this is the less necessary from the fact that the ground is very familiar and the facts cited quite obvious. It is necessary, however, to enforce in the light of them the statements made in the beginning. All the notions which have been quoted are of a general character; i.e. they relate to the general aspect under which human life was conceived. And therefore if it should appear that they differ considerably from modern notions of similar range, it would be necessary to infer a more or less fundamental difference of outlook. It is not like observing the difference between the *customs* of two ages, or the moral judgements over which change of mere custom can be supposed to have influence. The prevalence of these ideas means that upon all human life there rested a cloud of perplexity and failure. Men aimed high and thought deeply, but their speculations and hopes were vitiated by their limitation within the sphere of social and political experience; and this is another way of saying what has been already asserted in Lect. I. These thinkers, from the necessity of their position, misconceived the nature and value of ethical speculation, and were unable to enforce the generalizations they attained upon the human will, owing to the incalculable element of passion. They were without the guidance which comes from a view of human life in its true perspective in relation to its wider possibilities and its spiritual end[1]. The survival into modern times of principles and ideas such as those here described is almost always directly traceable to the continuance or the renascence of pagan ideas[2].

---

[1] Plat. *Pol.* p. 277 : Κινδυνεύει γὰρ ἡμῶν ἕκαστος ὥσπερ ὄναρ εἰδὼς ἅπαντα, πάντ' αὖ πάλιν ὥσπερ ὕπαρ ἀγνοεῖν.

[2] See Lecture VII.

Note 2 to Lecture I

NOTE 2.

'The true spirit of Judaism was enshrined in the Law.'

IT is perhaps a presumptuous thing to make any statement whatever as to the significance and order of the various elements in the Old Testament. It will be desirable therefore to lay down from the first that neither in Lecture I nor in the present note is any attempt made to review, still less to revise, the critical analysis of the Old Testament books. But in many cases this criticism is largely literary, and therefore concerns chiefly the actual history of the books themselves. Hence it may be possible to say something, without presumption, as to the effect upon our notions of Judaism of some modern researches. It is hoped that this will support and give clearness to the position adopted in the Lecture.

I. The chief difference between Jewish and pagan religions lies in the character of God, and not in the method by which He was approached. It is true that of the various religious practices which were followed by the neighbouring pagan peoples, only a certain number were authorized for the chosen people. There were limits, for instance, imposed upon the methods of seeking the will of Jehovah: certain types of magic and sorcery were forbidden, and human sacrifice was indirectly excluded. But prayer and sacrifice were for the Israelite, as for every other human being in the earlier stages of religion, the normal method of approaching God.

It is by no means a modern view that this was so. Several of the patristic writers, to whom all modern critical views would have appeared strange, are aware that there was a large element of concession to weakness in the Jewish ordinances. The early Christians were met by the two facts that the actual slaughter of victims, for instance, had ceased to be performed in the Church, and that the sacrifices of Jews and Gentiles presented many remarkable coincidences. Their sense of the continuity of Christianity with Judaism made it necessary for them to find an explanation of this circumstance. The generally preparatory character of the Jewish dispensation gives the key to the position. In some sense the Jewish sacrifices are explained and abrogated in the Christian order. But the exact form in which this truth was expressed varied somewhat. Some fathers saw in the particular details of the sacrificial code the outward form of a mystical system of religion and morality. This had been characteristic of Philo's exposition, and is followed by Origen[1] and by Augustine[2]. The allegorical method got rid of the difficulty caused by the apparent triviality of many of the enactments. As bare facts they had no importance, and it would be impossible to suppose that inspired writers should have recounted them for their own sake; as media of instruction they had their place. The difficulty of this view is that it does not adequately account for the historical facts of Jewish history: the moral instruction could have been conveyed without any actual historical presentation of the Law. But this objection does not lie against the other method of dealing with the Jewish dispensation. According to this view the Pentateuchal legislation was given because of the weakness and hardness of the heart of the people. According to Irenaeus[3], the Decalogue was to have sufficed for the people; but their immediate defection to an idolatrous worship showed their incapacity for so lofty a religion, and the sacrificial order was therefore instituted. St. Irenaeus cites in defence of this view the words of Ezekiel (xx. 25): 'I gave them statutes that were not good, and judgements whereby they should not live.' A similar view is expressed somewhat obscurely in the Epistle of Barnabas (ch. iv. § 8). The doctrine that the ceremonial law was a concession (without special reference to the scene of the calf-worship) occurs in Tertullian[4], and is

[1] *De Princ.* IV. 18.
[2] *C. Faust.* XII. chs. 38–40: where the authority of Philo is quoted.
[3] *Adv. Haer.* IV. 14–21.   [4] *Adv. Marc.* II. 18.

Note 2 to Lecture I

common in Chrysostom and Theodoret[1]. Both these methods of interpreting Judaism assume that it needs explanation, and the second, which is perhaps the most common, admits a considerable degree of kinship between Jewish and pagan religions.

Thus the Jews, acting in the way which all nations who had any religion at all would have been able to understand, sacrificed and prayed to their God; but they derived a very different result from it from any existing elsewhere in the ancient world. They approached God in the same way, but the God to whom they drew near was different. This method of approach is constant through all the history of the Jews. In all periods, under all the various conditions of their existence, we hear of sacrifices being offered as the natural and due means of approaching God and entering into communion with Him. In the earlier days of the patriarchs, throughout the period of the ministry of Moses, in the times of Judges and Kings, sacrifice was constant and natural. This does not mean that the central sanctuary at Jerusalem was always the rule or even the ideal of the Jewish people: upon this point the verdict of criticism may be accepted; but the fact remains that sacrifice existed as a practice—an obvious and necessary practice—during the whole known period of Israelitish history.

II. During the period of the prophets there is developed a strongly critical attitude towards the sacrificial method of appealing to God. The prophets are deeply moved by the thought of the holiness of God; indeed, this is to their minds the prominent divine character. They are impressed with a sense of the meaning of sin and its grave result in the separation of man from God. Life wears a deeper air of purpose and meaning than had been the case before. To their inspired prophetic glance the course of history, the whole movement of the world, depends rather upon moral considerations than anything else: even politics come to be in their minds a stage of probation on which the great issue of faithfulness or unfaithfulness to Jehovah is tried. The

---

[1] Chrys. *Adv. Jud.* IV. 6; Thdt. *Quaest. in Lev.* I.; *Graec. Aff. Cur.* VII. 16. 36. Cf. also Orig. *c. Cels.* II. 2 and 3, Hom. in Jer. v. 14.

unity of God has to be protected against the irreligious influence of polytheism. There can be no true religion, they feel, for persons who fly about from one shrine to another, in hopes of winning by flattery of one god what the capriciousness of another has denied. For the Jew there can be but one God, whose action is not governed by caprice or favour, but who has one rule and one interest in all His dealings with mankind—the desire for holiness. It is out of this sense of unity that the universalism of the prophets arises. The belief in one God who deals with all men on the same terms gradually makes the old tribal conception impossible. It seems also[1] to have led to the insistence upon a single central shrine. This was the outward, almost the sacramental, symbol of the unity of God. Hence the universalism of the prophets somewhat inevitably took the form of a general gathering of all nations to Jerusalem[2].

In contrast with this profound and spiritual conception of life, the ordinary attitude of men was light and trivial. Even their religious observances, when they were not liable to the charge of idolatry, rested upon a poor and ineffective idea of God. They thought that by ceremonial practices they could satisfy the God whom they so ignorantly worshipped. The prophets are, therefore, continually calling them away from this narrow and essentially pagan view of God to a higher one, continually reminding them that no sacrifices will avail them if they persist in a life of sin.

The very strongest language is used in condemning this abuse. The superior claims of morality are unhesitatingly asserted, and it is maintained without reserve that sacrifice in itself is of no avail whatever to bring men under the good pleasure of God. It is true that in many passages the language used seems to condemn the use of sacrifice altogether, and to put before the minds of the people a wholly 'spiritual' view of religion without any material element or form in it all. It seems as if the province of religion was to

---

[1] Cf. Wellhausen, *Proleg.* pp. 23 foll. Eng. Trans.
[2] Isa. xi. 10-16; Zech. viii. 20-23, &c.

be restricted to moral effort, and all outward manifestations to be denied to religious worship. The prophets seem to have looked not only beyond the position in which all religion then was, but beyond even the present dispensation, and to have caught a glimpse of a future in comparison with which even the vision of the Apocalypse would appear formal and exterior. Unless the interpretation which is thus hastily put upon their language be erroneous, they must seem to have anticipated the modern demand for a 'purely spiritual' religion.

It is difficult, however, not to believe that this interpretation is erroneous. In the first place, to place such a conception of religion as this in the age of the prophets is surely an anachronism. It could hardly have been expressed in any terms which the people of that day could have understood. And it must necessarily have failed hopelessly. We may doubt, indeed, whether this view of religion has ever been successful at any period of the world's history; but it certainly has formed the ideal of many Christians since the Reformation, and is often supposed to have been the guiding influence of the whole of that movement. It is probable that the transference of this conception from modern days to the age of the prophets is partly responsible for this interpretation of their language. But, as has already been said, it is difficult to see how this notion could have been made intelligible at that day. The prophets protest doubtless against the formal and ceremonial use of means in religious worship; they resent the essential frivolousness of all externalism. But it may be doubted whether they would not have assumed the continuance of sacrifice and other rites as the obvious conditions of religious worship, the abolition of which would never have been thought possible. They wrote, it is continually being pressed upon us, in the light of the problems of their own day and in terms of their own experience, and their language is only intelligible with reference to the whole of the life of their day. It is probable that the disappearance of sacrifice as an integral part of worship would never have been fully intelligible until after the Death and Resurrection of Christ. Though the use of sacrifice and such means of atonement seemed strange and inoperative to many who felt in themselves the sense of sin unrelieved, yet there was never any likelihood that the practice would disappear until the true substitute for it was found.

Secondly, there is no real inconsistency between the language of the prophets and the prevalence of ceremonial practices [1]. This is conclusively proved by the continuous prevalence of the Temple ritual in the period after the exile, which gave rise to many of the most spiritual of the Temple-psalms. The Law, for instance, so enthusiastically commended in Ps. cxix is the Levitical Law. If the extreme position be the true one, that all the Psalms as we have them come from the post-exilic age, then it will follow that all the most spiritual writings in that book must be conceived against a background of elaborate ceremonial. The Psalms of Solomon, which were a production of the years B.C. 70–40 and belong wholly to the Pharisaic party in its later days, show a continuance of the same combination. The Law and its due observance are continually alluded to: but, at the same time, the service is a spiritual and religious one—not a mere ceremonial observance [2]. In many cases it would be as difficult to infer this from the language of the Psalter as to infer the glories of the mediaeval Church from the staid severity of the *Imitatio*. In both cases the explanation is the same. The psalmists and, in their way, the prophets, like the author of the *Imitatio*, express one aspect of the life of their day, emphasize one element in their religious experience; and it is as erroneous in one case as in the other to take this one feature as exhausting their spiritual outlook [3].

[1] Cf. Prof. Cheyne, *Bampton Lectures*, p. 358, note *aa*.
[2] Cf. *Psalms of Solomon* : ed. Ryle and James, esp. p. xlix and reff.
[3] The last four verses of Ps. li. combine the spiritual and ceremonial elements in Judaism in a most striking way. If, as is frequently maintained, the last two verses are by another hand, it remains that the editor who

Note 2 to Lecture I

III. This view of the meaning of the prophetic utterances renders intelligible the state of things which followed the Captivity, to which we must now turn. The restoration of the worship of Jehovah was in reality a triumph of the prophetic spirit. The old tendency to fall away to the worship of other gods, against which the prophets had protested in vain, had been brought to an end by the lesson of the Captivity. The question for the restored Jewish nation was not so much whether Jehovah should be worshipped rather than any other deity, but *how* this worship should be ordered so as to keep its hold upon the people. This was a practical problem rising directly out of the teaching of the prophets, and it was the prophet-priest Ezekiel, according to the prevalent theory, who produced the first sketch of the new code which was to give the answer. From the time when the new order was established the disposition to lapse into heathenism was on the decline. It received a serious blow when Ezra forbids all inter-marriage with the people of the land, and is successful in carrying his prohibition into effect: and the successful revolt of the Maccabees protected the integrity of the Jewish spirit against the perilous assaults of Greek culture.

The breach of continuity caused by the Captivity makes it difficult under any circumstances to give an intelligible account of the new order. The task is made far more difficult if we are to assume that the prophets had always stood in violent antagonism to all external symbolism in religion. If that were the case, the rules devised by Ezra must be regarded as pure inventions of his own. They could have had no attractiveness to the people, and they would easily become confused with the rites of other nations; that is, they would have materially aided the result he was most anxious to defeat, the absorption of the Jewish individuality into the general mass of neighbouring peoples. For this reason alone it would seem very difficult not to hold that much of the ritual

attached them to the Psalm can have seen no inconsistency in them with the spiritual tone of vv. 1-17.

contained in the Pentateuch had a part in the consciousness of the people. It was modified, no doubt, to suit the new conditions; it was stereotyped. Different stages of it may still be traceable side by side in the written books; but still it remains that the people who were carried away captive retained enough sense of nationality to wish to come back again, and, as they owed the vitality of their national consciousness in great measure to the prophets, they would have been hardly likely to welcome a legal system devised to promote the practices which the prophets had condemned. A new code could have appealed only to a new people. Unless, therefore, the Jewish people had utterly lost all sense of their own past, the new law by which they were to live must have appealed to them through it.

And it is possible to go even further than this. The ritual enactments are archaic in type in very many cases. They go back to an extremely early period of religion; and, apart from this, many of them are inexplicable. The researches of Professor Robertson Smith have shown beyond dispute that the Levitical sacrifices are based upon ancient conceptions traceable throughout the history of the earlier Semites, and that though later ideas are found grafted on to the old sacrificial system, yet the basis of it all lies beyond the earliest history that we have of the Jewish people[1]. The relation of the sacrificial feast to the act of worship and the details of the ritual have no meaning that belongs essentially to the date of Ezra; they are explicable as being the traditional methods and assumptions of sacrifice which are adopted without question as obvious. Their presence in the code, therefore, implies a long and continuous traditional practice.

An incidental illustration of this point of view may be found in the much later writings of Philo. Philo is at considerable pains to explain the details of the Levitical Law, as men of his school had previously been at pains to explain traditional observances amongst the Greeks. In the two

[1] For the details of this argument see Robertson Smith, *The Religion of the Semites*, lects. vi, vii.

treatises, *De Animalibus* and *De Sacrificantibus*, he explains the various rules in a philosophical sense. The principles of his philosophy are set forth, he thinks, as in a figure by the sacrificial rules, and the due explanation of the sacrificial ordinance is not given till its philosophical significance is drawn out. It is not Philo's fault, though it may be his misfortune, that he had not the advantage of the anthropological explanation of these things; but it is at least remarkable that it never occurs to him to dispute or to hesitate about the reasonableness of the ordinances. They have never been questioned, and he is content with them.

So far it has been attempted merely to call attention to the continuity of the sacrificial idea through all Jewish history. This position is, of course, in no way novel. But it is important to bear in mind the significance of what has been said. The constant element in Jewish history is the presence of a priestly tradition, probably not at first written, which takes shape eventually in the Pentateuchal legislation. A more occasional element in Jewish history is the activity of the great prophets. These stand out from the prophetic class and appear as direct representatives of Jehovah, speaking immediately in His name, and giving authoritative directions as to matters of morality and politics. They at times appear in strong antagonism to the priesthood, condemn their misuse of their office, their immorality, or their avarice. But at the same time both parties alike trace their origin to Moses, and claim the respect which is due to them on that account. Both claim to stand in regard of the people as Moses stood, between them and God. The people themselves are not qualified to approach God: in one way or another an interpreter or intermediary is necessary: the true way of access is not open [1].

[1] The recently published work of Prof. Ryle on Philo's quotations from the Old Testament illustrates this point admirably. For Philo the Old Testament dispensation was contained in the Pentateuch. Far the largest number of his quotations comes from the Books of Moses. They occupy pp. 1-282 in Prof. Ryle's book, while the citations from the rest of Scripture cover only pp. 283-302. Again the Psalmist and the prophet Zechariah

This position of incomplete power of access, which is analogous to the sense of failure and perplexity so prevalent in the pagan world, is characteristic of the whole ancient dispensation, and is directly associated by St. Paul with the Law. To St. Paul's mind the disabilities involved in the legal position consist not merely in being commanded certain ceremonial practices and forbidden others, but in being commanded at all. The cases he chooses to illustrate the legal position are not the commands to sacrifice or to keep feasts, but the purely moral prohibition, 'Thou shalt not covet.' The prophets do not escape the legal position by saying, 'I hate your burnt-sacrifices; incense is an abomination to me.' Their high moral ideal has the same externality about it that belongs to the Law itself. It is imposed from without; it runs in the form of a command. And therefore it is perfectly justifiable to see in the Law—the Pentateuchal enactments of Ezra, if Ezra's they were—the most conspicuous embodiment of the most prominent characteristic of Judaism.

Hence, though the literary history of the origin of the books of the Old Testament may throw incidentally much light on the order of the ideas, yet it cannot reverse the old conception of Judaism. The Jews were, after all, the people to whom a Law was given. Though the prophetic writings may be prior in point of time, they do not alter the generally legal relation between God and man. The phrase, 'the law and the prophets,' expresses accurately the due relation between the two. The normal position of the Jew in regard of God was that of a man who had to approach his God in a particular way. And the definition of the right way was not within his reach. It had to be settled by some intermediary — priest or prophet — who revealed authoritatively what was right for him to do.

And again the evangelical value of Judaism depends not so much on the peculiar method of approach to God as on

are spoken of under the title 'one of the friends of Moses.' (Ryle, *Philo and Holy Scripture*, pp. xxvii–xxix.)

Note 2 to Lecture I

the character of God Himself. The modern reaction against ceremonialism *as such* has led to considerable misapprehension in this regard. It is true, of course, that the ceremonial law of the Jews was purged of much that lent itself to superstition. Even in cases where the ritual was archaic and ran back upon coarse and almost savage presuppositions, the coarseness and savagery were mitigated and their full results averted. For instance, in the case of the shew-bread or the sacrificial meals, where pagan deities would have been supposed to consume the food, the idea of consumption by God is absent, but the notion of communion is emphasized. But these and similar differences are really differences of detail. The decisive characteristic lies in the character of God developed to its highest by the prophets, but enshrined none the less in the Law. The love of God and His hatred of sin give their special character to the Jewish ritual and observances. The belief that God moves forward through history with a definite purpose of redemption—even though this should appear in the shape of a promise to rescue His chosen from foreign oppression—the sense that God must vindicate His righteousness openly before the world, these and the like of these are the really decisive and significant features of Judaism. The fault of Judaism lay not in the fact that it assumed a body of ceremonial ordinances, but in the fact that the thing to which all these pointed was not yet come about. The fault of the Jews lay not in the fact that they believed and rejoiced in their Law—no faithful Jew could have done otherwise—but in the fact that they evaded the true bearing of it, satisfied themselves with a mechanical following out of its precepts, and looked no further. They were right in holding that the Law was the essence and basis of Judaism, wrong in ignoring or forgetting the prophetic comment upon it, and upon the wonderful history through which their nation and its Law had come to be.

So it is that the Sermon on the Mount is rather a full statement of the full meaning of the Law than a complete breach with the legal dispensation. The Sermon reveals, as no part of the Old Testament had revealed, the nature of God and the demand it makes upon men. It declares the spirit which the external ordinances were meant to enshrine; it shows the level of obedience and the stretch of effort which God requires of men. And no one who thinks well of it as a moral code can afford to think disparagingly of the old Law; the two hang together inseparably, and form part of one providential scheme. The various strains of Jewish thought and aspiration find their true synthesis in the Law, and the final statement of the Law is to be found in the Sermon on the Mount.

LECTURE II

'Art thou he that cometh, or look we for another? And Jesus answered and said unto them, Go your way and tell John the things which ye do hear and see: the blind receive their sight, and the lame walk, the lepers are cleansed, and the deaf hear, and the dead are raised up, and the poor have good tidings preached to them. And blessed is he, whosoever shall find none occasion of stumbling in me.'—
ST. MATT. xi. 3-6 (R.V.).

LAST Sunday it was argued that there was a radical deficiency in the point of view of all ancient ethical systems. Both pagan speculation and Hebrew legalism had this point, at least, in common: that they presented a principle, or an ideal, or a code, which the will had to accept from without and put into practice as best might be. Even the Sermon on the Mount, though it transcends all previous thinkings upon the subject, runs still in the form of a law, and still leaves us, therefore, in face of the question how this law is to be obeyed. The question before us to-day is whether the ethical conceptions which sprang up together with Christianity supply any means of meeting the difficulties in which earlier speculations had left us.

I must first call attention again to certain points which we have already had occasion to notice. There was, we observed, a general consensus of opinion among ancient moralists in favour of believing in a moral ideal. The speculations of Greeks seemed almost of necessity to lead up to this conception, and it was the method in which they expressed to themselves their views of right and wrong. Further, various aspects of life were fixed upon as being the essential ones to every well-ordered character; men were exhorted to find their highest good in knowledge, in pleasure, in virtue, and so on. None of these intuitions were wholly wrong, however inadequate we may find them to have been. Knowledge *is* essential to all good life, because man is essentially a rational being. Pleasure *is* a constant element in all action, and every action is in some way affected by it. Virtue *is* obviously and necessarily associated with the highest life of a moral being. And among the various possibilities which human conditions offer, we should naturally anticipate that one way of self-adaptation to them would be better than all the others. We may, therefore, look to find all these preliminary efforts reconciled and confirmed in the true system of Ethics.

But as we pass into the region of the Gospels, we seem to change into a wholly different atmosphere from anything that has been familiar in Greek or even in Old Testament literature. Not only are such questions as those just named wholly absent, but there is extraordinarily little of positive moral exhortation in the Gospels. The Synoptic Gospels—to speak of them first—give a short and fragmentary account of the life of our Lord as it appeared to His contemporaries in Galilee. The events are not precisely defined in regard of time, and we cannot say exactly of how many of the days of our Lord's life we know anything at all; we may be sure that it is a very small number. There are discourses. There is the Sermon on the Mount, for instance, and some others more or less connected in character. But the longest, with the one exception of the Sermon, are occupied with parables of the kingdom, the charge to the apostles, and the eschatological discourse in the week of the Passion. They deal incidentally with moral questions; and they are used, of course, as an armoury of ethical precepts. But their first and most obvious meaning is governed by the circumstances out of which they arose. They have permanent moral value because our Lord always opened up the permanent moral meaning of the events upon which He made comment. He encourages or reproves some one with whom He is brought in contact; and His words display a profound intelligence of the ways of human wills, and we learn principles of wide application from them. Besides these there are histories of acts of healing and mercy, now and again containing some reflection upon the scene of distinctly ethical import. In the peculiar parts of St. Luke's Gospel especially we find searching comments upon life; and it is in St. Luke that the more profound moral problems are touched: such, for instance, as that of the victims of the fall of the tower of Siloam. But when all allowances have been made, the three Synoptic Gospels remain predominately historical, and there is comparatively little to be found in them of positive moral instruction, except in so far as the historical events give rise to it.

The Gospel of St. John preserves in large measure the historical character of the other three Gospels; the discourses described in it seem always to be primarily explicable out of the events which occasioned them, and are never purely speculative discussions which have no contact with actual history. But, of course, they enter far more profoundly than any of those in the Synoptic Gospels into the secret springs of moral action, and they come nearer to a systematic discussion of ethical problems. This is especially noticeable in regard of the contrast between Faith and Unbelief. Our Lord is continually dealing with this opposition and exposing its hidden grounds. But this, it must be remembered, is just one of the moral questions which the circumstances in which our Lord was placed forced forward most conspicuously. It arose whenever His claims were confronted with opposition, or He was required to produce credentials. He never deals directly with such demands, but explains instead the moral conditions of faith and its opposite. Thus the occasional character of our Lord's Discourses which we have noticed in the Synoptists is preserved in the Fourth Gospel.

Now all this means that the important element in the Gospels, from our present point of view, is the life historically described, rather than the moral precepts which emerged in the course of it. The discourses, the warnings, the prophecies, precepts, prayers, all have their place in the story in virtue of their relation to the life which is the central thread of them all. They all illustrate the mode in which Christ dealt with the circumstances in which He was placed, and therefore indicate indirectly the way in which the disciple should expect to be as his Master. Thus the life of Christ is presented historically, and is, as it stands, an embodiment of a moral ideal. The object of the compilation of these various collections of anecdote was to bring the force of His example to bear upon the minds and hearts of those who knew Him but by hearsay—to preserve the memory of that which all must regard as an ideal life. It is an ideal—and in this regard the old craving for a moral ideal was met and justified—but it was not an imaginative picture, drawn by the hand of genius on the model of actual experience; it was the historical account of one who lived and was active and died in definite historical conditions.

At first sight it might seem as if this were the real distinction between Christian and pre-Christian ethics, that in the one case the ideal was imaginary—a poetic construction for prosaic people to realize : while in the other the ideal began by being historic—presented in prosaic conditions enough—and only interpreted in its real significance by later hands. And thus we might be inclined to argue that the Sermon on the Mount might so be separated finally from all its pre-Christian forerunners, in that it was spoken with the living voice, and sealed by the death, of the Man in whom the ideal was actually embodied. But this impression would not last long. If the imaginary ideals of ancient days failed by being external to the will, the evangelical ideal would not succeed by being historical. The ideal figure of the Gospels might command more ready submission, by its simplicity and its unblemished perfection, but he would be a bold man who would embark unaided on the enterprise of imitating it. Do we not hear from time to time complaints made of the inaccessible heights to which the imitation of Christ would lead us, the impossibility of combining it with any serious attention to the ordinary interests of life? Is it not constantly maintained that harm is done by insisting upon so lofty a conception of right? that effort is paralyzed and progress checked by the constant presence of a notion of good and a rule of action quite beyond the power of man to fulfil? It would require more even than the telling fact that the ideal had been actually embodied to make it effective as the inspiration of the will.

Let us, then, look back again upon the history of the life of Christ, to see if any light is thrown by it upon the source of Christ's own power. He certainly makes no secret of it. It is by the finger of God that He casts out devils. It is His union with the Father who sent Him that accounts for and justifies all that He does. His last acts, His death upon the cross, are that the world may know that He loved the Father, and that as the Father gave Him commandment, even so He did. It was an exceptional relation that He claimed with the Father in heaven, and He claimed it throughout. It is suggested by the distinctive use of the phrase 'My Father'; it is asserted in His claim to be about His Father's business, in the parallel which He draws between the Father's ceaseless work and His own action in regard of the sabbath-law. It is put forward in the most startling way to the Jews in the words, 'I and the Father are one'; and to the chosen band of followers in the discourses on the last evening. And not only does He rest His account of His own power upon this basis; He also, on the other hand, condemns all self-imposed tasks which are not ultimately traceable to God. The Jews, He says, only understand the work of men who come in their own name—men who know not whence they come and whither they go; for these seek their own glory in a manner which those who do the same can easily understand: neither they nor their followers understand or care for the glory which cometh from the only God. So the whole course of His life, strange and hard and cruel as its conditions must have seemed to those who falteringly followed Him, is to Him sane and orderly and intelligible. He knows that He must suffer—knows that in the most obvious and material sense His mission must seem to fail. He looks forward to the future and sees the fortunes of His followers throughout the ages, and knows that their fate will in many respects resemble His. Therefore He warns them beforehand in the fullness of His knowledge, that when it happens they may remember, and not think it different from the regular and determined order which by the Father's will had governed His life. His whole course, with its achievement and its failure, as we speak, was explicable by reference to the Father's will.

The ideal figure of the Gospels differs from its ancient Greek precursors in being an attained, realized, historical ideal. The point last touched upon marks the difference between the Jewish moral consciousness and that which followed upon the appearance of Christ. The Jew, I pointed out last time, was for ever haunted with the impossibility of attaining to that spiritual communion with God for which his soul longed. And he knew that the cause of his failure was his sin. Christ was wholly independent of any such sense of failure. He shows no sign of any apprehension of error on His own side. The Son of Man goeth as has been determined. The prince of this world comes and has his hour of temporary triumph; but that is a thing to which Christ consciously and voluntarily gives way. It comes from no failure on His part—no mistake made by Him. He possesses, and has never lost, the perpetual consciousness of the Father's good pleasure. In the passage of strong emotion at the visit of the Greeks; in the agony in the garden; even when He takes upon His lips on the cross the awful words of dereliction from Ps. xxii—at the last pass, when the task of bearing the whole burden of the world's sin is almost over, and He has to face the horror of death under the conditions of sinful humanity —He expresses Himself in terms which involve a filial relation to the Father, and He dies committing His soul into that Father's keeping. Thus His sense of constant communion with the Father satisfies the anticipations and fulfils the hopes of the most spiritual among the Jews, or rather proves the possibility of such satisfaction; just as the historical character of His self-manifestation gets rid of the difficulty which always presses upon the ideals of the imagination, the doubt whether they are possible or not.

In the life of Christ, therefore, the conception of an ideal moral figure reaches its climax; the conditions of life are fully satisfied, and the whole spirit of the Law is embodied in it. The dispensation of externalism is explained and completed, and the new hope is raised that success may attend man's efforts instead of failure. An instance of true human obedience is now before the world, and men have at least that example to look to in their own lives. But still the history occurred in a definite place and time. The occasions which Christ had to meet were His own, and can never be precisely repeated. And, on the other hand, other men's lives are peculiar to them. Their circumstances and temptations are all their own: the plan of action which will suit one man will not suit another; the appeal which will affect one character fails wholly of its effect on another mind. The example of Christ must be translated into terms that all men can use throughout all time; the principles displayed in the various actions recorded must be laid bare; or it will sink back into the remoteness of mere past history, fainter in outline, requiring continually more elaborate study to keep it alive, as the years go on. And thus a new question arises, for the answer to which we must again look back to the records: Is there any force in existence which will preserve our ideal from fading away with age and losing hold upon our lives?

In speaking to the Jews of His communion with the Father, Christ always expresses Himself negatively. It is because they have no knowledge of, or true relation with the Father that they fail so hopelessly to understand the mission of Christ. He explains that as He declares in His actions His union with the Father, so they declare by theirs a lack of affinity with all divine things. But to the apostles in the last hours He speaks in very different terms. His state of constant communion with the Father is to be understood and partly, at least, attained by them after He has gone and the other Advocate is come. The Spirit of Truth will come, and will dwell within them, and will interpret their experience of Christ's earthly mission, will recall its details and explain the future, and will relieve the separation which at present pains them, and will be the medium of the realization of complete communion between God and them. Christ recognizes, in other words, the necessity of some application and extension of His life and work, of some link between it and the world in which its scene was laid. Its full power to help is not attained even in the experience of Christ's closest followers; it is to come when their weakness and half-knowledge is under the strong ruling of the Spirit of Truth. Then they will know, then they will experience the union of which at present they have seen only the outward signs, for they will be bound together by the Spirit in a unity of which the unity of the Father and the Son is the archetype.

This profound and precise teaching, which we find in St. John, is in harmony with the drift of the other Gospels. It explains the careful selection and trial of those who were to be the means by which the new truth was to be spread over the world. It explains, as has often been pointed out before, the gradual withdrawal of Christ from the crowds, His steady repression of their undisciplined enthusiasm, His anxious efforts to educate and discipline His followers[1]. He wanted something stronger than thoughtless admiration and unawakened partisanship. A new power was to be put into the hands of men, a new kingdom was to be founded, and a special character was required for the work. Christ might marvel at the faith of the Roman centurion—greater than any He had found in Israel— but it was not upon that that He built His Church. And His action is a practical comment upon the parables of the kingdom, with their emphasis on variety of character, on selection, on the gradual extension of the truth by regular growth from the centre where it was first planted.

Thus the tendency of Christ's teaching is to concentrate attention upon His own nature and the source of His moral activity. He represents Himself as acting in the power and under the direct ruling of the Spirit of God: and in regard of the future, He does not exhort so much as promise; He does not demand

[1] Cf. Holland, *Creed and Character*, Sermons iii. and iv.; Latham, *Pastor Pastorum*; especially chs. viii. and ix.

particular services so much as give assurance of general powers.

If I have been right in thus describing our Lord's work, and in the explanation I have given of His charge to His disciples, it becomes clear that the real centre of investigation into the ethical import of Christ's life must be transferred from the Gospel story to the time after Pentecost. It was then, when the promised outpouring of the Spirit came upon the Church, that the practical significance of Christ's life could be traced in the life of men; it was then, and not before, that the moral ideal He had set up before men's eyes could be made available for them. Before this His closest followers had found out only part of His secret; He was different, indeed, from themselves, with special relations to the Father in heaven, but living and acting and expressing Himself under conditions similar to their own. But His Resurrection and subsequent departure, together with the Mission of the Holy Ghost, changed everything for them. They were no longer weak and hesitating and puzzled, but they were ready to lay down decisively what was right and wrong in the interpretation of their commission, to explain precisely what it was they had to set forth, and so to start with clear and set purpose upon the conversion of the world.

At first there is an almost monotonous simplicity about the subject of their preaching. They preach simply Jesus. They are witnesses of His Resurrection. The single phrase, Jesus is Lord, seems to be the sum total of their creed. They baptize all who propose to join them without exception, even though in one case the Holy Spirit has already fallen upon the converts; they continue in breaking of bread and in prayer; they affirm their separation from worldly interests by community of goods, and by enduring persecution; and by degrees they spread the knowledge of that which they believe over a wide area. They seem to be filled with a new force of gladness and of hope, and they are convinced beyond all doubt that the faith which they teach, centering in Jesus Christ, is sufficient to save mankind. Moreover, their opponents recognize that their inspiration runs back in some sense upon the Crucified; they complain that the apostles will, if they are not silenced, bring this man's blood upon them. And so the new departure dates somehow from the life and work of Christ.

It would be tedious, and is unnecessary here, to trace the steps by which the various dogmatic and practical elements of the life I have just sketched separate themselves and become distinct. But without passing beyond the apostolic age, it will be easy to illustrate some of the ways in which these elements were brought to bear on practical life. The simple fact is declared first—the absolute sufficiency of the life and death and resurrection of Christ; and this is soon, but later, made articulate and explicit and applied to the practical needs of life.

I. The first point requiring consideration, in logical order, is the nature of Christ Himself. Who is He that His life and death should have such power? The answer is really given in that phrase already quoted, the assertion of which St. Paul restricts to those who speak in the power of the Holy Ghost—Jesus is Lord. This phrase seems (to judge from the use of the word Κύριος) to identify Jesus, in some way not as yet further defined, with the Lord Jehovah—the God of the old Covenant; and it is evidently a formula upon which a great deal turns. As the process of reflexion went on, and the necessities of controversy forced forward the need of definiteness, this identification expressed itself in the belief in Christ's mediatorial functions as between God and man. He had removed the barrier of sin which man had erected, and reopened the way of access from man to God. He had done what the Law could not do: He had obeyed, and made obedience possible. And all this came to pass in virtue of His unique relation to the Father, of His mediatorial position in regard of the whole scheme of things. Though identified in nature with God, He is not to be merged into the Being of God. He is the Image of the invisible God, in whom all things have their system; He is the Word, through Whom all things were made, Who by His coming in the likeness of sinful flesh has declared beyond all mistake or possibility of error the invisible God. Because He is all this, and because He has of right and necessity and nature the position of mediator between God and man, it was for Him, and for none other, to remove the disabilities of man by becoming man. The apostles, in accordance with their Jewish training, look upon sin as the real source of all man's failure, and therefore any account of things that shall satisfy them must be adequate to deal with this. It is the coincidence between the half-complete faith which they won through the intercourse with Christ, and the flood of light which this belief, when quickened and confirmed, throws upon all human life, that strengthens them in their preaching. They speak from sheer necessity that which they know.

The evidence for all this, to the mind of St. Paul, lay in the certainty of the Resurrection. This was the illuminating fact which brought into the clearest possible light the nature of Christ and the significance of His work. The prophet who was born of the seed of David, according to the flesh, was declared to be Son of God through the Resurrection. It was that fact that confirmed the impressions the apostles had already formed of their Master, which sealed His life and work with the good pleasure of God, and it was of that fact that they all were witnesses. And it was the ground of their conviction that the old order had passed away and a new period had opened. 'If Christ has not risen, ye are yet in your sins.'

It is St. Paul who lays most emphasis on the fact of the Resurrection, St. John on the fact of the manifestation of the Word in flesh, but both alike regard the work of Christ as forming a turning-point in the history of man. Morally speaking, the whole position of man is changed by the Incarnation and Resurrection. New possibilities are opened to him in this world, he has new certainty and a new interest in the next. Up to this date the purpose of life had been obscure, the future of man largely uncertain. Life had to be taken as it came, as an accepted fact, and made the best of from that point of view. But to the apostles, the Incarnation to a great extent rationalized and made it intelligible. Man was now brought into a true relation with God; death was annihilated, and man had attained a real and certain hold upon immortality. The very idea of life had now a wider range, and offered a wider field, therefore, for man's speculation. Christ had seemed to fail just like other men, but His followers knew that this was a false account of His life, because He had risen and revealed by His rising a whole new world of life. So that in order to understand the reality of His success, the whole view of life had to be shifted, and the presence of a new force admitted. Spiritual realities had to be considered as part of the ordinary furniture of man's life, things as necessary and obvious in all human judgement and activity, as the most indispensable facts of nature and society. Otherwise the old standards remained minatory, relentless, inaccessible as before.

II. Closely allied to this new conception of life, and rising out of the belief in Christ's relation with the Father, there came a new idea of the relation of man and God. The account of Christ's teaching in St. John's Gospel is specially marked by the insistence made upon the revelation of the Father. The Father is described as being practically unknown before, and revealed to those who would hear through the acts and words of Christ. Again, one of the promises made by Christ to His apostles in the last discourses is that the Father will love them and make His abode with them, and that the Spirit will continue the revelation of the Father thus begun. To know Christ is to know the Father : 'He that hath seen Me hath seen the Father.' A similar doctrine, asserted in a different set of circumstances, is found in St. Paul. St. Paul speaks of the return of men from the state of enmity in which they had previously lived to that of sonship. God is no longer a slave-master before whom men must crouch in fear ; He is known through Christ as the true Father of man, in relation to whom we stand in the privileged position of sons. The presence of this conviction alters all our methods of approach. We have boldness : we pray readily and naturally, trusting to the Spirit to interpret; we are easily able to understand even trouble and persecution, for it is but natural that a Father should chasten His children in His love ; we trust God against appearances—even when He seems to forsake or neglect us—because He is our Father, and because there is no power that can separate us from His love. He has commended His love towards us by sending His Son in due time, according to His pre-determined plan and counsel; we understand Him again ; He sees us in His Son, and our faith justifies us.

III. The two points I have just named bear on the general conditions of human life. But the effect of the new faith was not confined to these general conditions, it passed on and dealt with narrower questions of ordinary practice. The new facts which had entered into our human sphere through the life of Christ had freed us from sin's rule, and not only that, but also from the terror of the Law. Here then arises a question. Does the new position mean absolute freedom to do exactly as we like, or must we still be governed by the moral law? St. Paul, St. Peter, and St. John answer this question practically in the same way. The man who has accepted the new position cannot sin; not because anything that he does will be accepted before God, but because the Spirit of God Himself has come upon him and taken command over his life. Thus one function of the Holy Spirit in man is to guide his ethical life and affect his practice. And this indwelling of the Spirit, from the ethical point of view, has two chief characters. It forms a new spring of ethical activity; it is the actual means by which moral life is made possible—the way in which the life and example of Christ is applied to the individual soul. And it sharpens the perceptions of the conscience, thus bringing new moral ideas into view and widening the range of old ones. The idea of sin, for the person who is under the control of the Spirit, is defined not by any popular or legal standard, but by that which God calls sinful. The moral life is determined from within; the spirit of the man, moving harmoniously with the Spirit of God, is expressed in the form of a distinct moral character. The flesh, the principle of selfishness, transiency, discord, is subdued, and the fruit of the Spirit in all its various forms becomes manifest in consequence. Thus no Christian need suffer, or ought to suffer at the hands of the law, as an evil-doer; he is excluded from that by his Christian profession: so far, at any rate, he must satisfy the conditions of human society. If beyond that he is persecuted for his faith, that is not his concern; he may count it all joy. Moreover, the type of life which is set before the Christian as his ideal is indifferently described as the work of the Spirit, and as the interpretation of the example of Christ. The mind of Christ Jesus in which He emptied Himself, and was found in fashion as a man, not thinking it a thing to be grasped at to be equal with God, is the more excellent way of love, itself a fruit of the Spirit's guidance, which seeks not its own.

Under the influence of the Holy Spirit the whole notion of morality has moved inwards. The range of duty is not less precisely defined than before. But, as compared with the Law, the moral code of the New Testament tends to be positive in strictly moral regions where the Law was on the whole negative—repressive of instincts, preservative of rights—and to be negative or indifferent over all that ceremonial area which occupied so large a space in the ancient legislation. Further, the author of the Epistle to the Hebrews sees no limit to the possible adaptations of the new faith to circumstances. In times of exceptional trouble and alarm, he is confident that the faith of Christ will satisfy any demand that may be made upon it, and remain permanent whatever else may change.

IV. One further point there is which is of considerable importance. In speaking of ancient Greek moral systems, I mentioned the fact that in one class of them man was regarded as essentially a social being. This point of view reappears in Christianity. Man is treated as being always in some social relation with his fellows, and the strongest possible metaphor is used to express this unity—that of a body and its members. We see this conception of Christian unity arising in the Acts, we watch it in the Epistles, growing in intensity and definiteness; but we notice throughout that it concentrates itself upon the union of the Body with Christ the Head, and that it belongs essentially to the spiritual order. It is within this unity that the Spirit operates, giving to each his separate function; and this unity is the normal moral environment of every Christian soul. It is into this unity that every one is baptized, and the fact of admission supplies one important motive to moral action. Because we are thus baptized into the Death and Resurrection of Christ, we cannot sin. Because we are members one of another, we must put away lying, and speak every man truth with his neighbour. Because we partake of the loaf and of the cup of the Lord, the visible expression of our unity, we must examine ourselves and not come unwarily. These sacraments and this social organism—the city of God —form the new moral environment of man and illustrate its new significance. They emphasize the fact that man's life is a spiritual thing, of spiritual significance, so that his acts, however they may be regarded in the world, cannot be exhaustively judged within that limit. And this means not merely that when death is over the events of this life will be brought up against the man to his glory or his discomfiture. Such a separation of this life from the next is not scriptural. It means that man now and here lives his true life in a spiritual atmosphere, in a spiritual society. The springs of his life rise in heaven, where Christ is: and there too is to be found the goal of all his striving. But on earth no less than in heaven this same society exists and operates, transcending all the human bases of division that exist here, political or national, unmodified in its absolute unity, even by the impenetrable veil of death [1].

I must now attempt to focus the discussion of these two lectures, and define the differentia of Christian Ethics. It is manifest that all philosophy of whatever kind depends for its character upon its data. The theory or system which results from the philosophical process consists in an ordered statement of the facts taken into consideration. The difficulty attaching to ethical philosophy under the old conditions was, that it stated as its final results propositions which are obviously not an accurate or complete counterpart of moral facts, and was unable to suggest a means of realizing even these partial rules. The Law itself, though it came with divine authority, and was supported upon the highest sanctions, failed to produce the effect it contemplated. Christianity meets this difficulty not

[1] I am well aware that in thus describing the characteristics of the Christian Church in apostolic times, I must have seemed to assume unwarrantably a particular view of many disputed questions. But I venture to urge that the positions assumed which seriously affect the general doctrine are questions of criticism, relating mostly to the dates and authorship of books. It would be impossible for me, even if I were capable of doing so, to argue out these questions—which for my purpose are but side issues—ὅπως μὴ τὰ πάρεργα τῶν ἔργων πλείω γίγνηται. I have, however, endeavoured to avoid forcing the language of those books which the best information at my disposal enables me to regard as genuine and canonical.

by inventing a new theory, but by introducing a new life The previous failure was due not so much to faults of speculation as to a narrowed experience of life. Man's life was practically bound down to the space between the cradle and the grave, or at most closed by a hazy vision of a shadow-world beyond. And this narrow experience of life was due again to no fault of speculation, to no lack of care, or insight, or circumspection, but to an actual injury to life itself, a positive deformity which separated it from its true ideal, narrowed its outlook to its manifestations in the material world, and therefore left philosophy to form its ideals on incomplete data. But it is on the basis of a new life introduced and active in the world that all Christian ethical theory is erected. The human life under discussion is a fuller thing than had been supposed before, the area of human action is enlarged so as to take in the whole spiritual world, and a new certainty and clearness of meaning has been given to it. Christ has come into the world bringing the new life with Him, and it is to this that He endeavours to draw attention. So His moral teaching is fullest in His earliest days, and it sifts out of the crowd those who are capable of moving further. So far from trying by degrees to get a wider audience for His words, as the preacher of a new theory might have done, He draws away, as we have noticed, from the crowds and concentrates Himself by degrees upon the education of the disciples; even with them He continually asserts the preliminary character of all that He has to say, and points forward to a day when all that is obscure will be explained. His object is to let them see into the source and nature of His life. This view explains the fact, also, that the apostles in their epistles lay emphasis not on the words of Christ's teaching—think how few the certain references to His words are—but are anxious about those points which most definitely give evidence of the entry of the new life and the abrogation of the old—the Crucifixion and the Resurrection. This view, again, explains the novel character of the apostolic discussions about moral life and action. Of course, the apostles, who were bred under the Law, would naturally take the tone of command rather than that of reasoned exposition in the laying down of moral truths. But this does not explain all the difference of attitude between Greek moralists and, for instance, St. Paul. We cannot imagine St. Paul discussing the question whether virtue is pleasure, or knowledge, or life according to nature; that is not the way in which such questions arise before him. He does not crush the antinomian— the man who was for defying all law and living as he pleased—as Plato with playful sadness crushed his, by pointing out that the life of the tyrannical man was 729 times less pleasant than that of one who lives the life of justice. Nor is this because Plato was wrong in so doing, or because St. Paul has a different theory; but simply because St. Paul is dealing with a new set of facts, and his thought moves wholly in the new region. To his mind, outward morality is the necessary expression of a life already infused into the soul. Already, in part, the ideal of humanity is attained in every person who has come under the new dispensation. Already we have within us the firstfruits of the Spirit —the force that is to govern us and guide us into the very presence of God. This life here and that to come are parts of one whole; and virtue here is the natural expression of the one spiritual life of man in these earthly conditions, the earthly analogue of that more perfect compliance with the will of God which is to be attained at the consummation of all things. St. Paul's ideal is a spiritual one, formed upon the experience of a spiritual life; and the ancient ideals are earthborn, and earthy to the end.

It is not, perhaps, very easy to make this clear and convincing. For (1) the whole conception of the new spiritual life has been much modified in comparatively recent times, and various associations with the modified view hang round the language of the New Testament. And (2), still more, Christian and pre-Christian ethics cover a great deal of the same ground, and therefore the difference between them is apt to be minimized or ignored. I hope however to show in detail in the succeeding lectures of this course, that though it may be difficult sometimes to describe it, there is a very marked difference between Christian Ethics and all that went before; that Christianity has added definite ideas to the ethical consciousness, and that where it has adopted old ones it has gradually remodelled them in the process. But there is still a third reason why this position is difficult, one of a most serious kind, of which I will speak shortly here.

I have made the whole difference between Christian

and pagan ethical speculation turn upon the presence in Christianity of a new vital force, whose activities form the subject of a new ethical theory. And my further contention is that this essential difference saves Christian ethical theory from the failure which haunted speculations of this kind under the old conditions. Under the old circumstances ethical principles were thrust in upon the will from without, and could not be safely trusted to govern it securely. Under the new dispensation the will is seized upon by this new vital force which works from within outwards, so that instead of man's having to conform to a pattern outside him, his will, set in motion by its inward converse with the indwelling Spirit, expresses in outward action that Spirit's rulings. That is the theory. And it is confronted directly with the actual state of Christendom —with the spectacle of broken unity—of open sin in those who claim Christ's name—of more than half the world after all these years still unconverted, still lying in the evil one. War is still waged, in spite of the nominal reign of the Prince of Peace; and as we look out upon it all, it seems as if the night were deepening instead of departing, and the promise of day deferred past all hope. That is our difficulty. And it is a serious one, because it meets us just at the point where we thought we were the strongest. We claimed to rest our theory upon facts: the fact of the Incarnation and Resurrection, the outpouring of the Spirit, and the mission of the Church. And these facts, we thought, should force themselves into notice—should be effective, and should bring with them a manifest change in the world. Whereas it is just in the region of fact that we are assailed. We are reminded of facts open and notorious, which we cannot deny. What are we to say then? We must, first, confess sadly that the sins and the faithlessness of churchmen have hindered the work of Christ and delayed His coming. But though we confess this with shame and penitence, we cannot admit that there is any reason to suppose that the kingdom of Christ will be sudden in its coming, in such a sense as to supersede its normal method of gradual extension and growth. And we must, further, resolutely call attention to the partial and one-sided picture of Christendom that is frequently presented. No one who looks below the surface can deny that underneath all the confusion and disorder the new life is really at work, and really effective in producing the highest moral life. If you doubt this, go into any of our large towns, and follow some parish-priest whose heart is in his work in his rounds among his people. There you will see displayed, in plain prosaic fact, the power of Christ's risen life in the subjection of inveterate habits of sin, and the gradual conformation of characters of every kind, strong and weak, lettered and ignorant, laborious and leisured, to the type of moral action which Christ presented upon the earth and the Spirit still interprets. Such things are near us to-day, just as certainly as the strife and sin which shame us, and seem too massive to be ever overthrown.

And beyond this it is open to any one of us to find the assurance of Christ's present power in our own lives, though this is perhaps exceptionally difficult in academic life, especially for those whose path lies through the fields of ancient learning. Our studies here interest us deeply, perhaps even absorbingly. We read of the struggles of ancient men towards the light, and we think more of them, in a way, for failing so magnificently than if they had succeeded with less trouble and fuller knowledge. Life does not look very hard, and we seem to have all we need for it in the teachings of the ancient moralists. As a matter of fact, however, that is not the way, nor are those the weapons of the battle of life. When we rise up at last to a hand-to-hand encounter with sin, without any loss of admiration for those whose wisdom has enchanted us, we shall quietly lay aside the armour we borrowed from them, and deal with our enemy decisively with a sling-stone taken out of the River of Life.

LECTURE III

'But now abideth faith, hope, love, these three; and the greatest of these is love.'—1 COR. xiii. 13 (R.V.).

I HAVE endeavoured to show in the last two lectures that the characteristic feature of Christianity is to be found in the entry of a new spring of life upon the world. It was not merely that a new way came into vogue of describing and co-ordinating the facts: there was an enlarged conception of the range and the possibilities and the relations of human life.

The first form, therefore, in which men became conscious of this new ethical impulse was in direct experience. Those who came within the range of the apostles—who repented, were baptized, and received the Holy Ghost—were those who felt the force of the new order. It was an experience of a very clearly marked type, lying chiefly in the ethical and religious spheres[1]. They derived from it a sense of utter breach with their own past; they were delivered from a burden; they could look up and be glad, and face the future with new vigour. St. Paul is for ever congratulating himself and his converts upon this new creation

[1] The γλωσσολαλιά and other miraculous physical effects did not, apparently, last beyond the first age.

The Theological Virtues 75

—the new gift of moral life and health which had come to them.

The strength of the feeling of new freedom may be gathered from one curious feature of early Church life. There was no small danger in the suddenness and sharpness of the revolution of a real development of antinomianism. This is, I say, a curious feature. For the emphasis laid by the apostles in their preaching upon the necessity of repentance from sin, μετάνοια, as a condition even to the initiatory rite of Christendom, might have prevented, one would have thought, the notion that after this initiatory rite the commission of sin was indifferent. But it was not so. Among many of the early converts it was a real danger, and St. Paul is at great pains to meet it and to provide against it.

In a sense this was a very early and crude attempt to adjust the new circumstances to actual life. It was a very early and crude expression of the vivid consciousness of novelty. Old things had so completely passed away, the new life given was so completely effective, that the old restrictions upon self-expression might be regarded as vanished too. Jew and Gentile alike might easily argue that the dispensation under which they had lived before was in its nature transitory, and bound up with the conditions out of which it had arisen. So that a change in these conditions might easily be expected to lead to a complete change in the rules that governed life. It was, perhaps, a mistake not so very difficult to make; and it has been made with far less excuse many times since those days. But the apostles spoke in regard of it with no uncertain sound. Freedom, St. Paul maintains, means merely new capacity for service—a change of masters, not an unmodified exercise of individual liberty. Before, he tells the Romans, they were servants of sin; now, freed from that slavery, they are servants still, but servants of righteousness—capable of doing such service to God as He requires. The essence of the old disability was that they *could* not do certain things —through the weakness of the flesh—the things which God required. The essence of the liberation is not that they have won a loose, independent, purely self-determining position; they are freed, not in any and every sense, but freed just where they were bound before; they can, if they will, do the things now from which they were excluded before.

In various characteristic ways other New Testament writers express their views of the connexion of the new order with moral life. St. James speaks of the fiend-like character of faith which comes to nothing, which is mere belief without works. St. John warns his readers that he who commits sin is not born of God: as if there were an inexorable incompatibility between sin and the new birth. The author of the Epistle to the Hebrews in the most solemn way warns those to whom he writes that 'for those who wilfully sin after receiving the full knowledge of the truth there remains no more sacrifice for sin, but a fearful expectation of judgement and a fierceness of fire which shall devour the adversaries.' Other passages will no doubt occur to your minds in which this position is asserted.

But though they condemn the too hasty inference which was born of the new sense of freedom, the apostles provide no *system* of Christian duties: the new life will itself determine the will in relation to circumstances. They deal with ethical problems of directly practical character as they arise. They warn their readers against certain practices to which *some* are given. It is plain to be seen that the Gentile churches especially were under strong temptation to sensual and coarse sins, and these St. Paul denounces. Or St. Peter will remind his readers that if they must suffer—if the will of God be so—it should not be for civil crimes. These they need not commit; they cannot help it if their faith is held to be a crime. And besides these and similar warnings against sin, there is a distinct type of virtue encouraged, which includes many ideas that had not been before held necessary to a virtuous life. Thus St. Paul describes the fruit of the Spirit in the well-known list of virtues; and St. John lays open the necessity of love, the murderousness of hatred; and St. James condemns the double-souled and the selfish rich. But the moral utterances have almost always unmistakably written upon them the signs of their connexion with occasional circumstances. They refer to the condition of the churches to which they are written, and do not seem to spring from any consciously developed system of moral ideas.

But though the general character of the moral exhortations is incidental, it must not be supposed that there are no predominant ideas emerging from the surface. It is with the ethics as with the theology of the apostles. They deal with theology not from the point of view of a schoolman or compiler of a system, but with special reference to questions arising in the churches over which they held rule. Even so characteristic a doctrine as that of Justification by Faith in St. Paul, though it is possible to trace signs of its language in the speeches ascribed to him in the Acts, is yet developed and presented in something like completeness of detail for the first time in the Epistle to the Galatians—in conscious opposition, that is, to a theory of another kind. The circumstances make a demand for a more systematic enforcement of truths already taught, and thus the relative importance of various factors in the whole doctrine comes into view. Something of the same sort happens in regard to Ethics. There are frequent passages conveying warning or rebuke or exhortation which it is possible to refer at once to the condition of the Church at the time. But through these, or rather from a comparison of the various sections of practical import, it is possible to find certain typical moral ideas which have a wider range than the immediate circumstances of any one Church. They are certain general forms in which the new life is to find expression. As the doctrinal passages have to be taken not merely in isolation, but with reference to the substance of the apostolic preaching, which underlies and makes intelligible all the occasional writings which survive in our New Testament; so the comments upon moral questions seem to point to the operation of certain leading notions which were fitted to become the basis of a new and systematic treatment of human life from the point of view of the faith of Christ.

The most conspicuous among these constant moral ideas are the three which occur in the passage I have made the text of this lecture—Faith, Hope, and Love. This verse, indeed, is the most prominent of all those which contain an allusion to them. But it is by no means true that this is the only passage in which they occur. In several of the Epistles there occurs after the salutation a passage expressing St. Paul's thankfulness for the general condition of the Church to which he is writing. The character of this opening varies, of course, in different Epistles, but in 1 Thess.[1] these three virtues form the ground of St. Paul's thankfulness, and in several others there are allusions to them more or less clear[2].

Further, the ideas which are connected with these virtues are found in various places in close association. Thus, for instance, in Rom. v. we have access by *faith* to the grace in which we stand—we rejoice (or boast) in *hope* of the glory of God; and not only so, but we rejoice even in tribulations, knowing that tribulation works endurance, and endurance a tested character, and this again works *hope*, which cannot make us ashamed, because the *love* of God is shed in our hearts through the Holy Ghost who is given unto us.

---

[1] 1 Thess. i. 2, 3: εὐχαριστοῦμεν τῷ Θεῷ πάντοτε περὶ πάντων ὑμῶν ... ἀδιαλείπτως μνημονεύοντες ὑμῶν τοῦ ἔργου τῆς πίστεως καὶ τοῦ κόπου τῆς ἀγάπης καὶ τῆς ὑπομονῆς τῆς ἐλπίδος τ. Κ. ἡ. ᾽Ι. Χρ.

[2] For instance, Col. i. 3-5: εὐχαριστοῦμεν τῷ Θεῷ ... ἀκούσαντες τὴν πίστιν ὑμῶν ἐν Χρ. ᾽Ι. καὶ τὴν ἀγάπην ἣν ἔχετε εἰς πάντας τοὺς ἁγίους, διὰ τὴν ἐλπίδα τὴν ἀποκειμένην ὑμῖν ἐν τοῖς οὐρανοῖς.

Nor is the connexion wholly peculiar to St. Paul. In St. Peter's first Epistle, Christ is said to have been 'manifested for your sakes, who through Him are faithful in God who raised Him from the dead, and gave Him glory, so that your *faith* and *hope* rest upon God.' And then, in the next verse, he goes on with the command, '*Love* one another with a pure heart fervently.' So in the Hebrews (x. 22, &c.) we read, 'Let us approach with a true heart, in confidence of *faith* . . . let us hold the confession of our *hope* unwavering, for He is faithful that promised: and let us consider one another to provoke unto *love* and good works.'

The recurrence of this association in three of the authors of New Testament writings is sufficiently marked to arrest attention. It suggests an inquiry as to the meaning of these three terms and the grounds of their relationship. The first head of this inquiry brings very clearly to light the lack of system and technical precision in the usage of the words. Of the three, the word ἀγάπη is the only one which always means a moral condition. Whether applied in its natural sense to man, or by an extension of its meaning to God, whether used with subjective or objective reference, it always has the one meaning of a particular state of mind and will[1].

But it is different with πίστις and ἐλπίς. In the case of the latter of these, indeed, the ambiguity is but slight. The word varies simply between the two

---

[1] The one possible exception is the passage in 2 St. Peter (ii. 13), where it occurs in the plural. If the word is genuine in this place, which is more than doubtful, it will mean *love-feasts*. This is the only exception to the constant meaning of the word.

senses of a particular temper of mind and the objects upon which that temper rests. But with πίστις the ambiguity is somewhat more serious. Not only does it stand for the temper of the faithful person and the object of his feeling, but the character of the moral temper itself is not as clearly marked as that of the other two. The ambiguity proceeds from different causes. In the first place, the word means not only trustfulness but also trustworthiness. And even in those passages where the active sense seems to be necessarily implied, different writers attach slightly different meanings to the word. In St. James, for instance, in the notorious passage about the relation of faith and works, πίστις seems to mean little more than belief in a fact that is not subject to verification by means of the senses. In St. Paul, whose exposition of faith is verbally, at any rate, in flat contradiction to that of St. James, the word πίστις means much more than an intellectual acceptance of facts not sensuously verified. The typical case considered by him is that of Abraham, who accepted and believed without wavering in the promise of God that he should have a son. And the crucial point of his act lies in this, that he recognized[1] to the full the actual facts of the case. He saw all the physical conditions which made against the fulfilment of God's promise. Yet in full view of those, without any natural likelihood on the other side, he believed; that is, he trusted his knowledge of the character and power of God against everything else. His faith was akin to love, and

[1] Rom. iv. 19 (R.V.).

St. Paul naturally enough in another place speaks of faith being made active by means of love. In the Epistle to the Hebrews there is another slight difference of usage. This is made obvious and precise by the occurrence in the Epistle of a phrase which almost amounts to a definition of faith—'the substance of things hoped for, the evidence of things not seen.' In this case faith seems to mean the certainty which arises out of man's confidence in God, that his hopes will be realized[1]. It is characteristic of the man who endures as seeing the invisible; not merely the personal confidence in God of a man who simply trusts against the nearer evidence of that which he sees, but the quickened spiritual vision, which pierces through barriers of whatever kind, and enjoys, as it were, the certainty of the fulfilment of hope.

Here, then, we have three moral conditions which, in various forms, are inculcated upon, and regarded as generally typical of, the Christian life. All of them are unfamiliar elements in the language of ethical philosophy, and it is not, at first sight, an obvious thing that they should be so definitely treated as necessary factors in Christian life. But the reason of the place they hold in the minds of the New Testament writers is not far to seek. It is that they unite the Christian most closely with the central facts upon which the Christian dispensation rests. The result of the events of Christ's sojourn here was, as we saw, to place man in a new and spiritual order, filling him with new

[1] Cf. S. Chrys. ad loc. (quoted by Westcott): ἐπειδὴ τὰ ἐν ἐλπίδι ἀνυπόστατα εἶναι δοκεῖ, ἡ πίστις ὑπόστασιν αὐτοῖς χαρίζεται.

and spiritual life. Hence the primary effect of this new knowledge and inspiration must be to develop characters required by the new conditions. This faith which is so necessary and so significant is related directly to the Death and Resurrection of Christ. It is the way by which those facts are seen in their true significance as revealing God, and placed within the range of the spiritual life of each individual. They are not mere dead history; they are facts of spiritual import, and determine for ever and for all men the conditions of the spiritual world. And by faith they and all their spiritual consequences are brought within the horizon of the ordinary Christian. He partakes in the benefits of the new birth—the barrier thrown down, the power of sin overthrown, the force of new life made possible, the new and filial attitude towards God. So with hope; that virtue bears, as is natural, chiefly on the future, on the second coming, the consummation which God will put upon all His plans in history. That and the citizenship with the saints, begun upon earth indeed, but to be brought to its full richness of perfection after the Parousia, are the lively hope to which the Christian is begotten again, which steadies him even under the pressure of persecution. He is at home with the purposes of God; he understands what happens in the light of this hope; he lives with the firmness and decision of one who has a purpose, and is sure of the goal to which he moves. And so Christian love is a principle of filial interchange of communion between God and men. God beseeches them through His ambassadors to be reconciled with

Him; He commends His love towards us by having sent Christ when we were at enmity with Him. And we meet Him who first loved us with love, which grows continually towards the perfect state when the fear of man for God shall be finally cast out. From this union with God, which the Death and Resurrection of Christ have made possible and real, no power can sever us. In the strength of it we can look straight past death to the end when God shall be all in all.

There is, then, great reason for the recurrence in the New Testament writers of these three moral ideas, and the various kindred thoughts which are allied to them. For they are indeed in very close correspondence with facts and beliefs which formed a large part of the apostolic message to the world. These three virtues, in fact, concentrate in themselves the attitude of man towards the new truth conveyed by the Christian Church. Christian men are expected to produce them; they follow easily out of the new conditions in which men are placed by the new faith, and they form the mainspring (especially love, which is the greatest of them) of the type of life in the world of men which Christianity has done something to create.

But when we come to inquire what all this has to do with moral philosophy, what are we to say? It is granted at the outset that the writings of the apostles are unsystematic, and that the virtues upon which they laid so great stress connect themselves primarily rather with the facts of the Christian creed than with any strictly philosophical conceptions of life. Have

The Theological Virtues

they, then, no significance for ethical philosophy? Must we, speaking scientifically, treat them as belonging to religion as a purely optional province, and as having no place in the philosophical view of life? I think not. Rather I think that they carry with them serious philosophical consequences in two ways, and that these two consequences are two of the essential distinctions between the Christian philosophy of ethics and all others.

The three virtues of which I have spoken are all of them habits which take men outside the range of their own narrow individuality. They are not merely personal graces, but they force every one who possesses them into relation with a wider end than any which can fall within the sphere of a single life. The man who loves another, for instance, cannot stand alone; and so far as his love forms a part of the ideal character at which he aims, the good of others is an essential part of his ideal. Thus love saves him from purely self-regarding views of life. But this is by no means the whole significance of these three virtues, nor is their relation to the wider conception of mankind their distinctively Christian feature. All three of them have their real importance in the fact that they connect man with God and with a spiritual order in which man's life finds its place. And that means that in philosophical language a new end has been found for the life of man; in other words, the life which is ruled by them is shown to be rationally significant and, within necessary limits, intelligible.

This is a matter of very serious concern. For the

doctrine of the end of life is one of the most characteristic and distinctive elements in moral philosophy. In fact, the attempt to define the end of life is one of the chief objects of the existence of moral philosophy at all. I endeavoured to show in the first lecture the fact and the reason of the many failures of ancient times. I must now attempt the far more difficult task of indicating the reason of the greater success which belongs to Christian moral philosophy.

I. The end suggested by the three virtues of which I have spoken is the union of the soul with God in love. For the other two—faith and hope—are, in a sense, preliminary conditions of the third. It is upon the basis of faith in the atoning love of God and hope in His promises that the true Christian love of God rests. And hence union, free and unfettered intercourse, which is the ideal consummation of love, is the end to which all three converge. But the idea of union with God suggests at once a comparison with the mystic conception of Plotinus[1] and others of his school. Are we to say that the end of human life, as conceived by the Neo-platonists, is organically one with the Christian ideal now described? Is the Neo-platonist mysticism the Christian idea shorn of its Hebrew and materialistic associations? Is such a mysticism the true modern interpretation of the Christian goal of life? To these and all such questions the answer is emphatically No! These mystic ideals, though in some phases of society they exercise a wonderful control over minds of

[1] Cf. Enn. i. 2; Bk. xix in Kirchhoff's edition.

a certain order, have always one very serious defect. They involve the absorption of the individual life into the boundless sea of the Divine Being. They are not, strictly speaking, goals for human action and striving; they are rather a means of escape from the weariness of conscious life—a confession of its toilsomeness, and the ultimate doom of irrationality which falls upon those who enter upon such conditions of toil. No scheme of life can pretend to justify the facts of life to reason so long as the present order of things is kept out of relation with the end. Life is not rationalized so long as it is maintained that the law of universal effort has no meaning in the next world as well as in this. Or, to put the same thing in another way, it is no comfort to the man who strives while he is here, and strives, to all appearance, in vain, to tell him that this life and his own consciousness will be simply obliterated in the world to come. He wants to know that the pains he endures here have a meaning, that they are not merely inexplicable torture, but prepare him for a life in which, with his own self-consciousness fully retained, he will have power to act without the impediments which hamper him here. If the end of all is to be absorption, life is merely a disordered delirium which precedes a dreamless sleep indistinguishable from death. Such a hope supplies no true justification to any one, and it attracts none but the world-weary, and these it kills rather than cures.

Though, at various times, such a conception of the end of human life has been couched in Christian language and found its way into the Church, it is neither the true idea of the Christian end, nor indeed is consistent with it. Whenever it has appeared it has either come in with some foreign element such as philosophy, or has resulted from the exaggeration of the subjective aspect of the Christian conception of man and God. From first to last the Christian idea is social, and involves the conscious communion between man and man, between man and God. And no state of things in which the individual consciousness disappears will satisfy this demand. It may be difficult to picture the city of God—in which the citizens are in full and free intercourse with the object of their soul's desire—even symbolism can only help by giving pictorial form to principles; but so long as the language of social intercourse is retained, so long as we speak of the love of God and of the end as communion with God, so long we must retain the belief that the individual life is permanent through all phases of existence. This is a distinction which marks the essentially Christian ideal from all forms of mysticism wherein the individual disappears. It is a distinction which does not necessarily prevent much use of common language and some coincidence in thought. But it emerges at last as an irreconcilable incongruity, sufficient to mark off one point of view from all others of the opposite type. It is a difference not of detail but of general idea.

But it is not enough to call attention to the difference between the Christian ideal and that which resembles it most nearly in external character. Nor is the fact that it retains personal self-consciousness as a necessary and permanent element the only point which justifies the claim of Christian ethical ideas to be in truer correspondence with fact. It is true that no system to which personality is indifferent will ever explain life of which the basal characteristic is to be personal. But besides this, the state or activity which is assumed as the end of human action should bear some nearer relation to ordinary experience than is implied in just not omitting its central factor, it ought to bear more directly upon the contents and course of human life as we know it.

In more ways than one, I think, the Christian ideal, with its associated virtues of Faith, Hope, and Love, will be found to meet this demand. It must be remembered, of course, that all these three, converging as they do upon the love of God, which is the final end of human life, deal with the fundamental aspect of all human activity, and control the outward life of man by that means. They are states or conditions of mind which govern the general character of the actions of men; they do not enjoin particular and definite acts. It is true that in the later ethical literature of the Church it has been ruled that certain acts are excluded by them; for instance, love or charity is said to be incompatible with a deadly sin. But this is a negative and restrictive efficacy, and this is all that belongs to these three virtues in the immediate experience of life; their true value lies in the underlying attitude towards all action which they imply.

I have already in this lecture given a hint towards

the understanding of the force of these separate virtues, and I must now develop this in further detail. Through faith man approaches God with confidence and without fear. Though he sees all around him signs of alienation from God in the past, he accepts by his faith the assurance that the condition of hostility is at an end, for him actually, for all men potentially. This he does on various grounds. He receives the historical tradition of the life and work of Christ, he accepts the interpretation put upon it in the New Testament and in the Church Catholic, and he finds in this belief the justification and the impulse to his confidence in God, seeing that the whole drift and movement of history is changed by it. Faith is to him a continual habit of confidence in the Wisdom and Love which guide the course of the world. And therefore he is freed from the uncertainty and doubt which must have pervaded his mind apart from this faith of his. Neither his own actions nor the course of history can seem irrational or purposeless. For the facts in which he believes give the key to the explanation of history and human life. He knows as well as any one the difficulty and danger of life as it is; he understands the puzzled wonder of those who are without his faith. But he is saved from the paralysis of thought and will which come upon men who can see nothing all round them but inexplicable and irrational chaos; he has faith in God; he believes that in the due time God sent His Son; he can therefore go about his business in the world, sure that if he acts faithfully as in the sight of God he cannot fail. And let us notice that no mere aspiration, no vague wish or imagining will be satisfactory. Conjectures, vaticinations, hopes are just what the men of old possessed, which failed them in practice. Certainty and sureness of action can only come from certainty in faith. The man whose faith is weak will get along somehow, no doubt, but with many lapses and much of the bewilderment from which the follower of Christ should be free. But he is not the type of the faithful Christian. That type we shall find in the man whose faith never wavers nor hesitates, before whom mountains of difficulty and doubt depart like clouds before the sun.

The Christian virtue of faith, then, affects the general aspect of human life just where it is most necessary, giving decision and freedom in face of evil and human weakness. In much the same way hope also helps to determine the character of human life. This again is not a mere impulse or sentiment or passion : it is a habit of mind or character. Its first and most natural object is the fruition of the promises of God. To that, all who have faith look forward. And the certainty which belongs to Christian faith pervades also Christian hope. The delay of Christ's coming is not the cause of sickness of heart or of a growing anticipation of disappointment ; the heart knows in whom it has trusted, it is certain of the ultimate fulfilment of its longings ; it hopes therefore with full assurance, even though the outward aspect of things may be gloomy. It is not the hopefulness of complacent and shallow optimism, to which nothing is really evil or reprehensible. It recognizes the full truth of evil; it is undeceived; it does not veil any part of the full significance of sin, in this world and the next. But through all this it never hesitates to look forward to the gradual realization of the purpose of God and the complete triumph of good over evil.

This attitude towards the future in regard of the general order of the world necessarily affects the tone of a man's ordinary life. He learns endurance and self-control; he is able to avoid ill-balanced and hysterical excitement when he finds out evil; he keeps his head in times of perplexity and apparent ruin. The most desperate of all fears—that God has given over the world to pursue its own course, and that there is no rational and orderly climax to the course of human things—is taken away from him. So, too, he measures events and actions by reference to the object of his hope. They are good or evil according as they further or retard the process of God's providence—according as they advance or hinder the coming of the kingdom. That is the one object of his firm hope: to that he subdues all his other impulses and desires.

These two virtues, which determine so profoundly man's life in the world, are perfected in the still nearer intercourse with God in love. That man should attain to the love of God was indeed a new thing in history. It was commanded to the Jew that he should love the Lord his God with all his heart and mind and strength; and in the Psalms and elsewhere we can hear still the yearnings of those who sought to fulfil this command.

But the whole notion would have been strange to a Gentile, who stood to the object of his worship in a far more distant relation. To the Christian, who realizes in practice the possibilities of his position, it is permitted to live a life of silent and incessant communion with his Father in heaven. He will walk with God as a man with his friend. He will enjoy such intercourse not merely in rare moments of spiritual elation, as when the chosen three apostles saw the Lord transfigured on the mount, but as the normal and necessary atmosphere of his thought and action. He will have learnt to read the marks of God's love in history—especially in the story of the redemption of mankind—and he will respond to the love which has been thus displayed. And such a love cannot fail to govern his personal life. More even than faith or hope, it will control his will, guide his choice, colour his desires. As the love of a human friend insensibly moulds a man's nature into some conformity with the friend's character, so the love of God will draw out and fix all the potentialities in the man of likeness to God Himself. Through this love the problem of obedience will be solved. The law of God—the natural expression of the Moral Being of God—will tend to become the regular principle of action; the changeful, self-indulgent impulses which are alive within those who are without the love of God will cease to be attractive and lose their power to move. Without any need for removal from the current interests of men, such a man will find his life in the truest sense hidden with Christ in God; he will live and act among his fellows, but the real current of his being will run below the surface, where it is united with the Being of God. But it was to fulfil these demands—to guide the life of man to its due end, and to enable him to walk steadily through life—that ancient ethics spent so much labour, with disappointing result. The life of Christ, by opening up the vision of the spiritual order and concentrating man's efforts upon the love of God, gave him the guidance and stability he required. The desire to know the end was a true one, and was satisfied first by Christ.

II. I have endeavoured in this elementary way to put before you the outlines of the character of the Christian man in its inward aspects. It is a type of mind which depends strictly upon the existence of certain conditions—upon the presence of a particular end as the goal of life, and of certain virtues as means to its attainment. It is, of course, an ideal: indefinitely distant from the present level of attainment, but the guiding principle of all distinctively Christian development in morals. I have spoken of it in connexion with the end of life and the ordinary processes of human action; it remains to speak shortly of the effect of it upon the conception of human nature.

It must have struck many as somewhat strange that I should have spoken of these three types of character as virtues. They are, of course, well known under the name of theological virtues, but this seems rather a traditional name than a name which describes their character. Perhaps, however, it is not very clear what we exactly mean by *virtue*, and it may be worth while to consider this point very briefly. There are, of course, as many definitions of virtue almost as there are systems of philosophy, and I hope to append to this lecture some account of the variations in the meaning of the term. Here I need only name one general idea which seems to be necessarily involved in any conception of virtue. Whatever may be the particular form in which the idea is presented, this at least must always belong to the notion. Virtue must always mean the perfection and complete development of some power or some nature: that is, on the subjective side. From the objective point of view it may mean some particular course or type of action; but however this may be, it always implies that the course of action is the best that can be got out of the power or nature in question. This is the reason why in ancient times it seemed possible to talk of virtue as belonging to all kinds of things, animate and inanimate. And though we have restricted the use of the word to the perfect development of a moral being, we have not lost its central meaning. Hence, if we ask whether the three states described can be properly called virtues, we are thrown back upon the question of the nature to which they belong. And thus we are led to inquire whether the Christian point of view has involved any change in the general idea of human nature. It is obvious that if such states are to be called virtues at all— if they are to be in any way brought within the moral region—there must have been an alteration on the ancient philosophical view of man. In the first place, man's action is referred to an end beyond the existing order with a directness which has no parallel in the days before Christ. I have already dwelt on this: but it does not exhaust the points of difference. The virtue or character of faith involves a peculiar relation between the intellect and the will, which is an innovation upon ancient theory; and, further, the lower part of human nature enters in a new way into the important questions of moral and religious life. I will speak shortly of these two points.

First, it is obvious that faith is in large measure an intellectual character. It involves an intellectual relation to certain facts, but it differs from the simple processes of opinion and knowledge. These merely register and co-ordinate the reports of the senses: though not purely passive, they are not responsible for the facts with which they deal. These must be given and must be dealt with as they are. But it must have been already clear that the essential character of faith is somewhat different from this. The facts upon which faith relies, though some of them, as we believe, entered into the ordinary history of the world, are in many cases incapable of sensuous verification, and in all cases are interpreted with reference to a supernatural order. It is this which separates faith from the category of ordinary intellectual processes and brings it within the moral region. For the impulse which enables the intellect pure and simple to recognize and accept the facts and their interpretation comes from no scientific analysis but from the moral sense. The acceptance or rejection of these is a test of the state of the moral character, and of the relation of the individual to God; it is not merely the recognition or non-recognition of a certain state of the outer world, a process which may easily be morally indifferent. It is this fact which produces the peculiar difficulty and strain of faith. For the senses are powerful, and exercise a strong control over all our thinking. So that it is hard even for those in whom faith really dwells to live so completely in a spiritual atmosphere as to see the whole of life in the light of God's will and love. It is easier to break up experience into separate districts under the control of separate faculties. But this is to surrender the unity of life, the realization of which should result from the new conception of the end. Thus, in the later technical language of Christian ethical philosophy, faith is an intellectual virtue; it is the perfection or ideal of the intellect, which is rendered possible by the existence of a certain state of the will [1].

Secondly, it must appear strange to those who are familiar with ancient moral theory that the theological virtues of hope and love lie so near to the region of passion or emotion. Though temperance and courage are said to be virtues of the irrational part of the soul, their formal character consists in the control of reason exercised over the passions in a particular way. Whereas in the present case it is hope and love themselves that constitute the virtuous character, and not merely the control of these emotions by reason as an alien force. It is this that marks the point of difference. In Aristotle, for instance, hope occurs only as

[1] See Note 2 at the end of this Lecture.

the ground of a false form of courage allied to the courage of drunkenness. And love almost disappears from the moral sphere in the same author, though friendship, limited of course to the friendship for man, holds a high and important place in the system. In later Greek thought the emotional side of man's nature was still more contemptuously treated, and met with the unfavourable judgement that belonged to all the material nature. We are not concerned to deny the close connexion between these theological virtues and the emotions. It is both real and significant. It is real, for the manifestation of hope and love towards God must always have something of the nature of feeling, as do the hope and love which rest on our fellow man. They are enlightened and guided by the intellectual apprehension of their object, but they move and act like emotions; they sanctify and control the emotional nature; they are its regeneration and its virtue. And this connexion is significant. For the adoption of the emotional nature into the region of Christian morality, together with the new alliance between the intellect and the will, implies the redemption of the lower part of humanity and the restoration of complete unity into the nature of man. So long as the various elements in man are regarded in separation, conceived as aiming at separate objects—objects which may and often do conflict—there is but little hope of a uniform and balanced development of man towards a moral ideal. The passions may be silenced by the intellect, but they are not convinced that silence is their proper duty. They are present always, and are in close contact with the world, and have some influence and part in every act which man commits. No system of ethics will be satisfactory which ignores or denies this; and the fact that Christian thought has reinstated them, supplied them with their true object, and bound them up into unity with other faculties, is of no slight philosophical importance. It means that Christianity has brought into line the unruly element of passion with which Greek philosophers had found it so difficult to deal[1]. Thus from this point of view also life has gained in rational completeness; intellect, will, and even feeling are made to converge upon the one end of all effort—union with God in love.

The result of this somewhat incomplete inquiry is that with Christianity there came in a new view of human nature, which was rendered necessary by the new relations towards God demanded of man. It is not true that there were no anticipations of this position before, and no signs that something of the kind was required. But until the events of the life of Christ had made clear the true and spiritual meaning of man's life, there was no way open by which all the elements of the problem could be satisfied. It is contended that these three virtues are not mere optional graces which men can do very well without. Pre-Christian or non-Christian morality could perhaps do without them: but they are essential to the character of Christian moral life. They are necessary to the full realization of man's powers in this life; for they perfect him and satisfy him just where he is at a loss

[1] Cf. p. 31 above.

without them. In this life, at any rate, all three, in St. Paul's language, abide; they are the abiding conditions of complete moral as well as of spiritual or religious life. And if the full vision of that which is believed—the open and unfettered fruition of that which is hoped for—will mark the close of the operation of faith and hope, it will be because they have vanished into the closer union of love: for this is a virtue not of the way only, but of the country—of the fatherland to which, after our earthly pilgrimage, we hope by God's grace to return.

NOTES TO LECTURE III.

NOTE 1.

The History of the Word Virtus *and its Greek Equivalents.*

THE word *virtus* is used in ecclesiastical writers as an equivalent for two Greek words, which at first sight would seem unlikely to be confused, ἀρετή and δύναμις. The object of the present note is to call attention to the operation of this confusion, and to consider whether it in any way affected the notion of moral virtue. It will be necessary to speak first of the use in later Greek of ἀρετή and δύναμις.

Ἀρετή had meant primarily excellence of any kind, and was applied indiscriminately to all things capable of excellence. In later times it tends to be restricted to moral virtue, and in consequence its sense varies according to the different ideas of virtue prevailing in the different philosophical schools. The term was always more naturally connected with the idea of a state or fixed character than with a course of action. Aristotle distinctly asserts that virtue might exist and be ineffectual[1], and the identification of virtue with a passive condition of the soul was the prevalent doctrine in later days. Even though it proceeded from or gave rise to right action, it was in itself a passive condition of being. The emphasis laid by the Stoics on the negative conditions of happiness—the necessity of passive endurance and the like—bound the idea of virtue more and more closely to its associations with a passive state.

At the same time, this separation of the virtuous condition of mind from the active and practical results which it produced was rendered possible to the philosophers by the elaborate and precise vocabulary which they had acquired. The

[1] *Eth. N.* I. viii. 9; *Top.* IV. 5.

capacity for virtue which is present in every man (δυνατοὶ ἐσμὲν φύσει[1]), the confirmed habit of mind which is developed by moral practice (ἕξις), the moral activities in which this habit is displayed (ἐνέργειαι), are distinguishable indeed, but are, after all, aspects only of the single process called moral life. The distinction between them, however real, is not one which is likely to be for ever maintained. Though virtue might still be defined in terms of passive conditions, yet the word δύναμις, which of necessity enters into relation with ἀρετή, contains in it a suggestion of movement towards realization, and its allied sense of *faculty* distinctly contemplates activity. To this term we must now turn.

The term δύναμις, from the point of view of technical philosophical usage, is of the greatest importance. The well-known distinction between δύναμις and ἐνέργεια plays a large part in Aristotle's philosophy. The two terms are as a rule strictly relative. That which is δυνάμει ὄν is not as yet brought to perfection; when it is ἐνεργείᾳ ὄν its capacities, hitherto latent, are realized. So matter, which is capable of receiving form, is, in regard of that form, in a state of δύναμις; when it has been determined into the form of which it is capable, it has reached the condition of ἐνέργεια. The oak is present δυνάμει in the acorn; it is present ἐνεργείᾳ when it has attained maturity. This seems to be the relation ordinarily expressed by these two terms. There is, however, another use of the word δύναμις, according to which it is defined as ἀρχὴ μεταβολῆς ἐν ἄλλῳ ἢ ᾗ ἄλλο[2]. From this point of view the word seems to imply a definite capacity of initiating change, and not merely a passive condition antecedent to another, which other is strictly bound to its antecedent by a law of necessary evolution. The use of δύναμις in the writers later than Aristotle is somewhat ambiguous. It has been already said that in the Nicomachean Ethics a distinction is drawn between ἕξις and δύναμις, virtue being identified with the former. In the

---

[1] *Eth. N.* II. v. 5.
[2] Cf. *Met.* Θ. chs. 1-5, and Bonitz's notes, pp. 379 and following; Trendelenburg, *De An.* pp. 242, &c.

Note 1 to Lecture III.

Eudemian Ethics[1] ἕξις and δύναμις are used as alternative terms for virtue, apparently with the implication that virtue consists in the best state or method of using one's powers. In a passage in the *Magna Moralia*, I. ii. 2, δύναμις is defined as a possession of power which a good man uses well, and a bad one ill; so that wealth, &c. are δυνάμει ἀγαθά. These uses of the word are mentioned here because of their bearing on the connexion of the idea of δύναμις with that of virtue : and they seem to show that the active and passive senses (if the phrase may be allowed) of δύναμις entailed different statements as to the relation of ἀρετή and δύναμις. In the passive sense δύναμις is the natural antecedent capacity for virtue ; in the active, it is more like a force that can initiate change towards virtue. This ambiguity prevailed in the later philosophical use of the word δύναμις. Plutarch[2] uses it of virtue almost as a synonym of διάθεσις : and Plotinus recognizes the two meanings of the term. He denies[3] that his first principle is δύναμις in the sense of matter, the general indifferent substratum of all things : but in another place he denies that matter is δύναμις· τί γὰρ καὶ ποιεῖ ;[4]

The word had also another meaning or association : it was used for a military force or armament. This use is not uncommon in historical writers : in Herodotus, for instance, and Xenophon. It is probable that it was owing to this usage of the term that the LXX almost invariably translate the word צְבָאוֹת by δυνάμεις. The phrase, the Lord of Hosts, appears in the LXX as κύριος τῶν δυναμέων, and a reference to the Concordance of the LXX, now in course of publication[5], will show that while there are twenty-five Hebrew words and phrases represented by δύναμις, the word most commonly occurs in this sense.

It is probably by no means an accident that Philo, who seems to have studied the Old Testament in the LXX, should have selected the word δυνάμεις for the beings who surround

---

[1] *Eud. Eth.* II. i. 2.
[2] *De Virt. Mor.* ch. 3.
[3] *Enn.* V. iii. 15.
[4] *Enn.* III. vi. 7.
[5] Hatch and Redpath.

the supreme God, and act as intermediaries between His spiritual nature and the coarse material world. And in the use of this word Philo has combined several streams of thought. These δυνάμεις represent not only the angels who surround the throne of Jehovah, but are also conceived as the archetypal ideas on the basis of which the whole world was framed. Moreover, there is uncertainty as to the number of them. At times they are treated as the attributes of God, and equivalent to these in number; at times they are described as twofold, one representing the Goodness (ἀγαθότης), the other the Power (ἐξουσία) of God. Thus there is an opening for the association with the term δύναμις of the ideas of Goodness and Power as well as the metaphysical notion of cause or archetype. So far as the usage of Philo prevails, it is clear that δύναμις is on the way to a change of meaning.

Apart from Philo, the position as regards ἀρετή and δύναμις is fairly clear. The severe distinction laid down by Aristotle is hardly maintained, and the term Virtue, though usually defined strictly as a passive state in itself, was extended so as to cover some of the aspects or moral action which Aristotle excludes. The tendency therefore to confuse or identify it with δύναμις belongs rather to inaccurate than to scientific language.

In classical Latin the only word used for ἀρετή is *virtus*; but in a certain class of ecclesiastical writers the ordinary word for δύναμις is *virtus* also. This use seems to have begun with Tertullian, and to have connected itself with the classical use of *virtus* for strength and vigour. But it is chiefly noticeable in connexion with the LXX. So far as I have been able to ascertain, Tertullian habitually translates δύναμις by *virtus*[1]. In one place he explains it as meaning *vires*[2]: 'Nam praeter quod omnibus notum est orientis virtutem, id est enim vires, auro et odoribus pollere solitam, certe est divinis scripturis virtutem quoque ceterarum gentium

---

[1] This is not quite invariable. Cf. *Adv. Herm.* ch. xix, where δυνάμει is translated *potentatu*.
[2] *Adv. Jud.* ch. ix.

aurum constituere.' This use remains in the Psalter as it stands in the ordinary editions of the Vulgate. Out of the sixty times that δύναμις occurs in the Psalms, there are only four instances of the use of any other word than *virtus* to translate it. But in the rest of the Vulgate Latin Old Testament, Jerome, who has corrected it from the Hebrew, uses different words, according to the underlying Hebrew expression. In the New Testament *virtus* frequently stands as the equivalent of δύναμις, and survives in one place into our English Version (St. Matt. v. 30) ' He felt that virtue ($=virtu$-$tem=δύναμιν$) had gone out of him.' I can find no instance of *virtus* in this exact sense, still less in the sense of potentiality, in any writer earlier than Tertullian. Even Apuleius, who frequently anticipates usages characteristic of Tertullian, shows no instance of this.

It is some time before the philosophical sense of δύναμις finds its way into Latin. Probably Marius Victorinus, an earlier contemporary of St. Augustine, is the first to use it. At least he in his controversy with Candidus the Arian introduces and explains the word *potentia*, as if he could not count on its being understood. The idea of virtue seems to have remained fairly clear from all associations with δύναμις (in spite of the connexion already noticed between δύναμις and ἀρετή) until a comparatively late period. The Latin Church was predominantly practical in its interest, so that it was not naturally concerned with such ideas as those conveyed by δύναμις. Moreover, its contact with Greek philosophy was mediated through Augustine rather than Victorinus. Augustine had been influenced by St. Ambrose, and St. Ambrose, in his turn, by Cicero, so that the Ciceronian treatment of moral virtue was familiar[1], and the more strictly philosophical idea of δύναμις was largely out of view.

The appearance of the works of ' Dionysius the Areopagite ' in their Latin dress[2] brought back the possibility of confusion

---

[1] Cf. Ambr. *De Off.* I. vii. 24, and Paul Ewald, *Der Einfluss d. stoisch-ciceronianischen Morals auf die Darstellung der Ethik bei Ambrosius*; Aug. *De Div. Quaest.* XXXI. i.; *c. Jul. Pel.* IV. 19.

[2] Cf. Scot. Erig. *De Div. Nat.* III. 3.

between the two terms, and among the Schoolmen[1] we find the Aristotelian account of δύναμις forced to act as a definition of *virtus* in the moral sense. This later confusion seems to be due entirely to the accident, if it may be so called, by which the two ideas were expressed by the same Latin word, together with the scholastic disposition to force a strict uniformity of significance upon all words. They assumed that one word must necessarily correspond to one idea, and that the definition must cover all its uses. While Greek was still known with even a small degree of accuracy, confusion was prevented by the existence of the two Greek words with their separate associations. But this safeguard disappeared when Greek passed out of use.

The effect on the moral ideas was therefore less than might have been anticipated. St. Thomas defines Virtue in words which are closely parallel to a phrase quoted from Strato the Peripatetic in Stobaeus—τὸ τελειοῦν τὴν δύναμιν δι' ἣν τῆς ἐνεργείας τυγχάνομεν[2]. But this definition belongs in Strato to an account of the Chief Good, and is not therefore applicable to virtue. St. Thomas, however, uses it of virtue, and then proceeds to discuss and adopt the Aristotelian account both of Happiness and Virtue, without apparently recognizing any inconsistency in the juxtaposition. In short, it may be said on the whole matter that the confusion is a verbal confusion, and no more. It has left its mark upon philosophical technical language (e.g. in the expression *virtualiter* and the English virtually=δυνάμει), but in such a way that no serious misapprehension can easily result.

[1] S. Thom. Aq. *Sum. T. Theol.* Iᵃ. IIᵃ. Art. lvii. a. 4.
[2] Stob. *Ecl.* II. p. 80.

NOTE 2.

The Use of πίστις.

It has been urged in the Lecture that faith in the sense of a theological virtue is a moral temper affecting the intellect and its contents.

Modern discussions on the subject have proved clearly enough that the term is somewhat equivocal. It involves not only a particular intellectual attitude towards certain truths, or, at least, towards certain propositions which claim to be true, but also describes a moral temper. It happens not unfrequently that the moral temper is criticized in terms which belong properly to the intellectual attitude of mind: for instance, emphasis is laid on the insufficiency of given evidence to produce more than a partial conviction on the mind, and all activity on the part of the moral nature is denied. It is interesting to notice that the same difficulty prevailed in ancient days. A few illustrations of the use of the word πίστις and the discussions arising round it will make this plain.

In the ordinary usage of the Greek philosophical writers the word πίστις has an intellectual signification. It means that some position is accepted as true. At the same time there is a rather ill-defined distinction between πίστις and knowledge. Thus Plato[1] separates πίστις from μάθησις on the ground that πίστις might be false. In the *Republic* (534 A) πίστις is closely connected with εἰκασία, and in the *Timaeus* (29 C) it is said to stand to truth as γένεσις stands towards οὐσία; in other words, the contents of faith are fluid and alterable as compared with those of definite scientific knowledge. In the *Laws*[2] faith is spoken of in connexion with the Gods, but

[1] *Gorg.* 454 D. [2] P. 966: cf. Eur. *Med.* 417.

the word is still confined to the logical region. It is applied to the existence of the Gods, because the evidence of their existence is indirect, and the result of the evidence is faith rather than knowledge. There is no special significance attaching to faith in the religious region. As Dr. Robertson Smith pointed out, the idea of faith as a religious virtue does not belong to paganism [1].

In Aristotle a distinction is drawn between the bare cognizance of an idea and belief. Thus it is said [2] that a man may have ὑπόληψις and not πίστις. And in *Eth. N.* VI. viii. 6 [3] a contrast is drawn between the unintelligent repetition of ideas and the real belief in them (καὶ τὰ μὲν οὐ πιστεύουσιν οἱ νέοι, ἀλλὰ λέγουσιν). At the same time πίστις is less than demonstrative in its certainty: it performs in rhetoric the functions of ἀπόδειξις in strict scientific method [4]. This distinction of the degree or certitude implied by πίστις, as compared with more scientific grounds of conclusion, brings up the question of the criterion of truth and falsity, and the word πίστις naturally occurs in this connexion. It seems always to describe the state in which a position is accepted as true, but one which is not formally and scientifically proved. Thus in *De Caelo* πίστις is the word used by Aristotle (as before by Plato) for the belief in the Gods which depends on nature and the history of men. In other and later writers the same use prevails. The idea associated with πίστις is always an intellectual one, and its distinctive feature is that some truth or opinion is accepted on less than demonstrative evidence [5]. There seems to be no notion that faith can be

---

[1] *The Religion of the Semites*, p. 19.
[2] *Top.* IV. v. 3.
[3] Cf. the Paraphrast *ad loc.*
[4] Πίστις follows upon αἴσθησις, λόγος or ἀπόδειξις and ἐπαγωγή. *De Caelo*, I. iii. p. 270, b 13. *Phys.* VIII. 8, p. 262ᵃ, 18. *Post. An.* II. iii. p. 90, b 14. *Rhet.* III. xiii. p. 1414, a 34, and Spengel's note.
[5] Cf. Sext. Emp. *Adv. Math.* VII. 443, where τῇ περὶ τὰ παραδοχῆς ἠξιωμένα πίστει is contrasted with demonstrative knowledge; Plot. *Enn.* V. iii. 11, where πιστεύειν is used for the less certain method of reaching God. Cf. *Ibid.* § 7, *ad fin.*

Note 2 to Lecture III

a moral quality and reach truth in virtue of its moral character[1].

The adjective πιστός necessarily describes a character or quality, and its usage varies between the meanings *faithful* and *trustworthy*. It does not enter in any important degree into the present question.

When we turn to the New Testament and LXX use of the word πίστις we find ourselves in a very different atmosphere. The word which is the nearest equivalent to the Greek word πίστις in Hebrew has rather the passive than the active sense of that word; it means trustworthiness rather than trustfulness[2]. The translation of this by the Greek word πίστις produced some degree of ambiguity in the meaning of πίστις. The Hebrew word was distinctly and primarily the name of a moral quality; whereas the emphasis in the other case was, as we have seen, on an intellectual state. The way was therefore prepared for the growth of an idea in which intellectual conditions should enter definitely into moral questions.

To a certain extent this connexion was achieved by Philo, probably as an inheritance from his predecessors in the Alexandrian School of Jewish thought. He speaks in the highest terms of the virtue of faith, and Abraham is made the type of it by Philo as well as by St. Paul. In this, as in many other cases, it is very hard to say for certain what Philo's position exactly is. Dr. Lightfoot and, to a certain extent, Zeller regard Philo as having come very near to the Pauline estimate of the value of faith[3]. And it is true that he uses the very highest language in speaking about it. But it is difficult to believe that the superiority of knowledge to faith, which is undoubtedly insisted upon by Philo at times, is not most completely in harmony with his general view of the ideal of life. The essence of faith, to Philo's mind, consisted rather in the rejection of facts of sense in favour of the more

---

[1] But cf. Plot. *Enn.* II. ix. 15, where virtue is affirmed to be an essential condition for the knowledge of God: ἄνευ δὲ ἀρετῆς ἀληθινῆς θεὸς λεγόμενος ὄνομά ἐστιν.

[2] Lightfoot, *Galatians*, ed. 6, p. 155.

[3] *Ibid.* p. 160. Zeller, *Griech. Phil.* Bd. iv. p. 406.

certain facts of reason. And these required faith for their appreciation, because the soul is sunk in the flesh. Though profoundly important and valuable, faith was in no way the final condition of the mind.

Philo, in fact, is the first writer in whom we find traces of the modern opposition between Faith and Reason. And it is clear that the conflict is one which depends on the contact of Greek with Hebrew ideas. Philo's associations with Greek philosophy make him look with a depreciating eye on a state of mind which is certain without adequate scientific grounds of certainty: from another point of view he sees the religious and moral importance of such a mental attitude; he feels himself bound to explain why faith was counted to Abraham for righteousness. He sees the necessity of faith as a stage in the soul's progress. But still the joy which is typified by Isaac, and the vision of God which is implied in the name Israel, are higher conditions than that of Abraham.

This point will be made clearer still by means of illustrations from Clement of Alexandria and other Greek fathers who were specially concerned with the adjustment of Greek thought with Christianity. Before the date of Clement, as for instance in Justin, πίστις means, for the most part, belief in the historical facts of Christ's Life, and especially in the Resurrection. In Theophilus[1] it is described as a demand made by God upon men, and the wide range of its operation is affirmed[2]. With Clement of Alexandria we find ourselves in a much more modern atmosphere. The philosophers have already begun to criticize faith as an irrational principle, a method of accepting impossible things without proof. It is plain that Clement himself is under some confusion in regard of the word. He refers to passages in Plato where the univeral necessity of πίστις is asserted[3], but they only prove the anti-social character of lack of trustworthiness. In chapter iv of the second book of the *Stromata*, however, he shows that he has already found it

---

[1] *Ad. Autol.* I. 14.   [2] *Ibid.* I. 8.
[3] *Strom.* II. iv. 18, v. 23.

Note 2 to Lecture III

necessary to place faith in its due psychological position, and to this end he cites the verse in the Hebrews where it is approximately defined [1]. He describes it as πρόληψις ἑκούσιος, θεοσεβείας συγκατάθεσις [2], and explains later that 'it proceeds through the objects of sense, and then leaves judgement (ὑπόληψις) behind it, and hastens towards the infallible realities, and abides with the truth [3].' It has a moral value: it leads to remission of sins: men are responsible for their belief or unbelief [4]. It is essentially a gift of grace, and deals with spiritual things: at the same time materialism is the only logical result of denying its value; for it is necessary to prove the reality of everything that lies beyond the range of mere sense. Moreover, faith is liable to caricature: mere credulous conjecture (εἰκασία ἀσθενὴς οὖσα ὑπόληψις) is mistaken for it, though it is as far from it in reality as a wolf from a dog. It always involves knowledge, just as all knowledge implies faith; this separates it from its caricature [5].

These passages show plainly that the peculiar intellectual difficulty which is presented by faith had already arisen before the minds of people in Clement's day. He is, however, very far from having surmounted it. The philosophical tendencies of his education eventually gained the upper hand; and Clement maintains the position that faith belongs to a lower mode of life than knowledge. Its value is that it prepares the way for a state of things in which it is not required [6]. In other words, faith is still intellectual in its character: an intellectual preparation for intellectual and moral perfection.

Origen, as we should expect, comes nearer to a full and

---

[1] *Strom.* II. iv. 8; Heb. xi. 1.
[2] *Ibid.*
[3] *Ibid.* II. iv. 13: ἡ πίστις διὰ τῶν αἰσθητῶν ὁδεύσασα ἀπολείπει τὴν ὑπόληψιν, πρὸς δὲ τὰ ἀψευδῆ σπεύδει, καὶ εἰς τὴν ἀλήθειαν καταμένει.
[4] *Ibid.* II. iii. 11.
[5] πιστὴ ἡ γνῶσις, γνωστὴ δὲ ἡ πίστις θείᾳ τινι ἀκολουθίᾳ τε καὶ ἀντακολουθίᾳ γίνεται. *Ibid.* II. iv. 16: cf. the relation between faith and learning, *Ibid.* I. vi. 35.
[6] *Ibid.* VI. xii. 98, and throughout Books III. and IV. of *Strom.*

exhaustive conception of faith than was given to Clement. He rejects and condemns the philosophical criticisms upon the principle of faith. It is not, he urges, a blind confidence; it does not make impossible the fullest inquiry; and, moreover, the use of this principle is in harmony with the general order of life [1]. Beyond this, when he is speaking positively of the meaning of faith to the Christian, he distinguishes between perfect and imperfect faith [2]. Faith, he tells us, may be imperfect: that is, it may relate only to a part of the whole content of a true faith. The passage here quoted seems to imply that the natural object of faith is the creed. In this Origen reminds us of Justin (see above, p. 110); but it should be noted that the points he selects are those which bear most nearly on conduct. The beginning of the *De Principiis* shows that he regarded this factor as the starting-point of a scientific investigation, the end of which would be a complete articulation of the whole order of God's providence. The inferiority of faith to knowledge assumed by Clement tends, therefore, to disappear. Knowledge is faith, only in a more intense and complete form. Faith is transfigured and completed in knowledge [3].

That this discussion or difficulty between the Greek and the Christian conception of faith was a lasting one, is shown very clearly by Theodoret's work *Graecarum Affectionum Curatio*. This is a definite attempt to place side by side the Greek and the Christian point of view on various topics. The first book is devoted to a discussion on faith, obviously a question of some interest. After an attempt to set aside the objection raised to the Apostles on the ground of nationality, Theodoret defends the use of faith. He argues that all leaders of philosophical schools demand it from their pupils, and that it operates over the whole of human life— using an argument that Origen and Eusebius had used before

---

[1] Orig. *c. Cels.* I. 9-11.
[2] *Comm. in S. Joann.* XXXII. 9.
[3] Cf. Chrys. *In Gen.* xv. Hom. 36, p. 370 B, C; *In Psalm.* cxxvii. p. 360 B; Basil, *De Fide*, p. 224 C, ed. Bened. tom. 2, ep. 235, ch. 2.

Note 2 to Lecture III

him. But though he points out the necessity of faith as a preliminary to all knowledge, and gives as an illustration of it the confidence between a pupil and his teacher, he has fallen back from the level attained by Origen to a position in which faith is simply assent in anticipation of evidence.

The intellectual conception of faith, therefore, seems to have prevailed for the most part amongst the Greek writers. The moral aspect of it is more characteristic of the practical Western thinkers. Tertullian, for instance, in his paradoxical assertion of the independence of faith of all human laws of possibility or probability is giving expression not merely to a gratuitous paradox, still less making a statement gratuitously absurd[1]. He is declaring, against the Gnostics, that the character of God is the ground for accepting as true things which seem impossible to unprepared human eyes. And this estimate of faith is repeated in St. Augustine[2]. It is this indeed which makes faith a virtue.

[1] *De Carne Christi*, c. 5.
[2] In *Ep. Joh.* Tract. x. 2, Ep. cxx. (where the connexion of faith with reason and love is discussed) and many other passages.

LECTURE IV

[1] 'Wisdom reacheth from one end to another mightily: and sweetly doth she order all things. . . . If a man love righteousness her labours are virtues: for she teacheth temperance and prudence, justice and fortitude; which are such things, as men can have nothing more profitable in their life.'—WISDOM viii. 1, 7.

IN the last lecture I spoke of the due order of life conceived as related to God, who is its final goal and happiness: and of the transformation, resulting upon this view of man's nature, in the idea of virtue and duty. New ideas and claims, I endeavoured to show, fall upon man by reason of his relation to God; and a new view of the unity and activity of human nature depends upon the use (for the purpose of the higher end) of powers that had been neglected before. Such a view of life as is implied in the theological virtues is really essential to the full appreciation of man as a moral being. That is, it is not merely a decoration, an optional adornment to the social *human* life of man, but it is the firm foundation upon which anything like a true and adequate account of social morality must be raised. For morality is more than the due performance or avoidance of certain acts; it expresses the final constitution of the man; it is the most profound exposition of his inmost character. It is this

The Cardinal Virtues

inward side of things which the theological virtues most accurately represent.

I have now, however, to speak of man in his social environment, and of the effect of Christianity upon the existing conceptions of social order. Long before Christianity appeared men had reflected upon the conditions of their daily life, and had arrived at some definite view of right and wrong in regard to it. The difference between good and evil—the true and the false way of ordering desires and impulses—were already familiar subjects in the Western world, independently of the Jewish Law: and the most that Christianity could do in this connexion was to impress something of its own character upon that which was already in existence. The method pursued by the Christian Church, in regard of existing ethical philosophy, is of a piece with its treatment of all the other philosophical questions, of which it became gradually conscious. It finds certain terms and ideas in possession of the field of thought, and soon recognizes a certain amount of kinship in them to its own highest ideas. The terms are therefore accepted into the vocabulary of Christian writers, but their meaning is gradually modified. This took place in various ways. In some cases the appearance of actual heresy reveals some incompatibility between the associations of the language and its new context, as when it became necessary to distinguish the valid and the impossible uses of the word λόγος[1]. In other cases, and this is more especially true of moral ideas, the process of

[1] Cf. Eus. c. *Marc.* Eccl. Theol. II. xiii, xiv.

adaptation came with less strain and strife. Gradually, associations which the Christian sense found intolerable or inadequate were laid aside without any great alteration of vocabulary; but in the end the original authors of the phrases retained would have found some difficulty in recognizing their own ideas.

The best way of illustrating this point for the purposes of this lecture will be to select some distinctive Greek moral ideas and endeavour to show how, as a matter of fact, Christianity transmuted them. Of all those which we connect with Greek speculation in this sphere, the most characteristic are probably the four cardinal virtues, as they are now called, Temperance, Fortitude, Justice, and Prudence. These seem to be constant throughout the whole range of Greek ethics. In dialogues which all agree to be among Plato's earliest, these four virtues appear together, and are assumed as though already familiar. Two or three times some other name appears in the place of one of them, such as ὁσιότης or μεγαλοπρέπεια. But the connexion of the four is the regular usage in Plato, and his association of them in this manner seems to rise out of the general moral consciousness of Greece. A Greek seems to have been expected to develop these virtues, and Plato does not think it necessary to show the exhaustiveness or inevitableness of this classification. He takes them up out of the ordinary catalogue of moral ideas, and it is only in his later and systematic works that he attempts to show that they are the natural outcome of the regular Greek education, and correspond with the constitution of the soul. I need not remind you now of the part they play in the *Republic* and *Laws*, nor of Aristotle's treatment of them in the *Ethics*. Their history does not end there. In the Stoic schools, according to Diogenes Laertius, these four virtues were assumed to give an exhaustive account of that life according to nature which constitutes virtue; and other habits, such as μεγαλοψυχία, were forced into the scheme as subordinate species. Philo takes the four as describing the ideal of man, and he explains the four rivers of Paradise as being an allegorical expression of this truth [1]. Other virtues occur sporadically in Greek writers, and are recommended; but these are constant, and seem to be independent of the distinctions between one school of moral thought and another. Whether the final constituent of good was pleasure or knowledge or virtue, these four were the forms in which virtue was expected to be displayed. We are not concerned therefore in the least degree with any of the elementary problems as to the nature of virtue, upon which much discussion was spent, but only with the general character which the possession of all these four virtues was likely to produce.

The four virtues then give us the picture of a Greek acting in various circumstances, with reference to what modern language would call his various temptations. Instead of giving way to the inordinate desire for self-indulgence, he is temperate. Instead of giving way to the easeful vice of cowardice, he is brave. Instead of disproportionate self-assertion as against his fellows, in regard of the good things which the world

[1] Cf. Philo, *Leg. All.* i. 19, and see note at end of this Lecture, p. 158.

can give, he is just. And as a crown to the whole, instead of being morally stupid and blundering, apt to do the wrong thing, and incapable of guiding himself, he is a man who acts on principle, and is able to read the true character of men and things as they pass him ; for, in one word, he has prudence. I need not say that a person who had attained to such a character as this would have achieved no slight moral success ; none of the qualities described could be regarded as accidental, or unnecessary to the virtuous life. Nor does the ideal, however it may have been actually conveyed to the mind, relate to external observance only. It does more than regulate outward deportment. It lays its commands upon the will, just where control is needed, where the natural inclination to self-assertion is strongest. And it does this in the interests not only of the society, but also of the individual himself. Possessed as he is of various powers, and finding all round him the means of their gratification, he is likely to use his opportunities to the destruction of his own good as well as to the injury of his neighbour. The personal danger is provided against by the virtue of temperance in an especial degree, while fortitude and justice contemplate most obviously the good of the neighbour. Thus the general character of the ideal is one in which personal interests are curtailed and a certain degree of self-sacrifice is demanded. In the interests of the unity and harmony of the individual life, as well as the legitimate desires of other men, the natural tendency to unregulated self-assertion is restrained.

Hence, whether virtue be regarded as a mode or an effect of or means to pleasure, or as the most scientific method of dealing with life, its outcome as expressed in human life was to be a balanced and harmonious use of opportunities, an adaptation to the social environment which avoided friction and all savage competition of interests. The life it contemplated was bright and orderly: a state of things in which education and good breeding would tell, in which there would not be startling reverses or distressful situations. Even the Stoic, though he had given up all hope of his age and its life, looked forward in his heart of hearts to a life according to nature as his ideal—a life in which a rational order could be traced, in which the wise man would have less to put up with and feel more at home. It was only because the world had got awry that the Stoic ideal seemed grim and unattractive. There was for him no necessary connexion between virtue and misery; only the ideal of virtue was to be pursued without regard to untoward circumstances, however they might interfere with and mar his self-development[1]. Neither with the Stoics nor with any other of the Greek schools had self-sacrifice in itself any peculiar significance. It was required inevitably by the balance of varying impulses and the meeting of various individual interests. Any

[1] Cf. Epict. *Diss*. I. i. 23, xxv. 1, xxix. 12, xxx. 1–3, II. i. 17, III. vii. 29–36, IV. i. 68, and many other passages. There is educational value in ἄσκησις—separation from the interests of the ordinary world. See *Diss*. II. xviii. 14, and following sections—a very fine passage. The result of this ascetic separation is the true freedom. The attainment of this is the sole object of the sacrifice. Cf. Clem. Al. *Strom*. IV. iv. 14, vi. 29, xxii. 137.

one tendency or power, if it were allowed unrestrained sway, would produce a distorted individual life; and so the assertion of one man's desires to the detriment of those of other men would destroy the proportion and balance of the whole state. It was essential to the very existence of men in a society that they should make way for one another, and that the labours of one should be at the disposal of the many; while the Stoic would find that his pursuit of virtue and the life according to nature meant the surrender of much that would otherwise seem desirable. Thus there was a real demand for self-sacrifice: it was rendered necessary by the conditions of social life, and its object was the advancement of the individual perfection as well as the order of the whole body politic: it was inevitable, but not, in itself, virtuous.

It has indeed been pointed out that the demands of the Greek ideal were too high, and that it assumed the existence of slavery and other social conventions which diminish its moral value. But such criticisms touch rather its practical possibility, with which I am not immediately concerned. Speaking merely from the point of view of moral theory, it is unquestionable that the Greek conception of a life characterized by these four virtues is a very high and beautiful one. It aims, at any rate, at being the model of ordinary life, and is not a mere picturesque imagination; a person who was guided by it would have overcome many ordinary temptations, and would be living rationally and well.

On the other hand, when we come to consider the

Christian life or character as it is developed in the New Testament, some very marked differences appear. There is, in the first place, a tone of deeper seriousness and severity; there is a graver feeling about the way in which life is treated. The nearness and importance of the spiritual world accounts for this. And secondly, the self-sacrifice required is of a different and graver kind. It is not merely the necessary limitation of faculties and individuals that are mutually interdependent; its aim is not balance or harmony or adaptation to a complicated environment. It implies the facing of the fact that the true interest of man's whole life is not here at all, and that he may therefore, for his soul's sake, find himself obliged to give up the whole world. This world is not the area in which man's best activities are to move. But though this is so, the Christian's relation to the world is not one of mere submission to a cross-grained destiny. It may be that he is as isolated in it as the Stoic philosopher, but his isolation has a different meaning. The Stoic is oppressed by the movement of blind forces which from their nature take no account of an individual; the other is isolated because he is at war with the powers that be. The world might have been the true home of the man's spiritual impulses, but it is under the temporary sway of sin, and with this he is necessarily at war. Moreover, the Christian cannot fulfil his task by withdrawing into himself and simply enduring; for the warfare has to be waged also within him; the powers of evil have made themselves a home there too. And this fact reacts upon the character of the sacrifice demanded. The Christian has not merely to adjust the claims of his various powers and impulses, he must be prepared to cut off the offending right foot or hand.

It is this state of warfare (of which more will have to be said later) that determines the character of the Christian moral ideal as regards the world. It accounts for the extreme severity of much that we find within the Gospels. Everything that can be made a means of binding the soul to the things of this life falls so far under stern condemnation. Christ makes no concealment on this head; He is unmistakably, almost repellently plain. It is idle, He tells one, to take pride in keeping the commandments if you are not prepared to sell all that you have and follow. Short of this, riches are a snare, and may be an insurmountable obstacle to entering the kingdom of heaven. Even the sacred ties of family affection do not escape: the man who loves father or mother, wife or child more than Christ is unworthy of Him. Towards the world the Christian is to present only the appearance of relentless antagonism. He is to be suspicious of himself when men speak well of him, because he and the world cannot mean the same thing. As it hated Christ, so it must hate His followers; for the rule of life which obtains in it is self-assertion and hatred, and the Christian rule is self-sacrifice and love.

But though this separate and warlike attitude towards the world occupies a large area in the Gospels, it is by no means the whole of the Christian moral conception. We are shown the Christian life in other relations than that of defensive and aggressive warfare against an intruding hostile force. The true moral life of the Christian man is lived in the spiritual intercourse between himself and God, and in the warm and brotherly communion with the members of the body of Christ. It is in this region more than in the negative hostility to the world that we must look to find the source of the changes caused by Christian ideas.

I have spoken of the isolated and withdrawn life which belongs to the Christian. Such withdrawal is necessary in order to make a home for the Spirit of God. It is the Spirit Whom Christ promises to send, Who controls and guides the life from within. And the person who has yielded to this holy influence is no longer deprived of all living companionship. He has surrendered the world indeed, and may have found great pain in so doing: he may have isolated himself from the natural circle of his activity. But it is not the deadening and purposeless isolation of mere superstitious asceticism: rather, the companionship of the Holy Spirit quickens and intensifies all the best powers the man has. Nor is this warm spiritual life isolated through selfish desire for concealment. There is no effort made to conceal it; the world does not understand or appreciate it, only because the world neither sees nor knows the Holy Spirit. Among those who do, the bond of human friendship is drawn tighter than is conceivable upon any other terms. All alike are subjects of the Holy Spirit's indwelling, so that they are one, with something of the oneness which belongs to God. The social tie which holds all men together in some form or another, with varying degrees of stringency, is here transfigured. The Christian bond of union is more comprehensive than the tie of family or state, for the basis of it is the abiding in Christ and receiving His representative, the Holy Spirit: and this, as men soon found, left earthly and political associations wholly on one side. And this union is intenser even than the most vigorous forms of human sympathy, for it is independent of restrictions of matter, space and time, which limit and impede our earthly intercourse. Further, the expansive force of the Holy Spirit's operation is not restricted to those who are at any given time united together in spiritual fellowship. The privileges which belong to these are to be offered to the world. Through the first believers others will believe on Christ's name, when the newly founded Church takes on its function of making disciples among all nations. This Catholicity, which depends on the love of God for all men, modifies the position of extreme antagonism in which the Christian is placed towards the world. Though he is to be separate from it and all that is characteristic of it, though he is to expect nothing from it but hatred and hostility, he has a certain responsibility for those in it who have an affinity for the things of God. He is therefore bound to display his faith before the world in the interests of those who may be won to it, even though by so doing he seems to court persecution. It is part of the ready self-surrender which he owes to all men for Christ's sake, that he should risk incurring trouble or pain or death for the sake of proclaiming Christ's message.

I have endeavoured to restrict myself thus far to the language of the Gospels, and to derive from them the general outlines of the Christian character. As I had occasion to remark once before, the Gospels contain comparatively little in the way of ethical exhortation. Apart from the actual history of the Pattern Life and the exhortations to follow it, it is true rather that the foundations are laid upon which the typical Christian character is to be built, than that any complete articulation of it is given which would display it in its various relations in the world. But it requires no argument to show that such a character would at once involve itself in intercourse and communion with the world of men, and that its presence and activity under such conditions would lead to the development of some special outward form. A body of men drawn out of the world and bound together as Christ proposed to bind them in His last discourses, for whom the world as such was to have no overmastering attraction, yet who were bound to do all in their power to win the world for Christ, could not but appear as a distinctive body in the world, nor could they fail to produce a distinctive type of moral life. This process we find going on in the apostolic Epistles.

The conception of the Church as the new home is asserted with constantly increasing clearness in the Epistles of St. Paul. The breach with the old life and its sins is plainly declared, and the claims of the new social environment are asserted. The faithful are now 'in the Lord,' and their behaviour must be modelled accordingly. All forms of lustful and selfish sin are forbidden them as a matter of course; but also they are bound to a line of positive conduct as regards one another. As in the Gospels, so here in the Epistles, love is the basis of their action. And it takes the form among other things of a voluntary adoption of a restrained estimate of oneself. The disposition to respect and allow for the rights of others has been transformed into the duty of humility. This is essentially a social virtue. When St. Paul charges the Roman Christians not to think of themselves more highly than they ought to think, it is in order to impress on them the necessity of restricting themselves to the special functions committed to them by the Holy Spirit (Rom. xii. 3 seqq.). In the letter to the Philippians, humility is opposed to vainglory and the factious spirit of a hireling (Phil. ii. 3). And the effect of the presence of this virtue is that men are ready to do the work that falls to them without anxiously looking out for their own interests, and that they realize the privilege of being allowed to serve God at all in His Church. It is, of course, wholly distinct from diffidence—from the unrighteous refusal to accept God's call; it is not the fatal lack of enterprise which belongs to the man who hid his talent in a napkin: it is consistent with the loftiest positions which men may be called on to fulfil. But it implies the constant recognition that other men have interests and rights, and that the greatest of human lives is still only a single factor in a movement far more comprehensive than it. It includes the Greek conception of self-restraint, with the difference that it is based upon positive love to God and man.

Such a spirit of humility, of course, is not exhausted in its dealings with other men, even though in its essence it involves the realization of the littleness of oneself and one's own resources in contrast with the order of God's providence and the rival powers of one's neighbours. It is based upon a personal and subjective character of self-restraint and love. Humility, as a practical principle of life, is the social side or outward manifestation of the sense of unity and love which belongs to the body of Christ. It is impossible for one who does not love to be truly humble. For the absence of love makes the self-abnegation necessary for humility quite impossible: it makes it impossible to view men dispassionately and without anxious depreciation: it makes it impossible to endure the thought of a subordinate station or an uninteresting mission in life. For indeed there is no ground, except the sheer force of outward circumstances, for accepting or claiming less than the very utmost we want, save only the principle of love. Love is the force which holds society together: and humility is the form which it inevitably takes when life becomes complex, and interests conflict, and it is required to adjust men in due order for the purposes of life. We may see in the prominence given to this aspect of the virtue in the Epistles the beginnings of the adaptation of the Church to the idea of a long course of history in the world.

The contrast between the severe unworldliness of

Christ's teaching and the frank acceptance of social conditions by the Greeks, between the social polish which restrains desire within bounds and the Christian virtue of humility, has often been noted. And indeed it would not be easy to find two principles of life which differ, at first sight, more strikingly than the deep subjective Christian conception which I have endeavoured to describe, and the more objective rule of social life which formed the ideal of the Greeks. And it is necessary to recall the external and obvious difference, though it is not the most profound. Expressed in its ultimate form, the difference is nothing less than a difference in the value assigned to human personality. At first sight it might seem as if the Christian ideal tended to produce a dead level of indifferent insignificance: as if the strong insistence upon self-sacrifice and self-abnegation implied that the personal life were not in reality worth the saving. Whereas, on the other hand, the Greek ideal might seem to assume the presence of social conditions adequate to the development of the individual life to its highest point. For the ideal man seems hardly to have been expected to appear except in an ideal state, which is another way of saying that the true adjustment of the balance of personal powers implies a state which ideally serves the purposes of individual life. So that it might seem as if the true freedom of the individual would be found in the following of the Greek rather than of the Christian ideal.

But such an estimate of the difference would be

most inaccurate and superficial. I have alluded to it merely because, consciously or unconsciously, it does affect the ethical ideas of some in modern times, and in order to bring out more clearly the true point of difference between the one system and the other. This estimate then is superficial because it fails to give weight to the difference in character between the Christian and the Greek notion of personality.

Far from ignoring the importance of each single personal life, the distinctive feature of Christianity in the ethical regard is, as has often been pointed out, the new importance assigned by it to personality. In fact, it is hardly too much to say that in the ethical, as well as the metaphysical region, the idea of personality is the gift of Christianity to human thought[1]. It is the presence of this idea which gradually produces the marked change which occurs in the associations of the old philosophical language of ancient Greece; and it provides the key at once to the apparent contradictions in Christian ethical ideas, and to the effect of these upon the ancient doctrines then prevalent. It will be necessary to consider this point somewhat in detail.

I. In the first place, from the Christian point of view, there is an absolute value attaching to every human personality. Every human being as such is important enough to have an interest in the scheme of Redemption, quite apart from his outward circumstances or personal endowments. Every one who comes within the range of Christ's sacrifice is individually worth the sacrifice that saves him. In what-

[1] Cf. Illingworth, *Bampton Lectures*, p. 8.

ever sense the question may be decided as to the relation of the Fall to the Incarnation, whether we believe that the creation of man involved the Incarnation, or that it is merely the fact of universal sin that gives it its universal bearing, there is no doubt as to the equalizing effect of the Incarnation upon the individual lives of men. From this point of view there is no such thing as an unnecessary or unimportant person: all alike are the objects of the ineffable love of God.

This absolute value belongs to the life of man in consideration of his personal humanity, and nothing else. It is not merely that a scheme is devised which applies to the human race, and therefore incidentally to each individual in it. Each individual has his destiny and his hopes, his capacity for happiness hereafter, his part in the response of praise from the creature to his Creator: and therefore each individual life is, in a measure, complete by itself. This does not mean, of course, that man's social nature is ignored or denied, still less that he is saved apart from the Body, which is the Church, but simply that the social aspect of his life no longer sums up all that can be said of him. The individual interests and destiny of each man are important in themselves. Others may be related to the course of his life in various ways, they may enter into it and affect it. But there is no vicarious salvation. Every man lives a separate life and follows out a separate path through the world[1].

II. This fact explains the possibility of the ruthless enmity between the Christian and the world. The

[1] Cf. Clem. Al. *Strom.* IV. iv. 15.

old tribal and family associations clung still to the ancient religions, and man was not regarded as in himself a religious being. He accepted naturally the religion of his neighbours and of his state, feeling no call to content himself with the position of an outlaw rather than resign his religious ideas. He felt no responsibility for these; it would be waste of effort and unreasoning obstinacy to endure persecution for them. So it is said that Marcus Aurelius marvelled at the curious fanaticism of those who preferred to die, or surrender everything that makes life desirable, to surrendering their private beliefs and observances. He was living in an ancient circle of ideas. Hostility to the world was not required of the votaries of ancient faiths.

But it was required of all Christian men. Because their religion was based on a real and personal relation between the soul and God: and each man's personal destiny was involved in the maintenance of this personal intercourse. And this was the first necessity of the spiritual life. Family ties, friendship, the various links which bind men together in a state, were all of them secondary to this[1]. It might mean an agonizing wrench to relinquish the power of free association with fellow-citizens, and to take up voluntarily the position of the man without a city (ἄπολις); but no claims from the side of the world, however venerable, could stand for a moment before the counter-claim of God to the whole devotion of each single heart. The more successfully we throw ourselves back into the state of feeling on this point which prevailed in ancient days, the more

[1] Cf. Clem. Al. *Strom.* IV. iv. 15.

profound will appear the change which the new religion implied. It is true that the overshadowing unity of the Roman Empire was tending to diminish the force of local feelings, and already the Stoics had begun to talk of the citizen of the world. But it was the sense of personal responsibility for using or misusing the privileges to which God had admitted the followers of Christ, which made it possible to defy so successfully opinions which had come to look almost like necessary truth. And so the insistence upon the personality of man explains the possibility of the warfare with the world.

III. It is in the same direction that we look for the explanation of the modifying principle which, as I have indicated, must have seemed to stand in flat contradiction to this willingness to defy the world—I mean the principle of universal love, the missionary impulse to extend the faith to all. As it follows from the absolute value of the personality of man that he can never be merged in any political environment, so it is for the same reason that every man is worth trying to save, and has an actual claim to love. For the rights of a man increase in proportion as the conception of humanity grows in dignity. While men are looked at from the outside, and estimated according to the part they play in their society or the history of their time—while it is possible to despise slaves and foreigners and tradesmen, and all who fall below the level of a leisured class, there can be no idea of a universal claim of man on man, no possibility of even aiming at a universal love. That becomes possible and even necessary when a view of manhood is attained by which the possession of humanity, with all its capacities for intercourse with God, becomes the essential and primary dignity, before which all earthly distinctions pale and disappear. As beforehand men had claims to consideration according to the position that they held, so now all men alike have the claim which flows from the dignity of their manhood.

It is, of course, the strenuous assertion of the equal manhood of all men that saves Christian ethical theory from the charge of narrow individualism. It would have been conceivable that the relation of the individual to his God should have been exclusive and private, looking merely upwards towards God without any reference outwards over the hosts of men. Under such conditions the most hopeful result as regards mankind as a whole would have been indifference not unlike that of the Stoics: a very probable result might have been perpetual conflict of individual interests. It makes the whole difference that the relation between man and man is mediated through the intimacy of man with God. For thus the mutual kindness of men is brought within the range of religion: and not only so, the strong claim for sincerity which lies upon all man's dealings with God affects his dealings with his fellow-man. God requires the full utterance of his inmost self in love and worship; and man, who is or may be in full communion with God, has a claim to a love no less sincere, no less religious. Though it is true that unless we love the brother whom we have seen, the love of God is dried up in us, it is no less true that the final justification of the love of man is to be found in the one relation of sonship in which all men stand to God through Christ. For it is this that gives the human nature itself its dignity, and binds men together not by any terms of external association, but in the inmost centre of their nature, where are the springs of love. Thus the new conception of man combined the various tendencies in the new faith. Because man is created a person capable of intercourse with God, he can never satisfy himself with any lower end: any interests that conflict with this must be ignored. Because he is so created, he is capable of, and indeed required to take a part in the evolution of the Purposes of God—the salvation of the whole world. Again, because he is so created, he has his own part and no more: he does his own work, humbly, gladly giving what he can of service for the good of all for whom Christ died.

It has been necessary to allude to all these familiar truths in order to bring out precisely the nature of the problem that lay before Christianity when it attempted to adopt and mould to its own use ethical ideas already in existence. They were, as we have seen, the product of the social life of Greece, and they expressed this life in the form in which it had been familiar. Thus they fell in most naturally with the civic ideal, and they scarcely left room for the individual except in connexion with this environment. They represented an enlightened and cultured popular opinion[1], and made no provision whatever for independent advances be-

---

[1] Cf. Stewart, *The Ethics of Aristotle*, vol. i. p. 204.

yond the popular levels of thought. The universal individual responsibility for living the highest life was hardly admitted at all.

The problem before the Church was, therefore, one of very considerable difficulty. However sympathetic it might feel to that which was good in the moral life of the civilized world, it could never ignore the points of difference. For, indeed, these were not accidental; they followed from the fundamental character and constitution of the Church. The view of human personality which involved so much change was not a mere theoretical persuasion; it was an assumption underlying the chief fact in the religious experience of Christians. If we may believe the speeches of the apostles in the Acts to represent the early teaching of the Church, it claimed to present for man's acceptance a scheme or method of salvation. This was its starting-point, and it was owing to this, its special characteristic, that the special features which I have already noted in its moral theory were present. Men *must* be of infinite value as individuals: God had actually taken so much pains to save them. For the Church, therefore, to adopt any inferior view of mankind would have been to surrender its whole *raison d'être*. If, then, it is to adopt and to assimilate any of the existing data of moral theory, it is bound to impose upon them its own sense and dovetail them into its own system.

We naturally expect to find that such a process as this took some considerable time. And this expectation is fulfilled by the facts. There were, of course, elements in Christianity as it had been presented by the apostles which lent themselves readily to a sympathetic contact with Greek ideas. The social aspect of man was the chief of these. The man who had been received into unity with Christ was thus made a member of a vast society: he became a fellow-citizen of the saints, and of the household of God. And in the earliest days—in the writings of St. Paul and St. John—there dawned a vision of a great heavenly city in which citizens were enrolled from every nation and tongue. For long years this seemed to be but a vision of future glory. To the persecuted and despised the inheritance of their kingdom seemed to be a hope merely to lighten the toil of pilgrims through a strange land to their proper home. But as the days went on and Christianity became more and more unmistakably a permanent factor in the world, it came to be within the range of hopefulness that a Christian society should be firmly established in actual reality. The Empire itself, so long hostile, became christianized after a fashion; and at length St. Augustine attempted to lay down the principles of the city of God just at the moment when it had become plain that the kingdom of Christ had more lasting power in it than Rome itself.

The contrast between the two Empires has often been drawn, and I need not dwell on it further. Through their contact there came to light a mediating idea between the old morality and the new. For a long time in Christian writings we hear chiefly of virtues and vices that belonged to the inward course of Christian life[1]. Later on, when the Christian commonwealth had already been founded, and Christians had freely adopted prevalent methods of education and thought, we begin to hear again of the four virtues in which the ideal civic life of Greece had taken shape. It is recorded of Origen[2] that a course of ethical study formed part of the instruction he gave to those who were his pupils, and that this centred round the four cardinal virtues of ancient Greece. Their appearance at all in this connexion is significant, though, unless Gregory has greatly misrepresented his master, the interpretation Origen put upon them is not distinctively Christian. Courage, which is described as the preserver of all virtues, is the habit of abiding by the true laws of life in spite of every temptation to the contrary. Justice is, as of old, the habit of restraint within one's own limits, avoiding all trespass upon another's rights. And it is applied with special emphasis to the soul, to take due care of which is the truest justice. Prudence is the science or special knowledge that deals with good and evil. Temperance, closely allied with it, is the virtue which guides desire. Such expressions as these go but a little way, if at all, beyond the language of Plato; and Gregory himself finds the chief difference between Origen and some modern philosophers in the fact that Origen practised all these virtues while the others did not. In fact they were necessary for Christians to practise who lived in the world, and they were good in themselves. But they have not yet come under any transforming influence.

[1] Cf. Herm. *Pastor*.   [2] Greg. Thaum. *Or. Pan.* ch. ix.

A marked change has taken place when we reach the time of St. Ambrose, the teacher of St. Augustine and the author of the first treatise on Christian Ethics. A large portion of Ambrose's book, *De Officiis*, is devoted to the consideration of these four virtues. It has been maintained that this book is little more than a reproduction of Cicero's book similarly named. There is undoubtedly a close resemblance between the two, but the fact that St. Ambrose's book is intended especially for clerics leads one to anticipate peculiarities of treatment. And the expectation is not disappointed. The treatise assumes the validity of the classification under the head of the four cardinal virtues, and St. Ambrose almost apologizes for not beginning his book with the discussion of them. He first searches for them in the lives of Old Testament heroes, and, with some forcing of the words of Scripture, succeeds in finding them. This done, he expounds his own theory of their nature. They are not referred to any one principle, though they are decisively connected with Christian ideas. Prudence is treated as supplying the necessary intellectual basis to all moral action, and as being, therefore, the most fundamental of the virtues. Justice, which comes next, is affirmed to be a social virtue. Ambrose complains that it has been largely represented as a self-protective retributive principle, and this he maintains is an inadequate view of it. It rather implies that the just man is bound to use duly that which is his own, property being but a loan from God. Somewhat curiously he bases it upon faith, by which he seems to mean that it is a great social bond which holds men together in Christ's Church. The discussion of fortitude follows familiar lines, except that this virtue is described as being the great bulwark against avarice; for avarice, according to St. Ambrose, is the vice which most often and most easily breaks down a man's resolution[1]. Temperance is more like a tactful ordering of life as a whole than anything which we associate with the name.

Thus this earliest treatise on Christian Ethics adopts, with some slight modifications, an older theory of life. There are signs in it that the time has come when a new spirit is to be poured into the ancient doctrine and new application made of ancient principles. This is especially prominent in the passage where St. Ambrose reviews these virtues in the light of clerical life. But it is in the writings of his great pupil St. Augustine that the step is taken which separates the newer theory most completely from the old. The names of these virtues are continually appearing in St. Augustine's writings from the earliest date after his conversion onwards. He asserts their prominence in all current ethical teaching, and in one place expresses a wish that they were as prevalent in practice as they are in theory[2]. But what is still more important, he gives them a new definition. He connects them closely with the true end of man's existence, viz. the vision and the love of God. And he makes love the point of contact between them. Thus, temperance is the whole-hearted love of God which

[1] Cf. Ar. *Eth.* III. vi. 4, where Aristotle speaks of boldness in connexion with the expenditure of money. Cf. also Clem. Al. *Paed.* II. xii. 129.
[2] *De Mor. Eccl. Cath.* I. xiv. 25.

displays itself in the control of all bodily passions—the readiness to surrender for God's sake all that is of the world and might divert the interest of the soul[1]. Fortitude is the submissive endurance of all that crosses the will and tries the temper for the sake of the object of love. The difference between them lies in the fact that temperance sustains a man in the contest with himself, fortitude in his contest with the outer world[2]. Justice, once the virtue which gave man his own, is now described as the love which serves God alone and wishes no evil[3]. And, lastly, prudence is the wise selective principle which enables the soul to guide its steps safely through the tortuous courses of the world.

This interpretation of the four virtues set the tone of all subsequent thought upon the subject in the West. It is possible to trace the effects of it in the writings of Gregory the Great: his frequent use of allegory to show that the four virtues are inculcated at every turn in Job and other such books proves how readily he assumed them. Also, there is a far more fixed and stereotyped system of moral virtue in St. Gregory than in St. Augustine; in fact, one might almost say that Gregory occupies an intermediate place between Augustine and Scholasticism. But when we come to read the greater schoolmen, especially of course St. Thomas Aquinas, we then realize the effect of St. Augustine's speculation. A great deal has happened by the way. There has been a long period of

---

[1] Cf. *De Mus.* VI. xv. 50; *De Mor. Eccl. Cath.* I. xv. 25.
[2] *De Lib. Arb.* I. xiii. 27.   [3] Cf. the same passages.

ignorance and scantiness of thought. But at last men have gone back to the old sources of ancient moral speculation, and Aristotle has been raised to a position of unquestioned supremacy. But it is Aristotle read in the light of Augustine who rules the schools. Aristotle's language reappears in St. Thomas: his divisions of the soul and his doctrine of the mean. But his four virtues are referred to the supernatural end of the life of man, and they are said to follow from the presence of the gift of love. The virtues are recognizable indeed; there can be no question but that they are true lineal descendants of those of Aristotle. Fortitude is still the cool, steady behaviour of a man in the presence of danger, the tenacious preservation of that which is dearer to him than his life. But its range is widened by the inclusion of dangers to soul as well as body; it is the bravery of one who dwells in a spiritual world. Temperance is still the control of the bodily passions; but it is also more positively than negatively the right placing of our affections. Justice is still the negative of all self-seeking—of all angry conflict with the interests of others; but the source of it all, and the ground of its possibility, lies in giving God the love and adoration which are His due. Prudence is still the practical moral sense which chooses the right course of concrete action; but it is prudence of men who are pilgrims towards a country where the object of their love is to be found. The four are recognizable, then, as I have said, but they have suffered serious change.

It is not that the Christian can afford to neglect them

and do without the temper they imply. But they had been defined in relation to an environment which once seemed the whole field of the operations of man. This point of view has changed. As we saw in the last Lecture, man's life has been related to a new end, and his social being has entered upon a wider life. The other world is now an element in all his experience. Man is revealed to himself as a spiritual personality living in a spiritual society. The temptations to cowardice and lust and covetousness and folly are seen to be in their ultimate form spiritual temptations: an effort on the part of the prince of darkness to break the link which binds man to his God, to split and shatter into fragments the close unity of the body of Christ. The virtues, therefore, which are to stand against this assault will still wear much of their ancient look; but they will spring from one source—the one source of all spiritual strength—the steady love of God, which is the duty and the virtue and the glory of the nature which God made for communion with Himself.

NOTE TO LECTURES III AND IV.

THE two preceding Lectures have been concerned with the effect of Christianity on moral life and theory in two special regards. It has been argued that the appearance of the three theological virtues points to a changed conception of morality which affects the whole of life : that a new end has been assigned to human endeavour, and a new principle of unification applied to the various elements in human nature. Further, that the old social idea of virtue expressed in the four cardinal virtues incurred certain necessary changes in view of the new associations of the new society—the Church.

The Church passed into the possession of a consciously elaborated moral theory by slow and gradual movements. As has been remarked in the lectures, its interests at the beginning were wholly practical, and it is only by accident, as it were, by the pressure of circumstances, that it enters upon the task of definition and systematization of its ideas. The position maintained here is that, in spite of the numerous forces existing and in operation all round it, in spite of the fact that the Church has always been careful to use for its own end the material supplied by its environment, the resulting moral philosophy was distinctive, and that this effect was due to the distinctive elements which were involved in Christianity and were peculiar to it.

In order to make this position plain it will be necessary to enter at some length into the philosophical conditions of the early centuries of the Christian era. It was not only in the Christian society that efforts were being made to satisfy the problems of life. Nor again was it only in the Christian society that the stern monotheistic morality of Judaism was being used for the purposes of a Gentile world. On the one hand, the Greek philosophical schools were still developing the lines of thought which they had inherited from Plato, Aristotle, Zeno, Epicurus. And on the other, Philo of Alexandria had made a serious effort to combine the legal system of the Pentateuch with a sort of eclectic philosophy of which Platonism was the chief ingredient. For our present purpose, Philo and his ethical philosophy are of primary importance. Attempts are constantly being made to show that Christianity contained nothing but what was already before the world. Judaism, interpreted no longer according to the letter, combined with a selection from the higher elements of Greek philosophy, is thought to be sufficient to account for it all. It is denied that there was any decisive breach with the past, any new knowledge brought into the world, or any new departure made which cannot be explained in terms of natural evolution. Pre-existing material was redistributed, and that was all.

It would be a serious obstacle to the success of such a theory as this, if another case could be found in which the same elements were dealt with by a thinker with a different result. For it would then be necessary to show that the difference of the result turns simply upon a difference of attitude towards the elements utilized by both. Philo is such a case, and his philosophy does provide an important foil to the actual work of the Christian Church. Philo was deeply learned in the Law, though for the most part he seems to have been dependent on the LXX version of the Hebrew scriptures. He has evidently drawn much inspiration from the philosophies of Plato and the Stoics, and he believes profoundly in the moralizing power of the study of philosophy. But the result in his mind is startlingly different from that which obtained in the Christian Church. He is essentially eclectic: he reproduces with very small modification the systems and ideas with which he is familiar: but he does no more. His thoughts reappear in Christian writers, and he has had influence upon Christian development; but he is still of the old order, he represents fairly what might have been the world's fate if

Note to Lectures III and IV

Judaism and Hellenism had combined without the illuminating power of the Spirit. To make this plainer it will be necessary to discuss Philo's ethical theory at some length, and to endeavour to show the relation that it and the kindred system of Plotinus bears to Church-writers, and especially St. Augustine. The gap in the argument of Lectures III and IV will then, it is hoped, be filled up. For Augustine is the most important of all influences upon the drift of Western speculation.

In the first place it will be necessary to allude to certain well-known difficulties in the interpretation of Philo. His works consist for the most part of comparatively short treatises bearing on the history or the enactments of the old covenant. The authenticity of some of them is doubtful, but Philo is not rigidly consistent with himself throughout those which are recognized as his. (1) The language of Philo, though full of technicalities, is hardly to be called technical. It is difficult, if not impossible, to lay down beyond the possibility of discussion the meaning to be assigned, for instance, to the various names of his virtues. Even when there are quasi-formal definitions to be found, the author does not always adhere to them. There is for instance a tendency to confusion between $εὐσέβεια$ and $δικαιοσύνη$ [1]: the good man is occasionally called ὁ ἀστεῖος [2] : and this word is used as a synonym for σπουδαῖος or ἀγαθός. Moreover the list of virtues and vices is uncertain. It varies in fullness from the simple list of cardinal virtues and their corresponding vices to the tedious prolixity of the lists in *De Mercede Meretricis*. At the same time Philo's writings are full of technical expressions borrowed from the various systems of philosophy with which he was familiar. (2) His style has a strongly marked tendency to diffuseness. He heaps up epithets and metaphorical expressions in his efforts to describe the Supreme Being, or the order of the world and such abstruse ideas, in a manner which became characteristic of Neo-Platonist writers, and was carried to its extreme point

[1] Cf. *De Praem*.c.9, II.416 M. [2] Cf. *De Abrah*.cc.19, 23, 46, II. 14, 18, 39 M.

of tediousness by 'Dionysius the Areopagite.' It is, of course, impossible with such a method as this to preserve complete consistency. The metaphors and epithets suggest different ideas and associations, and the subject they are meant to illustrate tends to be clouded over and concealed. An additional source of obscurity lies in the fact that Philo was not strong enough to force the various elements of his thought into complete unity. He never attains to a complete mastery over them all, but draws upon them singly from time to time, so that there is no consistent principle to which all his utterances must be referred for explanation. (3) Philo supplies a large stock of quotations. It is always easy to get from him phrases and short passages which seem to breathe the spirit of Christianity. The phrase 'God is Light' occurs in Philo[1]. There are many passages which suggest St. Paul. In the book *De Judice*, c. 3, we read that the love of money is ὁρμητήριον τῶν μεγίστων παρανομημάτων[2]. In *Quod Omnis Probus Liber*[3] Philo makes reference to the energy of those who contend for crowns of parsley, and the glory of their death if they die in their attempt, and urges that the desire for the true freedom of the wise man should be at least as eager and effectual. So again in *De Praemiis et Poenis*, c. 20, we are told that 'the intellect of the wise man is the palace and home of God[4].' Thus his isolated phrases encourage more hopeful anticipations of his philosophy, and suggest a closer kinship with Christianity than his works as a whole maintain.

Yet in spite of this and many other sources of difficulty in the interpretation of Philo, it seems possible to get from him some indications of a definite position—a position which is intelligible as a result of his environment, but was not strong enough nor new enough to do the work of the Christian Church. For there are certain points of view which are constant in Philo through all his uncertainties and eclecticism: these must just be mentioned here, in order to lead up to his view of the function of man.

I. God is for him always a transcendent Being, whose

---

[1] *De Somn.* I. xiii. I. 632 M. [2] II. 346 M. [3] c. 17, II. 463 M. [4] II. 428 M.

Note to Lectures III and IV

existence it is possible to demonstrate from the order of nature, but whose character and attributes lie far beyond the range of human speculation[1]. He uses continually of God the term τὸ Ὄν, which belongs to the vocabulary of philosophy, and implies that the ground of all existence is to be found in God. But he goes much further than this. He asserts that God is beyond the highest reach of man's conception. He is δραστήριον αἴτιον (a Stoic phrase)—the effectual cause of all that is; but simple beyond all possibility of complexity, 'higher than virtue, higher than science, higher also than αὐτὸ τὸ ἀγαθὸν καὶ αὐτὸ τὸ καλόν[2].' In this last passage Philo has taken a long stride towards the negative conception of God, afterwards produced by Plotinus.

In close connexion with this point of view, which is, as already observed, constant throughout Philo, stands the account given of the relation of God to the world. He created, not the world we see, but the archetype of it, the original of which this world is but a copy. This sensuous world seems to have been created by the mediate activity of the Word of God or the Powers of God. For on this head Philo is closely connected in thought with Plato. The Supreme God is capable only of good actions and of dealing with good things. Hence He may be said to make the stars, which are free from all evil whatsoever: 'they are living things, and living things with reason, or rather each is reason absolutely, good throughout and incapable of all evil[3].' But man's nature is capable of opposite activities. He has the gift which enables him to be temperate, brave, and just; but he can also choose the opposite course. Hence for his creation God takes on helpers who are responsible for the evil possibilities in his nature[4]. Moreover when evil has actually been committed, God is still entirely separated from it. It is not strictly true, it is 'economical,' the language of condescension, to say that God is angry or repents. Moses attributes to God ζῆλον, θυμόν,

---

[1] *Quod Deus Immut.* 13, I. 282 M; *De Praem. et Poen.* 6, II. 414 M; *De Mon.* I. 5, II. 217 M; *De Mundi Opif.* 2, I. 3 M.
[2] *De Mundi Opif.*, c. 2, I. 3 M.   [3] *Ibid.* c. 24, I. 17 M.   [4] *Ibid.*

ὀργάς, ὅσα τούτοις ὅμοια, ἀνθρωπολογῶν (by an anthropomorphism); and, if asked questions, answers that His object is to benefit all who come under the influence of His law. Some who have been initiated into the true mysteries of religion will never apply to God qualities that imply change: but those whose minds are duller and more inert require the medical aid, as it were, of law-givers, who devise the proper treatment for the affection under which they labour[1]. So again God gave the Ten Commandments Himself, but left His prophet or law-giver to develop them into their various details. And in the Decalogue there is no mention of punishment. It was fitting for God to appeal only to man's highest and most rational disposition—to call him to obey and not to threaten him. Threats and punishments and such things should be entrusted always to subordinates[2].

These passages are typical of many others in Philo. The doctrine they contain is a necessary consequence of the assumption of a transcendent God who is out of all direct relation with human and inferior things. They are not complicated by the difficulties which press seriously on the interpreter of Philo—whether the Supreme God is personal or not, whether the Divine Logos is or is not personal: and again whether the Logos is or is not distinct from the Powers. These are questions which it is hard to settle finally, because Philo is inconsistent in regard of them. And his inconsistency is easily explained. The points at which it arises all belong to the debateable land in which the frontier of Philo's Judaism and Hellenism lie. His language takes one character when the Judaistic influence is strongest, and another when Plato has most firm possession of his mind. Whereas there is never any doubt as to the transcendence of God; and it is obvious that this assumption must affect Philo's moral theory.

II. A second doctrine or conviction which meets us in many connexions, and has an influence upon the ethical beliefs of Philo, is that by which the world is represented as

---

[1] *Quod Deus Immutabilis*, cc. 13, 14, I. 282 M.
[2] *De Decem Oraculis*, c. 33, II. 209 M.

Note to Lectures III and IV

a great πολιτεία or state. This is, of course, a metaphorical way of describing the order of the world, and is suited both to the Jewish and Hellenic tendencies in Plato's mind. He may have derived it from the Stoic schools. Among them it was a common phrase indicating the relation of the individual to the world in which he was placed and the supreme power which placed him there. To be the true κοσμοπολίτης—the citizen of the world—who was wise enough not to expect to have things all his own way, but would rest contented with whatever happened, feeling sure that the reasonable order of the world required it—was the ideal or the boast of many a Stoic[1]. And it may have been from this point of view that Philo approached the idea. But, on the other hand, it is in close sympathy with a distinctively Jewish type of faith. The God of the Jews was before all things a ruler, the natural head of the Jewish state, and maintaining all things in due order by the exercise of His Wisdom. From the point of view of the Divine Wisdom the truly holy and religious man could be well described as a citizen of the world, and the whole world the state which the Divine Ruler administered.

It is true that the passages of Philo in which this idea occurs are mostly such as to suggest a Greek parentage rather than that of the Hebrew philosophers. But the other alternative must not be wholly excluded; the fact that the idea would lend itself to Jewish associations would no doubt give it a value in Philo's eyes. Thus in the first chapter of *De Mundi Opificio*, Philo contrasts Moses with other writers who have dealt with the history of law, in that he neither contents himself with a bare statement of customs, which would be unphilosophical, nor invents myths of the origin of society, but begins at the true beginning, the creation of the world, 'on the ground that the world is in harmony with the law, and the law

[1] Cf. Epict. *Diss.* I. ix. 1 and 2: εἰ ταῦτα ἐστὶν ἀληθῆ τὰ περὶ τῆς συγγενείας τοῦ θεοῦ καὶ ἀνθρώπων λεγόμενα ὑπὸ τῶν φιλοσόφων, τί ἄλλο ἀπολείπεται τοῖς ἀνθρώποις ἢ τὸ τοῦ Σωκράτους μηδέποτε πρὸς τὸν πυθόμενον ποδαπὸς ἐστιν εἰπεῖν ὅτι Ἀθηναῖος ἢ Κορίνθιος ἀλλ' ὅτι κόσμιος. Cf. *Diss.* II. v. 26, x. 3, xxiii. 42.

with the world, and the law-abiding man, who is the true κοσμοπολίτης, guides his actions with reference to the will of nature (πρὸς τὸ βούλημα τῆς φύσεως) by which the whole universe is ordered.' So in a long passage[1] he works out the idea more fully, referring it to Greeks and others who are ἀσκηταὶ σοφίας. He describes their way of life, their separation from the petty quarrellings of ordinary men, their peaceful habit of contemplation, their earnest inquiry into the order of nature, and their careful training of the soul away from the coarse things of sense to the contemplation of the higher powers; and then he says these have 'looked upon the world as a city, the followers of wisdom as its citizens whom virtue enrols—virtue which has been believed to preside over the common constitution of things (τὸ κοινὸν πολίτευμα).' This order Philo connects with ἰσότης, and argues that as equality and balance produce the order of nature, so in a state they produce democracy (ἡ εὐνομωτάτη καὶ πολιτειῶν ἀρίστη), and in the human body health[2].

These passages—and many others could be found—are sufficient to show the prevalence of the idea in Philo's mind. It will be clear at once how important a bearing it has on his ethical tendencies. We have already seen how closely his theology connected itself with his physical theories; it is now clear that his ethics follow suit. The pursuit of virtue is a process by which men's individual efforts forward, or at least come into sympathy with, the forces of nature. Nature is the true object of the peaceful contemplation of men, and the inevitable regularity of its movements gives the rule for their moral life. They must accept cheerfully and without protest the results of its providentially guided movements;

---

[1] *De Sept.* c. 3, II. 278-279 M.
[2] Cf. *De Just.* c. 14, II. 374 M. Further references to this idea will be found in the following passages: *De Spec. Legg.* III. 34, II. 330-332 M. This is a long and important passage, describing what Philo conceives to be the whole history of speculation in the mind. *De Praem.* cc. 4, 5, 6, II. 412-414 M; *De Dec. Orac.* cc. 20, 29, II. 197, 205 M; *De Mon.* I. 1, II. 213 M; *De Abr.* 13, II. 10 M; *De Jos.* 6, II. 46 M: ἡ μὲν γὰρ μεγαλόπολις ὅδε ὁ κόσμος ἐστὶ καὶ μιᾷ χρῆται πολιτείᾳ, καὶ νόμῳ ἑνί.

Note to Lectures III and IV

for God is good, and as He has not grudged existence to the formless floating matter of which the world is made, so His order will necessarily be the best possible. This is Stoic asceticism touched with the personal interest which the Jewish faith could add to that philosophy.

III. There is one more common character in Philo's work of which we must now speak. This is his interpretation of the Law. In his dealings with the Old Testament, Philo is chiefly concerned with the Pentateuch. As Professor Ryle's book will have shown conclusively, far the largest number of quotations come from this part of the Old Testament Canon. And the assumption of his whole method is that these Mosaic books must in some way be made to speak in the language of Greek philosophy. In the books of Moses, Philo recognizes two elements, the historical and the legislative : and he maintains that the object of the former is to illustrate and develop the meaning of the latter. Hence the histories are narrated not so much for the interest of the individual patriarchs and heroes as to supply types by which men shall be able to mould their own lives. In other words, the histories have to be treated as allegories. The enactments of the Law are at times subjected to the same treatment, but not always.

It is not easy to say precisely how much faith Philo had in the historical character of the stories he relates and allegorizes. In *De Mundi Opif.* c. 56 he protests against the idea that the story of the Fall is a myth (Ἔστι δὲ ταῦτα οὐ πλάσματα μύθων, οἷς τὸ ποιητικὸν καὶ σοφιστικὸν χαίρει γένος, ἀλλὰ τρόπον τύπων ἐπ᾽ ἀλληγορίαν παρακαλούντων κατὰ τὰς δι᾽ ὑπονοιῶν ἀποδόσεις)[1]. But, on the other hand, in *De Abr.* c. 11 he speaks as though the historical reality of the occurrences were completely indifferent to him (Προσηκόντως οὖν καὶ τὴν τῶν τριῶν λόγῳ μὲν ἀνδρῶν, ἔργῳ δέ, ὡς εἶπον, ἀρετῶν οἰκειότητα συνῆψε φύσις, μάθησις, ἄσκησις ... ἵνα καὶ τὸ αἰώνιον ὄνομα τὸ δηλούμενον ἐν τοῖς χρησμοῖς μὴ ἐπὶ τριῶν ἀνθρώπων μᾶλλον ἢ τῶν εἰρημένων λέγηται δυνάμεων, ἀνθρώπων μὲν γὰρ φθαρτὴ φύσις, ἄφθαρτος δὲ ἡ τῶν ἀρετῶν)[2]. What is clear is that the allegorical

[1] I. 38 M.   [2] II. 9 M.

method is relied on to educe the moral and theological significance of the words of the Old Testament.

In dealing with the Law, Philo shows a disposition to allegorize and sometimes also to rationalize particular enactments, such as that of circumcision[1], or the use of the blood and fat in sacrifice[2]. But in the long series of tracts which bear on the provisions of the Decalogue, he traces the complex system of enactments to the principles involved in the commandments themselves. In doing this, Philo was the forerunner of all those who have taken the Decalogue as a complete canon of life and applied its various precepts by means of expansion and analysis. Thus it is argued at somewhat considerable length that the law of murder covers various forms of death which are not carried out by open violence, such as poisoning by means of incantations; the law relating to involuntary destruction of an opponent is explained, and other similar enactments are discussed. The nearest approach to an ethical extension of the Law is found in the beginning of the exposition, in which Philo connects the prohibition of murder with the sin of sacrilege. The true name of the action is ἱεροσυλία καὶ ἱεροσυλιῶν ἡ μεγίστη, διότι τῶν ἐν κόσμῳ κτημάτων καὶ κειμηλίων οὐδὲν οὔτε ἱεροπρεπέστερον οὔτε θεοειδέστερόν ἐστιν ἀνθρώπου, παγκάλης εἰκόνος πάγκαλον ἐκμαγεῖον ἀρχετύπου λογικῆς ἰδέας παραδείγματι τυπωθέν[3]. In one connexion (the exposition of the third commandment[4], Philo makes use of an expression which suggests comparison with the Sermon on the Mount. 'It would be best, most profitable, most completely in harmony with a rational nature, never to swear at all: a word should be as good as an oath.' It is the second-best course to be trustworthy on oath, ἤδη γὰρ ὅγε ὄμνυς εἰς ἀπιστίαν ὑπονοεῖται[5].

In these and similar passages Philo shows clearly enough where he stands in regard of the Jewish Law. It is for him complete and final; he has no new message. The things he

[1] *De Circumcisione*, c. 1, II. 211 M.
[2] *De Concupiscentia*, cc. 10, 11, II. 356 367 M.
[3] *De Spec. Legg.* III. 15, II. 313 M. [4] *De Dec. Orac.* c. 17, II. 195 M.
[5] Similar advice is given in the treatise, *De Spec. Legg.* II.

does not understand at all, he allegorizes: that is, such provisions as seem to be purely positive enactments, of which, as Butler says, it is not possible to see the reason. These lose all meaning when their material form is cut away, and their supposed symbolic implication is alone drawn out. In no case does Philo approach what Christ, interpreted by St. Paul, has taught us to call the spiritual meaning. Allegory does not necessarily lead to a spiritual exposition. Its value depends entirely upon the character of the system of thoughts to which the material emblems are referred. Those who extracted the principles of Conic Sections out of Homer, or who in these days obtain prophecies out of the Great Pyramid, are obliged to use an allegorical method of interpretation. But neither interpretation is spiritual: in one case it is mathematical, in the other it is purely imaginative. In the case of Philo it is often metaphysical, sometimes ethical. But it does not reach beyond the ethical code already present in Philo's mind, and this is the code of the Law adjusted to the demands of Greek philosophy. Again, in cases where the method of allegory is not used, Philo appears rather in the character of a judge or casuist applying a rule of law to a variety of cases than of one who puts an altogether new and wider sense upon the claim of the Law. And then he does not as a rule get beyond the original reference of the Law: he expands it, as a general term may be shown to cover in detail certain particular instances. That is the full effect of the application of the law of murder to various kinds of killing. Philo only verges on the spiritual significance of murder when he explains it as a form of sacrilege. For it is in this and in such cases that he comes nearest to referring the whole of man's life to some wider conception of his nature and position. Philo treats the Law, as has been already noticed, as complete and final; he does not take the whole of it up into some wider system, which is the function of a prophet with a new message.

IV. But it is time to come now to the consideration of Philo's actual system or scheme of virtues. And this is by no means an easy task. The terminology of the moral philosophy of the Greeks was partly technical and partly popular. The four virtues—called by later thinkers the cardinal virtues—hold the first place. But there are always a number of other names of virtuous habits which appear from time to time in philosophical writings. Various virtues over and above the four are mentioned both in Plato and Aristotle, and Plutarch [1] accuses Chrysippus of having introduced 'a swarm of virtues neither familiar nor known.' If this was a true charge against Chrysippus, it lies with great force also against Philo. While there is constant reference to the four, there is always a list of other habits ready, sometimes a very long one [2]. Hence it is not easy to determine from the lists of virtues what the type of life is at which Philo aims. There is, however, one thing clear on the whole, namely, that εὐσέβεια—the right religious relation towards God—is the supreme virtue. Yet even this cannot be asserted quite without qualification, as Philo occasionally places some other virtue in this position.

The keynote of all Philo's ethical theory lies in the word *separation*. His scheme of human life consists in the gradual withdrawal from all earthly things and concentration upon the supreme existence, the source of all good and all blessing. It is clearly difficult for Philo to unite the various elements of his thought at this point. For the tendency of Jewish thought was certainly not ascetic by nature. The law of the Nazarite was almost the only feature in it which did not contemplate the ordinary practical life of the world. It was to be a life in which the presence and pressure of religion were to be continually felt, but it was still a life of an ordinary citizen. He would keep feasts and fasts, accept the rules of clean and unclean, and fulfil ceremonial obligations, but he would not be separated from the ordinary ways of men. On the other hand, the Hellenic view of life as governed by the speculations of Plato and the Stoics did carry with it a large element of asceticism. The dualism between soul and body which

[1] *De Virt. Mor.* c. 3.   [2] Cf. *De Poen.* c. 2, II. 406 M.

was characteristic of Platonism, the despair and perplexity which marked the Stoic view of life, were both disposing causes in the direction of separation. The wise man did not expect to find himself at home in the world; he expected rather to feel a stranger, and to live his truest life apart from his fellow-men.

So far as this doctrine depended upon a definite theory of the soul and the body, it was not particularly easy to Philo. His sense of the goodness and wisdom of God exercises considerable control over him; and his theory of the due order of the world stands against a doctrine by which the actual sensuous life is evil. At the same time there are passages in which the body is represented on a distinctly inferior level. Thus in *De Agric.* c. 19[1] he comments on the prohibition to go to Egypt for horses; he identifies Egypt with the body, and explains that to go the road to Egypt is to become fond of pleasure and emotion rather than of virtue and of God. Thus again, changing his metaphor, he speaks of the soul overwhelmed by the pressure of emotions and injustices, and sinking into the depths; and winds up with the words, 'the depth into which it sinks and is swamped is the body, itself likened to Egypt.' In the same work he speaks of the soul in the body in the phrase νεκροφοροῦσα. There are some, he says, who are uninitiated in the psychical agriculture, which sows and plants virtues, and reaps the happy life as a harvest from them; these men tend most anxiously the body—τὸν ψυχῆς ἔγγιστα οἶκον, ὃν ἀπὸ γενέσεως ἄχρι τελευτῆς —ἄχθος τοσοῦτον—οὐκ ἀποτίθεται νεκροφοροῦσα [2].

These and similar passages indicate the gloomy position occupied by the soul in the bodily life. In this doctrine Philo is in harmony with the Alexandrine author of the Book of Wisdom; that is, with the later and partially Hellenized Judaism rather than with the simpler faith of the Old Testament. But it would be an error to suppose that the position is wholly dismal. In every one's life there come occasional glimpses of the vision of good; no one is wholly left without

---

[1] I. 314 M. [2] *De Agric.* c. 5, I. 304 M.

some inspiration sent from God. Τίς γὰρ οὕτως ἄλογος ἢ ἄψυχος ἐστὶν ὡς μηδέποτε ἔννοιαν τοῦ ἀρίστου μήθ' ἑκὼν μήτ' ἄκων λαβεῖν; ἀλλὰ γὰρ καὶ τοῖς ἐξαγίστοις ἐπιποτᾶται πολλάκις αἰφνίδιος ἡ τοῦ καλοῦ φαντασία, συλλαβεῖν δὲ αὐτὴν καὶ φυλάξαι παρ' ἑαυτοῖς ἀδυνατοῦσιν[1]. But at the same time the true object of every soul is to still the passions and arouse the reason, and lead it to dwell on the perfections of God. In order to do this it is necessary first to receive the call or the inspiration of God. To ignore this is a grievous and foolish sin. Πτωμάτων ἀργαλεώτατον Θεοῦ τιμῆς ἀποπεσεῖν ὀλισθόντα, στεφανώσαντα πρὸ ἐκείνου ἑαυτόν, καὶ φόνον ἐμφύλιον ἐργασάμενον. Κτείνει γὰρ τὴν ἑαυτοῦ ψυχὴν ὁ μὴ τὸ ὂν τιμῶν ὡς ἀνόνητον αὐτῷ γενέσθαι παιδείας τὸ οἰκοδόμημα[2]. So God, wishing to purify the soul of man, calls upon it to make a threefold sacrifice (typified by Abraham's giving up his country, his own people, and his father's house)—the sacrifice of the body, the senses, and the discursive reason (λόγου τοῦ κατὰ προφοράν, that is, the reason which is exercised upon mere experience)[3]. The result of this call, if it be accepted by the soul, is to turn it away from the transitory and sensuous, and fix it upon the eternal. It means that the soul should forsake the body and its pleasures (τὸ παμμίαρον ἐκφυγὼν δεσμωτήριον, τὸ σῶμα), should draw back from the leading of the senses, and put no faith in the disquisitions of the ordinary reason (ἵνα μὴ ῥημάτων καὶ ὀνομάτων ἀπατηθεὶς κάλλεσι τοῦ πρὸς ἀλήθειαν κάλλους ... διαζευχθῇς)[4]. The method by which this separation is to be achieved is chiefly education. For ἀπαιδευσία τῶν ψυχῆς ἁμαρτημάτων, εἰ δεῖ τὸ ἀληθὲς εἰπεῖν, τὸ ἀρχέκακον, ἀφ' ἧς ὥσπερ ἀπὸ πηγῆς ῥέουσιν αἱ τοῦ βίου πράξεις[5]. Certain suggestions are found as to the course which this education should take. Children, says Philo, are fed on milk, and so

---

[1] *De Gigantibus*, c. 5, I. 265 M.
[2] *De Agric.* c. 39, I. 326 M. This passage comes, oddly enough, as a comment upon the injunction in Deuteronomy xxii. 8, to put a battlement or parapet on a new house. The new house is the οἰκοδόμημα παιδείας, which a man must not claim for himself.
[3] *De Migr. Abr.* c. 1, I. 436-437 M.   [4] *Ibid.*
[5] *De Ebr.* c. 3, I. 359 M.

Note to Lectures III and IV 157

minds which are untrained should receive γαλακτώδεις τροφαί; they should be instructed in τὰ τῆς ἐγκυκλίου μουσικῆς προπαιδεύματα[1]. The instruction in virtue (αἱ διὰ φρονήσεως καὶ σωφροσύνης καὶ ἁπάσης ἀρετῆς ὑφηγήσεις) are for mature men[2]. In this regard Philo's scheme somewhat closely resembles Plato's. But he is aware of certain dangers connected with some of the subjects in which Plato had faith; even dialectic and geometry do not in all cases contribute to the improvement of character. Hence the method commended by Philo is rather that of the Stoics than that of Plato, philosophy being divided into the three parts, physics, ethics, and logic. But still it contains the ordinary elements of education: reading, writing, the study of the poets, geometry, and rhetoric. It is after these that the occasion arises for developing the virtuous habits. In the work *Quod Omnis Probus Liber* Philo gives an account of the methods of the Essenes, who represent his ideal of the virtuous life. From this it is possible that we may get some notion of the method he would have pursued in this kind of education. It seems that the education consisted partly in the practice of moral duties, partly in exhortations. They use three rules—the love of God, the love of virtue, and the love of man. The former leads them to purity, truthfulness, and the conviction that God is the cause of good only. By the second they forsake the love of money, ambition, love of pleasure, and acquire continence, simplicity, modesty, firmness, and so on. The love of man produces kindliness, equality, and a general community of all goods. The *De Vita Contemplativa* (a work which has been long doubted, but is now ascribed to Philo by its most recent editor, Mr. F. C. Conybeare) gives a more particular account of the practices of those, whom the author calls Therapeutae and seems to regard as a more severe type of Essene. These are a body of men and women whose chief object is contemplation. They forsake all worldly goods and live in a community, fasting and praying continually, meeting only on the seventh day. These are the people

[1] *De Agric.* c. 2, I. 301 M.   [2] *Ibid.*

whom Philo (if Philo be the author) regards as following the ideal life; they alone are truly free, and they alone are truly happy. Their whole life is spent in following the highest knowledge, and in sustaining communion with the source of all things. This is, of course, an ideal to which the generality of men cannot attain, but it fixes, on the whole, the lines of Philo's views on morality. The four cardinal virtues, if they are active, require the aid of circumstances to bring them into operation[1]. And when in operation they are σωτήρια τῆς διανοίας[2]; they preserve the mind which the intoxication of folly destroys. So it would seem that they belong more naturally to the outward political or social life of man, which is dealt with by παιδεία rather than by reason alone. There are, says Philo, two parents of the true life, ὀρθὸς λόγος and παιδεία; the former exhorting to the following of nature (the principle of the life of the Essenes[3]), and the latter commanding the due use of the conventions and enactments of the state[4]. Yet even this division returns upon the ascetic ideal. In a later chapter (c. 20) of the tract *De Ebr.*, Philo cites Jacob as an instance of the man who combines the merits of ὀρθὸς λόγος and παιδεία, and represents his change of name as the moment of his attainment. Jacob is the name of learning and advance, powers dependent on hearing (that is, attained by education); but Israel is the symbol of perfection, as the name means the vision of God: for what can be more perfect of all the results of virtue than to see the truly existent being (τὸ ὄντως ὄν)? Thus the ordinary course of education when perfected ends in the ascetic contemplation of God[5].

The Garden of Eden represents the ideal order of the moral life. There is a river to water it, which breaks into four streams. The great river is virtue in general (ἡ γενικὴ ἀρετὴ ἣν ὠνομάσαμεν ἀγαθότητα). This rises ἀπὸ τῆς 'Εδέμ, that is, flows out from the Wisdom of God. It is in fact the Word of God,

[1] *De Sobr.* c. 9, I. 399 M.   [2] *De Ebr.* c. 6, I. 360 M.
[3] *Quod Omnis Probus Liber*, c. 22, II. 470 M.
[4] *De Ebr.* c. 9, I. 362 M.
[5] Cf. *Leg. Alleg.* I. 17, I. 54 M, where the position of πρᾶξις is contrasted with that of θεωρία.

Note to Lectures III and IV

and constitutes the four cardinal virtues. Of these each is chief in its own province. Φρόνησις fixes rules for things to be done; ἀνδρεία for things to be endured; σωφροσύνη for things to be chosen; δικαιοσύνη for the things involving others[1]. But φρόνησις reigns supreme over all, keeping the balance between the three parts of the soul. In this Philo follows Plato closely, and adds little to the conception of the four virtues already prevailing. In the tract *De Justitia*, he twice uses language implying the doctrine of the mean.

In this region of speculation Philo does little but maintain the Greek conception of virtue, giving it a bias in the direction of ascetic and philosophical piety. But there are certain conditions belonging to the moral or religious nature on which he lays emphasis, and is probably original in so doing. It is difficult to find a word to represent exactly what they are. In the treatise *De Praemiis et Poenis* they are described as *rewards* bestowed by God on certain individuals. In the *De Abrahamo* they seem to be the characteristic features of certain lives. The first of these states or rewards is *hope*, ἐλπίς, of which Enos son of Seth is typical. This is the great incentive to virtue as to all other things. It explains the long endurance and labour which men undergo who seek gain or glory: 'it is the hope of happiness which inspires those who are zealots for virtue to be philosophers, as by this they will be able to see the nature of things and do that which agrees (with this knowledge) with a view to the completion of the best lives, theoretical and practical, which he who gains is straightway happy[2].' Next to this comes μετάνοια, or repentance, ἡ ἐπὶ τοῖς ἁμαρτανομένοις μετάνοια καὶ βελτίωσις, which is typified by Enoch. For Enoch was translated; he was removed from a lower to a higher grade of being. The modes by which repentance is carried out are ἀποικία, change of place, and solitude, μόνωσις. A man must leave his country, his kindred, and his father's house, else he may find it im-

[1] *Leg. Alleg.* I. 19, I. 56 M.
[2] *De Praem.* c. 2, II. 410 M. Cf. *De Abr.* c. 3, II. 3 M (ἡ ἐλπὶς) ἦν ἐπὶ θύραις οἷα πυλωρὸν ἡ φύσις ἱδρύσατο βασιλίδων τῶν ἔνδον ἀρετῶν, αἷς οὐκ ἔστιν ἐντυχεῖν μὴ ταύτην προθεραπεύσαντας.

possible to break through the chains of habit. In a small work, *De Poenitentia*, Philo adopts the position that repentance is always the second-best course. The ideal thing is to do no wrong, though when wrong is done the best thing is to repent. At the same time there are very few whom God so graces as to keep them free from all evil, voluntary or involuntary[1]; and therefore Philo is perhaps not inconsistent in making μετάνοια the second of these states.

The third of these states (typified by Noah) is somewhat oddly called Justice, a term which one would naturally have expected to find used only for the virtue. Very little is said upon the subject in *De Praem.* (c. 4), but the life and significance of Noah are treated at some length in *De Abr.* (cc. 5–8). Two different translations of the word Noah are given, Rest and Justice, and their fitness is explained by reference to the life of Noah. In contrast to the other two, Enos and Enoch, he is the person who has attained, and is perfect and well-pleasing to God. These three—Hope, Repentance, and Justice or Rest—are the first or lowest triad.

Above them comes a higher triad, standing to the lower as the severer athletic trials of a man stand to those of a boy. It is typified by Abraham, Isaac, and Jacob, who in another place[2] are said to represent three types of virtue, διδασκαλική, φυσική, and ἀσκητική. Abraham stands for faith, Isaac for joy, Jacob, as before, for the vision of God. The quality of faith is obscurely described, but it seems to consist in a rejection of all worldly methods, and an approach to God by blind confidence in God alone: it consists, among other things, in a bettering of the 'soul, which rests upon the cause of all things, who can do all things, and wishes all that is best[3].' Joy is the natural outcome of faith, and is indicated by Isaac's name, which means laughter. The climax is attained by Jacob, whose name Israel means the vision of God, but does not imply the vision of God as He is: man

---

[1] *De Agric.* c. 40, I. 328 M.   [2] *De Jos.* c. 1, II. 41 M.
[3] *De Abr.* c. 46, II. 39 M; and compare note on Lecture III above (pp. 109, 110).

Note to Lectures III and IV

can only know that He is[1]. It should be further noticed that Philo expressly admits that these various qualities are not the exclusive possession of these patriarchs[2], and that he ascribes others to Abraham, such, for instance, as φιλανθρωπία[3]. This is described as ἡ πρὸς ἀνθρώπους δεξιότης, and is almost identified with δικαιοσύνη.

In addition to these social or moral virtues Philo makes allusion to the true form of polity. Politics is one subject of the education of the Essenes[4], and in a way forms the climax of the good man's thought. But it has a somewhat shadowy existence, and it is difficult to see why Philo should recur to the true constitution, if it were not that politics formed part of every Greek philosopher's speculations. Philo has no doubt as to the nature of the true constitution: it is democracy. This constitution flows from the principle of equality[5]; it is the original constitution of the whole world[6]; it is symbolized by the orderly arrangement of the senses in the soul[7]; its most dangerous opposite is mob-rule (ὀχλοκρατία)[8], which is indeed simply a caricature of it[9]. But the democracy in the created world is really a theocracy. This is the meaning of the first commandment—'that there is one cause of the world, one leader, and one king, who guides and governs all things in the way of salvation, having driven out from the heaven, the purest of things[10], oligarchy and mob-rule, traitorous constitutions which have sprung up among the worst of men out of disorder and covetousness.'

Besides all this there is a type of political virtue—the virtue of a ruler—which is represented by Joseph. In a certain sense such a man is an appendage or addition, as is implied by the meaning of the Hebrew word Joseph. Προσθηκαὶ μὲν γὰρ οἱ κατὰ πόλεις νόμοι τοῦ τῆς φύσεως ὀρθοῦ λόγου· προσθήκη δέ ἐστι πολιτικὸς ἀνὴρ τοῦ βιοῦντος κατὰ φύσιν[11]. The

---
[1] *De Praem.* cc. 5, 6, 7, II. 412-416 M.   [2] *De Abr.* c. 11, II. 9 M.
[3] *Ibid.* c. 37, II. 30 M.   [4] *Quod Omnis Probus Liber,* c. 12, II. 458 M.
[5] *De Just.* c. 14, II. 374 M.   [6] Cf. *De Sept.* c. 3, II. 278 M.
[7] *De Abr.* c. 41, II. 34 M.   [8] *De Agric.* c. 11, I. 307 M.
[9] *De Conf. Ling.* c. 23, I. 421 M.   [10] *De Dec. Orac.* c. 29, II. 205 M.
[11] *De Jos.* c. 6, II. 46 M.

life of Joseph indicates the demands made upon the ruler. He is first given the rule over sheep, then over Potiphar's household, and then is tried under the temptation of Potiphar's wife. He is thus ποιμενικός, οἰκονομικός, and καρτερικός [1]. His triumph over this seduction marks him as ἐγκρατής. Philo explains the story in the sense that the political ruler must resist the seductions of the mob: he knows that the people are supreme, but he is not prepared to give way to them contrary to his idea of right. He is pure and free [2]. As Joseph interpreted the dreams of Pharaoh, so the politician will be ὀνειροκριτικός. He will interpret human life, which is but a semblance—a dream without reality. In all the confusion he will keep his head, and be able to say what is right and wrong, and give sound guidance in life [3].

The various characteristics of Philo's philosophy, so far as they are required by our present purpose, have now been set forth. It is hard to derive any very connected theory from Philo's writings, for reasons which have already been mentioned. But it is urged that if Philo had any definite meaning at all, it approached the position here described. For the ideas and principles illustrated are not isolated expressions of passing opinion: they are views which continually reappear throughout Philo's writings, and the position they expound is easily explained out of the certain historical associations of Philo's life.

The most important of the principles noticed so far is that of the ascetic separation of man from the ordinary interests of life and his concentration upon the knowledge of the Supreme. This is no isolated idea or vague impression: it is reiterated in every possible form, and runs through the majority of his works. And it is not of Jewish origin. Its

[1] The first of these requirements reminds us of Plat. *Polit.* p. 261. The second is based upon a reason apparently accepted by Plato (*ibid.* 259 B), but which Aristotle, at any rate, would have rejected with scorn, viz. that a household is πόλις ἐσταλμένη καὶ βραχεῖα καὶ οἰκονομία συνηγμένη τις πολιτεία, ὡς καὶ πόλις μὲν οἶκος μέγας, πολιτεία δὲ κοινή τις οἰκονομία. *De Jos.* c. 8, II. 47 M. Cf. Ar. *Pol.* I. i.

[2] *De Jos.* c. 14, II. 51, 52 M.   [3] *Ibid.* c. 24, II. 61, 62 M.

history lies in Greek thought, and it falls into its due place in the evolution of Greek moral speculation. The ecstasy of Plotinus, in which the soul, after abstraction from all the pressing claims of the body, at last enjoys the sense of communion with the primal cause, is organically continuous with the asceticism of Philo.

Moreover, there are other signs of Philo's close connexion with the particular development of philosophy prevalent at the Christian era. At that time the Academy—the school which professed to have descended in direct line from Plato—was sceptical. They doubted the evidence of their senses, and had not as yet done full justice to the positive and constructive sides of Plato's thought. This aspect of his philosophy was coming to the front, and is the motive force in all the subsequent developments of Platonism. Philo shows signs of both influences. He quotes and is influenced by the language of the *Timaeus* and *Phaedrus*, and at the same time he shows a tendency to deny the reality of all sensuous facts. The passage concerning the politician as an interpreter of dreams (which is a very fine one) conspicuously embodies this view, and there is another long discussion upon the same point in *De Ebr.* c. 39 and following chapters.

The views of Philo, therefore, have considerable interest for us. He had absorbed the philosophical learning of the Greeks in the receptive Jewish way, and attempted to amalgamate this with the utterances of the Jewish Law. It was a time when new efforts were to be made to solve the problems of life and existence, and Philo was on the field early. He had in his hands two of the influences which were to combine in the later doctrines of the Church—philosophy and the Law: yet he did not succeed. It is not very hard to find the cause of this failure.

His doctrine of ascetic separation was inadequate on two grounds. First, it was primarily an intellectual movement. It depended on the intellectual distinction between the real and the false, and ended in an intellectual realization of the presence and power of the Supreme Being. The life of ordinary virtue was second to this divine philosophy, and was hampered by its relations with the material world. But it was the ordinary life of virtue that now required consideration and help.

And, secondly, the asceticism had really very little to say about practical duties. Not only was the life it commended chiefly intellectual, but it tended to bind down the life of the individual within himself and relieve him of the trouble of performing ordinary moral duties. The entire separation of the Therapeutae might be exceptional, and not for all; but the Essenes, who represented the practical rather than the theoretic life. were still separated from the world. It may be said that in all the discussions on the Law Philo deals with practical questions; and this is true of a large number of the treatises which are based on the Decalogue. But it remains that the value of a moral system depends very largely upon the ideal it sets before men, and Philo's was an unpractical ideal. It appealed to the good as Celsus tells us the Greek mysteries did, and it could never have been open to the charge of filling the kingdom of heaven with cobblers and other low and ignorant people[1]. Though Philo rightly resented the doctrine that nobility depends on the family in which a man is born, it was still the wise man alone who is truly noble, and he had a right to the name whatever the circumstances of his birth. In advance of his age Philo extended his patent of nobility to women[2], but he rests their right on the same philosophical ground. He has missed the opportunity of dealing with sin, and hence his system fails in comparison with the more seasonable suggestions of St. Paul.

This conclusion as to the importance of Philo is borne out by various facts: (1) by the generally metaphysical character of the influence of Philo and of Platonism upon the Church-writers; (2) by the drift of moral speculation itself within the Church. We must now illustrate these two positions. (1) The region in which the influence of Platonism was soonest and most effectively felt was Alexandria. And the two names

---

[1] Cf. Orig. *c. Cels.* III. 55.   [2] *De Nob.* c. 6, II. 443 M.

Note to Lectures III and IV

most closely connected with the Platonic theology are those of Clement and Origen. We shall do well, therefore, to speak of them first.

The philosophy of Plato, as has already been noticed, was resuming its more positive aspect in the period just preceding Philo, and had found affinities, born of controversy, with the morality of the Stoic. It would seem that Philo had but a small influence upon his age. Probably his intense interest in the Jewish Law would have made him unintelligible to many of his contemporaries. Hence he must not be regarded as contributing in any notable degree to the development of heathen Platonism [1]. But though this is true of his general relation to his successors, it remains that Philo anticipated the movement of Platonic thought in several important particulars. His conception of the nature of God and the mode of attainment of communion with God foreshadowed, as we have seen, the 'ecstasy' of Plotinus: and the emphasis laid by him on knowledge as the means of a virtuous life fell in with the Platonic tendency to regard evil as a mere mistake. Also the contrast drawn in Philo between the ideal life of knowledge and the lower life of mere virtuous practice anticipates the contrast between Gnôsis and Pistis—the esoteric and exoteric doctrines—of which we hear in the later schools and in Gnosticism [2].

---

[1] Cf. Bigg, *Neoplatonism*, p. 123.

[2] All these points of view are to be found in Philo; but it does not necessarily follow that they are original in him, or that, if they were original in him, it was from him that they percolated through the Platonic schools. It must always be remembered that those whose works are preserved to us, as one may say, accidentally, wrote in an atmosphere of philosophical discussion, and in the presence of a school of philosophical thinkers. In all these schools there were philosophical traditions—doctrines which would have been accepted by all who followed a particular line. This has to be borne in mind with special care in dealing with Clement and Origen. Clement (150–213 A.D.) could certainly never have come across Plotinus (205–269 A.D.), and Origen (185–254 A.D.) would probably have never known him as a teacher. Between Philo and Plotinus there is no philosopher of the first rank whose works have come down to us in any large quantity. Hence, though Clement was undoubtedly influenced by

Clement of Alexandria is of the greatest importance in this connexion. His knowledge of classical and philosophical authors was very considerable, and his method of using his knowledge is such as to make unusually plain the relation in which he stood to them. He constantly cites Plato and other philosophical writers, and explains the grounds on which he agrees with or differs from their opinions. He avows openly that in philosophy he is an eclectic, and that there are some philosophical positions that he cannot tolerate[1]. Hence we are not dealing with a writer whose literary antecedents require to be traced with difficulty; his indebtedness to philosophy, and especially to the philosophy of Plato, lies upon the surface. His attitude to pagan thought was, it would seem, somewhat novel, and excited some degree of suspicion. So he complains that some of his contemporaries are terrified at the Greek philosophers, like children at μορ-μολύκια, and expect to be led away from the faith by them[2]. To Clement's mind, on the contrary, philosophy is a gift from the Word of God: it is a preparation given to the Gentiles for the full light of Christianity, as the Law was given to the Jews[3]; and he is therefore fully justified in using such parts of it as help to clear up the Christian position. If it is not necessary to establish the truth, it may be a useful weapon of defence[4]. We may reasonably anticipate that it might be difficult to adjust the claims of the Greek philosophers and Christian theology; and so, no doubt, it proves. But though this is so, there is no mistake about the loyalty and complete-ness of Clement's adhesion to Christianity. Clement, though he must have been in some measure a student, had still an eye for what went on around him. He sees that the ordinary type of social life is coarse and vulgar, and he feels that in some way it is Christianity that has revealed this fact to him. Owing to the teaching of Christ the Paedagogus, he has learnt

Philo, yet a large allowance must be made for the growth of a tradition within the Platonic schools which will be the proximate cause of the peculiar type of Platonism found in Clement.

[1] *Strom.* I. vii. 37, xi. 50, and following sections.
[2] *Ibid.* VI. x. 80. [3] *Ibid.* VII. ii. 6, iii. 20. [4] *Ibid.* I. xx. 100.

the beauty of simple life and manners. He claims, therefore, that the Christian should be simple in all respects, in all the various regions in which the multitude of possessions makes ostentatious magnificence possible and easy. In these recommendations, which occur chiefly in the last two books of the *Paedagogus*, he does not pass very far beyond Plato. But the motive which he alleges is different, and it was probably more effective: the call of Christ finally disjoins men's minds from the more sordid interests in life; they seek simplicity naturally[1]. The same rule will obtain in every other case where luxury is possible; but always the object is not to destroy the various impulses of human nature, so much as to impose measure and order upon them, to keep them in their place with a masterful hand[2]. It is virtue only that is the cause of beauty, in man as in everything else[3]. These and other regulations, of which there is a large number in the *Paedagogus*, show clearly enough what was the nature of one of the effects, at least, which Christianity was having on the life of the later second century. The incidental descriptions of the existing practices of the rich heathen strike one at first as verging on satirical exaggeration. It is possible that they may be slightly exaggerated; but they certainly do not go beyond the accounts of writers in whom no Christian bias can be suspected—Lucian, for instance, or Plutarch. But there is very little severity in Clement's tone. He does write from the decidedly Christian standpoint; but, as has already been said, he does not regard heathenism as all irredeemably bad.

[1] *Paed.* II. i. 10 : οὐκ ἀφεκτέον οὖν παντελῶς τῶν ποικίλων βρωμάτων, ἀλλ' οὐ περὶ αὐτὰ σπουδαστέον· μεταληπτέον δὲ τῶν παρατιθεμένων, ὡς πρέπον Χριστιανῷ, τιμῶντας μὲν τὸν κεκληκότα κατὰ τὴν ἀβλαβῆ καὶ ἀπροσκορῆ τῆς συνουσίας κοινωνίαν, ἀδιάφορον δὲ ἡγουμένους τῶν εἰσκομιζομένων τὴν πολυτέλειαν, καταφρονοῦντες τῶν ὄψων, ὡς μετ' ὀλίγον οὐκ ὄντων.

[2] *Ibid.* v. 46 : ἁπλῶς γάρ, ὁπόσα φυσικὰ τοῖς ἀνθρώποις ἐστί, ταῦτα οὐκ ἀναιρεῖν ἐξ αὐτῶν δεῖ, μᾶλλον δὲ μέτρον αὐτοῖς καὶ καιρὸν ἐπιτιθέναι πρέποντα.

[3] *Ibid.* xii. 121 : τὸ γὰρ ἑκάστου καὶ φυτοῦ καὶ ζῴου κάλλος ἐν τῇ ἑκάστου ἀρετῇ εἶναι συμβέβηκεν. ἀνθρώπου δὲ ἀρετὴ δικαιοσύνη καὶ σωφροσύνη καὶ ἀνδρία καὶ εὐσέβεια. καλὸς ἄρα ἄνθρωπος ὁ δίκαιος καὶ σώφρων καὶ συλλήβδην ὁ ἀγαθός, οὐχ ὁ πλούσιος.

168   *Christian Ethics*

The attitude of Clement is clearly shown in the *Paedagogus*: and, if it were to the point here, it would be possible to illustrate much more fully the external contrast between Christianity and Paganism. We are concerned, however, more immediately with his general moral theory, and to this we must now turn. Clement wrote in full view of Gnosticism—a way of thinking which exercised considerable attraction over some minds. And this means that he was writing in view of a particular moral problem—the question of evil. Gnosticism in one respect resembled Christianity: it offered a theory of evil and a way of salvation from sin. But it differed in almost every other possible detail. The theories of evil offered by the various sects of Gnostics were almost always mechanical; and the way of salvation was rarely attainable by all men. A few—those who were capable of attaining the ideal of knowledge held out to them —were those who were in the way of salvation in the best and highest sense; the others lived on a lower level, and attained a poorer result. It is one of Clement's objects in his *Stromateis* to deal with this prevalent line of thought as a critic, but not as a merely unfriendly critic. Hence he accepts the term *Gnostic* as describing his ideal man; and he distinguishes two lives—a higher and lower—both of which are possible in the Christian Church, to both of which he promises salvation. The true Gnostic is wholly separated from the world. The attainment of γνῶσις is like death[1]. He is absolutely without passion of any kind; even the love, in which his character finds its complete satisfaction, is separated from all emotion[2]. It is also wholly disinterested. The Gnostic loves God because to do so is absolutely the most perfect realization of human life, not because it gains him any certainty of salvation, or because of any benefits that he has

[1] *Strom*. VII. xii. 71 : αὐτίκα ὡς ὁ θάνατος χωρισμὸς ψυχῆς ἀπὸ σώματος οὕτως ἡ γνῶσις, οἶον ὁ λογικὸς θάνατος, ἀπὸ τῶν παθῶν ἐπείγων καὶ χωρίζων τὴν ψυχὴν καὶ προάγων εἰς τὴν τῆς εὐποιίας ζωὴν ἵνα τότε εἴπῃ μετὰ παρρησίας πρὸς τὸν θεόν, ὡς θέλεις ζῶ.
[2] *Ibid*. VI. ix. 73.

Note to Lectures III and IV

received[1]. 'I will be bold and say that it is not because he wishes for salvation that he will choose γνῶσις who pursues it for the sake of divine knowledge alone.... Indeed, if any one were to offer to the Gnostic, as a test case, his choice between knowledge and eternal salvation (supposing these were separated which are really in closest union), without any hesitation he would choose the knowledge of God, judging that property of faith, which passes up through love to knowledge, desirable for its own sake[2].' Love, indeed, is hardly distinguishable, on these high levels, from knowledge[3]. Love has a suggestion of passion or emotion, which must be given up. The Gnostic will love mankind and try to save them: οὐδὲ ἄρα φιλεῖ τινα τὴν κοινὴν ταύτην φιλίαν, ἀλλ' ἀγαπᾷ τὸν κτίστην διὰ τῶν κτισμάτων[4]. He will be virtuous, but in his own way. As he has no base desires, his virtues will not take the form of a severe control over unruly impulses; he will differ from the lower type of virtue in having the supreme motive of all action present before him, the disinterested love of God[5]. His life will be spent in continuous silent intercourse with God; even if he uses the ordinary fixed hours of prayer, he will still live in ceaseless adoration of the God who reads the heart.

For all this the lower life is a kind of preface or introduction[6]. As the life of the Gnostic is characterized by knowledge and love, so that of the lower attainment is ruled by fear and faith. And yet this represents no slavish superstitious fear, which Clement regards as a πάθος[7], but rather a fear of falling away from God. ὁ τοῦ ἀπαθοῦς θεοῦ φόβος ἀπαθής, φοβεῖται γάρ τις οὐ τὸν θεόν, ἀλλὰ τὸ ἀποπεσεῖν τοῦ θεοῦ. It is a state

---

[1] *Strom.* IV. xxii. 137, 138.
[2] *Ibid.* 138.
[3] *Ibid.* VI. ix. 73.
[4] *Ibid.* 71.
[5] *Ibid.* VII. x. 59; and cf. Arist. *Eth. N.* X. vii., Of the gods and their relation to virtue.
[6] Πρόκειται δὲ τοῖς εἰς τελείωσιν σπεύδουσιν ἡ γνῶσις ἡ λογική, ἧς θεμέλιος ἡ ἁγία τριάς, πίστις, ἐλπίς, ἀγάπη, μείζων δὲ τούτων ἡ ἀγάπη. *Strom.* IV. vii. 55.
[7] *Ibid.* II. viii. 40.

which falls short of the full certainty of the Gnostic, though it is, as it were, a stage in the direction of the Gnostic's ideal. And faith is a summary and imperfect realization of that which the Gnostic knows[1]. For this life the ordinary education and virtue is suitable and sufficient. But though the Christian is continent and possesses all the cardinal virtues, his acts fall short of the absolute ideal, because he has not the true motive of all moral life, the disinterested and passionless love of God. This point of view is developed at length in regard to the virtues in *Strom.* VII. xi., and of this we need say no more. But it is desirable to add a few words concerning ἐγκράτεια, or self-control. This state was excluded from the class of virtues by Aristotle, on the ground that it was transitional and incomplete[2]; and in the special treatment given to it in *Eth. N.* VII the logical difficulties are discussed chiefly which can so easily be raised round a moral state which is transitional. There are occasional reminiscences of this logical aspect of ἐγκράτεια in Clement[3]. But, for the most part, ἐγκράτεια has acquired a much loftier position than it had ever occupied before. It is, according to Clement, inculcated in the Law as the basis of all virtue[4]; a superior level of it is attainable than any that was reached by Greek philosophy[5], and its character is more positive than before, seeing that it now forms the basis of reasonable self-limitation in regard of all the passions or desires. The cause of this

---

[1] *Strom.* VII. x. 47: ἡ μὲν οὖν πίστις σύντομός ἐστιν, ὡς εἰπεῖν, τῶν κατεπειγόντων γνῶσις, ἡ γνῶσις δὲ ἀπόδειξις τῶν διὰ πίστεως παρειλημμένων ἰσχυρὰ καὶ βέβαιος διὰ τῆς κυριακῆς διδασκαλίας ἐποικοδομουμένη τῇ πίστει εἰς τὸ ἀμετάπτωτον καὶ μετ' ἐπιστήμης καὶ καταληπτὸν παραπέμπουσα. καὶ μοι δοκεῖ πρώτη τις εἶναι μεταβολὴ σωτήριος ἡ ἐξ ἐθνῶν εἰς πίστιν, ὡς προεῖπον, δευτέρα δὲ ἡ ἐκ πίστεως εἰς γνῶσιν, ἡ δὲ εἰς ἀγάπην περαιουμένη. This state of things he compares (*ibid.* I. viii. 42) to the condition of true opinion as described by Plato, in which a man holds what is true on the authority of some one else, and does not know the reason.
[2] *Eth. N.* IV. ix. ad fin.
[3] E.g. *Strom.* IV. iii. 8: ἐγκρατεύεσθαι μὲν γὰρ ἀγαθοεργίας κακίας ἔργον, ἀπέχεσθαι δὲ ἀδικίας σωτηρίας ἀρχή. Cf. Ar. *Eth. N.* VII. cc. i. ii.
[4] *Strom.* II. xx. 105. [5] *Ibid.* III. vii. 57.

Note to Lectures III and IV

improved conception of ἐγκράτεια is probably due in part to the less hostile attitude taken by Christianity towards the body and the emotional nature than that which prevailed before.

Together with this account of the course of the Christian life, there are in Clement constant references to the life of Christ. The whole purpose of the *Paedagogus* is to show the effect of the teaching of Christ on life, and there are many passages in which reference is made to the example of Christ. We have to imitate the love of Christ, who came down to save us, and to follow His commandments[1]. Moreover, He displayed all virtues in their highest and most perfect combination: His life was the universal archetype which we can faintly copy in part; for no man probably can succeed in being absolutely virtuous in every connexion[2]. Even the remote and passionless apathy of the Gnostic is regarded by Clement as being an imitation of the life of Christ. 'It would be absurd,' he says, 'in the case of the Saviour, that His Body required necessaries like a body to sustain it in being: He ate, not for the sake of the Body which was supported by divine Power, but for fear that it should occur to any of his companions to think wrongly concerning Him— just as some have since supposed that He was manifested in appearance only:—He Himself was absolutely free from passion, nor did any motion of passion, either pleasure or pain, make way into Him[3]. Such language as this seems perilously near to Docetism. And, in truth, it must be confessed that Clement, though he stoutly affirms the reality

---

[1] *Paed.* I. iii. 9: ἄγωμεν οὖν τὰς ἐντολὰς δι᾽ ἔργων τοῦ κυρίου (καὶ γὰρ ὁ λόγος αὐτὸς ἐναργῶς σὰρξ γενόμενος τὴν αὐτὴν ἀρετὴν πρακτικὴν ἅμα καὶ θεωρητικὴν ἐπιδεικνὺς [? ἐπεδείκνυ]) καὶ δὴ νόμον ὑπολαμβάνοντες τὸν λόγον, τὰς ἐντολὰς καὶ τὰς ὑποθημοσύνας αὐτοῦ τὰς συντόμους ὁδοὺς καὶ συντόνους εἰς ἀϊδιότητα γνωρίσωμεν. πειθοῦς γὰρ ἀναπλέω, οὐ φόβου τὰ προστάγματα.

[2] *Strom.* IV. xxi. 132.

[3] *Ibid.* VI. ix. 71. This condition of freedom from feeling Clement ascribes to the apostles after the Resurrection. One may wonder how he brought his belief into harmony with the history of St. Peter and St. Paul in the Acts and the Epistle to the Galatians.

of the Incarnation, is more naturally drawn to the philosophical idea of the Logos in the world, revealing the Father. This is the side of Christian theology which Clement obviously thinks most suitable to the Gnostic; and he does not seem to feel that his doctrine of the Incarnation runs any risk of inadequacy. Yet it is partly owing to this lack of decision in regard of the Incarnation that his moral theory reveals certain inconsistencies. Enough has been said to show that Clement's aim, so far as that was definite, was a high one. It was, indeed, that which has been set forth here as essential to Christian ethical theory—to show that the belief in Christ Incarnate is the true and sure ground of successful moral effort. Christianity, by virtue of the life and death of Christ, is to succeed where the Jewish Law and Greek philosophy have failed. But then we are faced with a separation between the higher and lower life, such as was familiar to philosophy and characteristic of Gnosticism. It is true that this is represented by Clement as a stage in preparation for the ideal state; but it remains that πολλοὶ μὲν ναρθηκοφόροι, βάκχοι δέ τε παῦροι [1]. And, after all, the ground of the division is not one which, strictly speaking, ought to separate Christians; it is not spiritual, but intellectual. And thus, though Clement regards all men as called to be philosophers, and extends the possibility of the highest life to all men and women, even slaves, the introduction of a distinction which does not belong to Christianity at all, spoils his account both of the Incarnation and of Christian moral life [2].

The other great Alexandrine theologian, Origen, is a man of very different character. Clement, as has been already said, takes an easy eclectic view of life and philosophy, and fails to face all the problems which naturally arise in these regions. Origen, though he is quite as learned, and quite as fearless in accepting the truths which pagan thought had suggested,

---

[1] *Strom.* V. iii. 17.

[2] This conclusion is still further supported by Clement's account of evil. It has seemed better to put this under its proper heading in the note to Lecture V.

is in no sense an eclectic. He is the first of those who have endeavoured to form a complete scheme of the world, which should include Christianity. His reason has attempted to grasp the whole order of the Divine Providence, and justify the ways of God to men. Hence the interest of his ethical doctrine lies on the universal side rather than in details. If we may believe the statement of Gregory Thaumaturgus (already quoted in Lecture IV), Origen's own moral teaching centred round the four cardinal virtues. Of this there are traces in the writings of Origen. Thus in the Commentary on the Epistle to the Romans these four virtues are mentioned as obvious instances of ordinary moral ideas[1]. More frequently Origen includes in lists of virtues εὐσέβεια, which, as we have seen, Philo placed at the head of all the virtues; or some definitely Christian type of action, such as humility or purity and the like. Origen is perhaps too serious and introspective to dwell on the outward appearance of the life produced by Christ's tutorship so carefully as Clement. But he is no less certain than Clement of the supreme influence of the faith upon the character and the will. This point comes out most strongly in the discussion with Celsus. Celsus has the educated and polished disgust for all that is low and sordid and generally inferior. It is a complaint with him, therefore, against Christianity that it admits into the Church, and even welcomes, the foolish and the wicked. Origen's answer to this criticism is complete. He points out that the Church has no pleasure in the foolish, or even in sinners, as such; but that it receives these as well as others, and is successful in dealing with them. The foolish and the wise alike are called, for Christ is the Saviour of all men[2]; and it is far from being

---

[1] *In Ep. ad Rom.* III. p. 164, ed. Lomm. : 'Similiter et prudentia per boni et mali scientiam constat : et temperantia quae eligenda et cavenda sint, novit ; et fortitudo non ignorat, quae ad formidinem spectant. Ita et justitia.'

[2] *C. Cels.* III. 49 : τούτους μὲν καλεῖ ὁ λόγος, ἵνα αὐτοὺς βελτιώσῃ, καλεῖ δὲ καὶ τοὺς πολλῷ τούτων διαφέροντας. ἐπεὶ σωτὴρ πάντων ἐστὶν ἀνθρώπων ὁ Χριστός, καὶ μάλιστα πιστῶν, εἴτε συνετῶν, εἴτε ἁπλουστέρων, καὶ ἱλασμὸς ἐστὶ

true that education is held to be a disadvantage[1]. Again, though it is true that the philosophical schools do not call to their side the same sort of people as the Church of Christ, it is certain that they would do so if they could. With their lectures and commentaries they aim at spreading a knowledge of God, and dissuading men from sinful courses. καὶ οἱ φιλόσοφοί γ' ἂν εὔξαιντο ἀγείρειν τοσούτους ἀκροατὰς λόγων ἐπὶ τὸ καλὸν παρακαλούντων[2]. To achieve this end a complete change of life is required, and this is what appears to Celsus most difficult, if not impossible. The faith of Christ makes it not only not impossible, but not very difficult to get rid of vice, even though it be ingrained in the nature[3]. In his controversial work Origen describes this moral change in general terms; it consists in trusting oneself to God (πιστεύειν δεῖ ἑαυτὸν τῷ θεῷ) and doing all things with a view to the pleasure of God. And as for the possibility of such a change, Origen maintains that it is absurd that men should be able by practice to change their bodies to all sorts of ingenious acts, while they have no capacity for attaining their highest possibilities in the region of morality[4]. But this is by no means all that he has to say upon the subject. The change, the possibility of righteousness, depends entirely on the sacrifice of Christ upon the Cross. This is brought out with great clearness in the Commentary on the Romans. For instance, in explaining the meaning of 'dead to sin and alive unto God,' he says:

πρὸς τὸν πατέρα περὶ τῶν ἁμαρτιῶν ἡμῶν. οὐ μόνον δὲ περὶ τῶν ἡμετέρων, ἀλλὰ καὶ περὶ ὅλου τοῦ κόσμου.

[1] *C. Cels.* III. 49: οὐ κωλύει γε πρὸς τὸ γνῶναι θεόν, ἀλλὰ καὶ συνεργεῖ τὸ πεπαιδεῦσθαι, καὶ λόγων ἀρίστων ἐπιμεμελῆσθαι, καὶ φρόνιμον εἶναι.

[2] *Ibid.* 50. Origen notes that the Cynics are the only sect who follow the practice of popular preaching in any way at all similar to the Church.

[3] *Ibid.* 69: Ἡμεῖς δὲ (μίαν φύσιν ἐπιστάμενοι πάσης λογικῆς ψυχῆς, καὶ μηδεμίαν φάσκοντες πονηρὰν ὑπὸ τοῦ κτίσαντος τὰ ὅλα δεδημιουργῆσθαι, γεγονέναι δὲ πολλοὺς κακοὺς παρὰ τὰς ἀνατροφάς, καὶ τὰς διαστροφάς, καὶ τὰς περιηχήσεις, ὥστε καὶ φυσιωθῆναι ἔν τισι τὴν κακίαν·) πειθόμεθα, ὅτι τῷ θείῳ λόγῳ ἀμεῖψαι κακίαν φυσιώσασάν ἐστιν οὐ μόνον οὐκ ἀδύνατον, ἀλλὰ καὶ οὐ πάνυ χαλεπόν.

[4] *Ibid.*

Note to Lectures III and IV

'Vivere autem dicitur Deo, ut et nos non nobis, neque nostrae voluntati, sed Deo vivamus ut ita demum in vita ipsius salvi esse possimus, secundum eum, qui dixit: "vivo autem, iam non ego, vivit vero in me Christus." Quod vero similiter ut in superioribus posuit: "non solum autem, sed et nunc gloriamur in Deo:" et nihil addidit ad "non solum autem," similiter ut superius intelligendum est de his dictum, quae supra comprehensa sunt: id est, quod non solum, cum "inimici essemus, reconciliati sumus Deo per mortem Filii eius," et non solum in vita ipsius salvi erimus, sed et "nunc gloriamur in Deo per Dominum nostrum Iesum Christum, per quem reconciliationem" accepimus. Non autem sine causa addidit "nunc" cum potuisset dicere "sed et gloriamur in Deo per Dominum nostrum Iesum Christum per quem reconciliationem" accepimus: sed ut ostenderet gloriationem nobis non solum in futuro, sed et in praesenti datam de agnitione Dei, et emendatione vitae, et errorum correctione, sicut et in aliis idem Apostolus dicit: "spem habentes et praesentis vitae et futurae:" praesentis, quod honestior et emendatior est: futurae, quod aeterna est [1].'

Thus the acceptance of the salvation which is in Christ not only affects our eternal destiny, but also affords a basis for real moral advance. And Origen leaves us in no doubt of the fundamental nature of this salvation. We are justified in the end by the Blood of Christ alone. By a somewhat peculiar interpretation of St. Paul's language Origen maintains that there are two modes of justification: by faith, and by works [2].

[1] *In Ep. ad Rom.* IV. 12, pp. 314, 315, Lomm.

[2] 'Per omnem itaque hunc locum (i. e. Rom. iv. 1–5) Apostolus hoc videtur ostendere, quod duae quaedam sunt iustificationes, quarum unam ex operibus nominat, aliam vero ex fide. Et illam quidem, quae ex operibus est, dicit habere quidem gloriam, sed in semet ipsa, et non apud Deum: illam vero, quae ex fide est, habere gloriam apud Deum, utpote apud inspicientem corda hominum, et scientem quis est, qui credit in occulto, et quis est, qui non credit.' *In Ep. ad Rom.* IV. 1, pp. 232, 233, Lommatzsch. We are not, of course, concerned here with this theory of justification, as such; still less, with its relations to the doctrine of St. Augustine.

But neither of these stands alone or operates apart from the sacrifice of Christ: it is this which both gets rid of past sin, and enables us to do better in the future [1]. Hence it is clear that the basis of moral achievement is found in the acts of Christ our Saviour.

This aspect of morality is not, however, quite sufficient to cover the whole ground. On the lower practical levels, men are moved to virtue by varying motives. In this connexion there reappears the old distinction of the higher and lower Christian life which we have observed in Clement. The lower life, though it is really Christian, is actuated by motives of fear. Celsus condemns the use of this motive, and even that of hope; but Origen defends it on the ground of its result in producing definitely Christian virtue, thus showing that he looks with a kindly eye even on this less aspiring life [2]. It is a really Christian life, different from, and more successful than, the ideals of philosophy, but there are still greater heights open to the followers of Christ. The three

---

[1] 'Ex quo ostendit, quod neque fides nostra sine Christi sanguine, neque sanguis Christi nos sine fide nostra iustificat: ex utroque tamen multo magis sanguis Christi nos, quam fides nostra iustificat. Et ideo mihi videtur, cum in superioribus simpliciter dixerit : " iustificati ex fide " hic addidisse " multo magis ergo nunc iustificati in sanguine eius " : ut doceret, quod ab ira ventura etiam si fides nostra nos salvet, etiam si opera iustitiae, super haec tamen omnia multo magis sanguis Christi salvos nos faciat ab ira ventura.' *In Ep. ad Rom.* IV. ii. p. 309, Lommatzsch. In this case also we are only concerned with the fact of Origen's judgement on the matter: it is not necessary to attempt to define the exact way in which he thought the Blood of Christ was made available for us.

[2] *C. Cels.* III. 78 : Οὗτοι γὰρ (i. e. οἱ ἁπλούστεροι) φόβῳ τῷ περὶ τῶν κολάσεων τῶν ἀπαγγελλομένων, κινοῦντι αὐτοὺς καὶ προτρέποντι ἐπὶ τὸ ἀπέχεσθαι τούτων, δι' ἃ αἱ κολάσεις, πειρῶνται ἐπιδιδόναι ἑαυτοὺς τῇ κατὰ Χριστιανισμὸν θεοσεβείᾳ· ἐπὶ τοσοῦτον ὑπὸ τοῦ λόγου κρατούμενοι, ὡς φόβῳ τῶν κατὰ τὸν λόγον ὀνομαζομένων αἰωνίων κολάσεων, πάσης τῆς παρ' ἀνθρώποις κατ' αὐτῶν ἐπινοουμένης βασάνου, καὶ μετὰ μυρίων πόνων θανάτου καταφρονεῖν· ὅπερ οὐδεὶς ἂν τῶν εὖ φρονούντων φήσαι πονηρῶν προαιρέσεων ἔργον εἶναι. Πῶς δ' ἀπὸ προαιρέσεως πονηρᾶς ἐγκράτεια καὶ σωφροσύνη ἀσκεῖται, ἢ τὸ μεταδοτικὸν καὶ κοινωνικόν ; Ἀλλ' οὐδ' ὁ πρὸς τὸ θεῖον φόβος, ἐφ' ὃν ὡς χρήσιμον τοῖς πολλοῖς παρακαλεῖ ὁ λόγος τοὺς μηδέπω δυναμένους τὸ δι' αὐτὸ αἱρετὸν βλέπειν, καὶ αἱρεῖσθαι αὐτό, ὡς μέγιστον ἀγαθὸν καὶ ὑπὲρ πᾶσαν ἐπαγγελίαν. Cf. *ibid.* I. 9.

Note to Lectures III and IV

theological virtues are in one place described as grades in the attainment of divine knowledge[1]. This passage however does not define the relations between the various stages with any great clearness. The Prologue to the Commentary on the Song of Songs is more precise. Origen argues that the three works passing under the name of Solomon represent the true order of various pursuits of men. At the lowest grade stands moral philosophy—'per quam mos vivendi honestus aptatur, et instituta ad virtutem tendentia praeparantur.' This is represented by the Book of Proverbs. Next comes natural philosophy, set forth in the Book Ecclesiastes[2]. Highest of all comes the contemplative science (called inspectiva) 'qua supergressi visibilia, de divinis aliquid et coelestibus contemplamur, eaque sola mente intuemur, quoniam corporeum supergrediuntur aspectum[3].' This is figured in the Song of Songs under the imagery of love, and is identified by Origen with the virtue *caritas*. But it is from another point of view knowledge—the wisdom which comes from loving intercourse. In the Commentary on St. John Origen describes the way in which the growth in faith is possible[4]. In this passage Origen speaks of the various articles of the Creed as being the object of faith; and it is somewhat difficult to see how they bear on the practical conduct of life. It is important, therefore, to remember that he also regarded all virtues, of whatever kind, as being, in

---

[1] 'Et puto, quod prima salutis initia et ipsa fundamenta fides est : profectus vero et augmenta aedificii spes est : perfectio autem et culmen totius operis caritas : et ideo maior omnium dicitur caritas.' *In Ep. ad Rom.* IV. 6, p. 271, Lomm.

[2] Natural philosophy has a somewhat different meaning from that which is familiar to us. It implies the discussion of the nature of things, but with a practical object : 'quo nihil contra naturam geratur in vita, sed unumquodque his usibus deputetur, in quos a creatore productum est.' *Prol. in Cant.* p. 308, Lomm. Ecclesiastes is connected with this subject of study, because it distinguishes useful and useless things, bids men shun vanity, and pursue what is useful and right. It is thus a higher type of moral speculation.

[3] *Prol. in Cant.* p. 308, Lomm.   [4] *In Joh.* XXXII. 9.

a sense, a participation in the Son[1]. 'Every wise man, in so far as he holds wisdom, has a share in Christ, as He is wisdom.' So with power, sanctification, and redemption. If therefore growth in the knowledge of God is to be regarded as the climax of human life, and Christ is in truth the wisdom of God, then the full acceptance of Him will be necessary to lead to the attainment of that which is possible to man. In this regard Origen distinguishes between various titles of the Son. As Sanctification and Redemption He belongs closely to our life; but in knowing Him as Wisdom and Power we know something of the nature of God, through Him[2], and the end of all human life is to be admitted into the fullest possible participation of the Divine Nature according to the image and similitude of which man is made[3].

We have now spoken of those writers in whom the Platonic influence was strongest. It will have been made clear by this time that the region affected by the philosophy of the schools of the second century was primarily the metaphysical region. In the moral world there was already a new force at work. The underlying assumption of the Christian Church distinguished virtue from knowledge. The end of life was indeed the knowledge and the love of God; but even in Clement there are signs that this was not attainable in the ordinary philosophical way, by means of geometry and music. These and the usual philosophical curriculum might be good for the Christians to begin upon, as Origen seems to have taught, but the whole conception of the human nature was being gradually changed. And it is clear that the doctrines of the Incarnation and Redemption had the primary influence in causing this change. Men who had continually to be defending the reality of our Lord's body, who had to explain to their contemporaries the reality and dignity of His sufferings, who were forced by the primary assumptions of their creed to seek a moral motive for the Creation and Incarnation, could

---

[1] *In Ev. Joh.* I. 39. [2] *In Joh.* I. 39, 40.
[3] *De Princ.* IV. 37.

not put up any longer with the purely philosophical conception of God and of life. Though the writings of the great Alexandrines reveal the influence of Greek philosophy and retain some of its less felicitous features, yet their works mark far more truly the victory of the Christian spirit over the moribund forces of heathenism. When men educated like Clement and Origen found themselves in face of an alternative between Christianity and Platonism and chose the former, it was clear that the day of the latter was at an end.

The next person of supreme importance whose work and influence we must consider at length will be St. Augustine of Hippo. And seeing that in his writings the most important step in the way of systematization of ethical teaching was taken, we can afford to deal briefly with later thinkers. The Church, by the time of his death, had fixed the outlines of its own philosophy and ethics, and the principles which marked its final departure from ancient philosophy were fully and finally declared. St. Augustine, as every one knows, was born in Africa, and his earliest impressions of Christianity must have been those produced by the African Church. But the scene of his conversion was not in Africa, but in Italy—at Milan; and the immediate cause of his finally embracing the Catholic faith was Ambrose, the great Archbishop of Milan. Hence it will be necessary to speak of the characteristic features of the African Church, and to endeavour to estimate the influence of St. Ambrose, before we discuss the contribution of Augustine to the subject in hand.

The African Church was marked by very strong and characteristic features. Its general tone was practical, and not speculative; and its moral attitude was more stern than that of any other Church. These features are displayed in the most unmistakable form in Tertullian and Cyprian, its two greatest writers previous to Augustine. From their works it is not hard to get a picture more or less clear of the state of Christianity in the second and third centuries. In spite of persecutions, the Church had multiplied its members. Though Christianity was still legally under the ban of the

Roman Empire, persecution was practically far from being continuous; and there were therefore intervals during which those who professed the faith could display their way of life unmolested. The increase of numbers and the improvement of the position of the Christians laid the Church open to the perils which come of prosperity. Persons became outwardly Christians who had no moral sympathy with the Church, and raised perplexing problems by their actions. Further, in the easier times, men who were in fullest sympathy with the Church looked more narrowly at their own lives, and inquired more anxiously than before at what points the taint of the world was liable to affect them And besides these matters, serious difficulties arose in connexion with heresies; which, according to Tertullian, sprang up when the fire of persecution was fiercest, as scorpions are most plentiful in summer-heat [1]. Throughout the whole period the polity of the Church was growing in firmness, and the order of its ministers, &c., was being irrevocably fixed.

From these facts it follows that we have, as we should expect, casuistical discussions in plenty, controversial works dealing with the theories of the heretics, and tracts and letters relating to questions of outward order [2]. It will not be necessary to make an elaborate analysis of the works of Tertullian and Cyprian; such an attempt would carry us beyond our purpose. But there is a distinct result traceable to these African writers which entered into the stream of history and has contributed to the conclusions arrived at on ethical questions. Of this, something must be said briefly.

1. One point which the danger of persecution especially helped to bring out was the separateness of the Church from the world. It is easy to understand how the desire to avoid giving unnecessary offence may have led some Christians into perilous compliance with worldly customs: how they may have thought it desirable to enter as far as possible—as far,

---

[1] *Scorp.* c. 1.

[2] In all these matters Tertullian's later works, after he joined the Montanists, are of less importance and authority than the earlier ones.

Note to Lectures III and IV

perhaps, as their inclinations would have led them—into the life of the day. Thus it seems to have been a question how far Christians could safely go to the shows at the theatres. Both our writers condemn such a practice. Tertullian shows how the origin of all the various performances is religious, and involves an indirect homage to the pagan worships. It is not a case in which the argument can be used that it is well to enjoy what God gives. The whole thing is tainted by its history and its associations, and Christian men who have broken off from all the heathen past have no right to allow themselves in such dangerous pursuits. Cyprian will not allow a professional actor, though he has ceased to perform, to remain in communion with the Church so long as he continues to keep a school of acting[1]. If the resignation of this profession brings him to poverty, he can be supported like other men by the funds of the Church, but he cannot be permitted to dishonour the Church by supporting so corrupt a profession. In sterner tones Tertullian forbids[2] various trades, such as that of the classical schoolmaster or the vendor of incense and other sacrificial requirements. They are infected with the idolatrous taint. The schoolmaster has to know and teach the names and histories of the corrupt heathen gods; the incense-seller and similar purveyors support the sacrifices which, as Christians, they are bound to condemn. Such trades must, therefore, be relinquished: 'fides famem non timet.' In like manner, while the corrupt morals of the age are condemned, a contrast is drawn between the virtues of the Christian and those of the philosopher. Both Christian and philosopher aim at patience, for instance. But Cyprian claims that the Christian succeeds where the philosopher fails[3]; and Tertullian, who laments sadly the small amount of patience he possesses himself, declare that the 'patientia gentilium' is 'falsa, probrosa'—a mere indolent acquiescence in evil[4].

[1] *Ep.* II. c. 2.
[2] *De Idol.* cc. 9–11.
[3] *De Bono Patientiae,* c. 2; cf. Tert. *Apol.* c. 46.
[4] *De Pat.* c. 16.

2. On the other hand, there is an intense feeling of the unity and fellowship which is involved in the Christian brotherhood. The life of the Church, its history, its doctrines, its hopes, are sufficient to every true Christian without the false excitement of theatrical displays. The true tragedy, as Plato said of old to the poets, is the reality of life. 'Si scenicae doctrinae delectant, satis nobis litterarum est, satis versuum est, satis sententiarum, satis etiam canticorum. satis vocum, nec fabulae sed veritates, nec strophae sed simplicitates. Vis et pugillatus et luctatus? Praesto sunt non parva et multa. Aspice impudicitiam deiectam a castitate, perfidiam caesam a fide, saevitiam a misericordia contusam, petulantiam a modestia obumbratam, et tales sunt apud nos agones, in quibus ipsi coronamur. Vis autem et sanguinis aliquid? Habes Christi [1].'

So the history of the Church is continuous from the days of Christ through the apostles. It has a single tradition, speaks with one voice, rejects innovations in doctrine or discipline, takes pains to guarantee the fitness and faithfulness of its ministers [2]. It is a society that has its own laws and principles, planted in among the nations of the world, with the command laid upon it to baptize all the nations in the threefold name. To give way to sin in this society is an act of treachery, a breach of the union between the individual soul and Christ [3], which may indeed be irreparable on this side of the grave. 'Christi nomen induere et non per Christi viam pergere quid aliud quam praevaricatio est divini nominis, quam desertio itineris salutaris?' With such a society the fact of persecution and sorrow in this life is as nothing, seeing that to it belong unchangeably the certainty of the Resurrection of Jesus Christ and the sure hope of immortality with Him.

These are ideas which constantly recur in the writings of

---

[1] Tert. *De Spec.* c. 29.

[2] Contrast lax discipline of heretics, *De Praescr. Haer.* c. 41.

[3] The question of sin and its varieties will be more carefully treated in the note appended to Lecture V.

Note to Lectures III and IV

Tertullian and Cyprian, and it is easy to see how naturally they arose out of the situation in which the writers were placed.

3. There is another important feature of their teaching which is more directly theological: in this also they are more closely in contact with the Alexandrine theologians than in their discipline. This point arises out of the controversy with Gnosticism. In the teaching of several of the Gnostic sects there was a disposition to erect an impenetrable barrier between the Old Testament and the New. The God of the Old Testament was represented as a principle of evil, whose work was set aside or at least wholly reorganized by the good God revealed in the Gospels. This is the point seized upon by Tertullian in Marcion's heresy, and it leads to a very important discussion. Tertullian aims at showing at considerable length that in the moral nature of God is found the only key to the whole process of revelation from the beginning of things onwards. The cause of all this discussion was, of course, the problem of evil. It seemed impossible to account for the presence of evil in the world if the Creator had been really and wholly good. Tertullian is perfectly aware of this. He describes Marcion as 'languens (quod et nunc multi, et maxime heretici) circa mali quaestionem, unde malum . . . alium deum praesumpsit esse debere[1].' In the first book Tertullian occupies himself largely in proving the absurdity of Marcion's conception of God by means of certain rules or canons or axioms which declare what the nature of God must be: 'regulae certae ad examinandam Dei bonitatem[2].' We need mention two only out of this list. According to one, Tertullian lays down the rule that the goodness of God, if there at all, must be rational[3]. 'Exigo rationem bonitatis, quia nec aliud quid bonum habere liceat quod non rationaliter bonum sit, nedum ut ipsa bonitas irrationalis deprehendatur[4].' In another of his canons Tertullian defends the use of such language as that of anger, judgement, &c., of God on the ground that without this we

[1] *Adv. Marc.* I. 2.   [2] *Ibid.* 22.
[3] *Ibid.* 23.   [4] *Ibid.*

cannot understand His goodness. 'Nihil Deo tam indignum quam non exequi quod noluit et prohibuit admitti: primo, quod qualicunque sententiae suae et legi debeat vindictam in auctoritatem et obsequii necessitatem, secundo, quia aemulum sit necesse est quod noluit admitti et nolendo prohibuit. Malo autem parcere deum indignius sit quam animadvertere et quidem deo optimo, qui non alias plene bonus sit, nisi mali aemulus, uti boni amorem odio mali exerceat, et boni tutelam expugnatione mali impleat [1].'

In the second book Tertullian endeavours to meet the criticisms of Marcion on the Old Testament history. He has but little difficulty in arguing the goodness of the original creation, and for the origin of sin he falls back on the freedom of the human will [2]. He defends the long-suffering and severity of God, maintains the high moral import of the Law (c. 27), has something to urge even in favour of the minutiae of the ceremonial (c. 19), and makes a somewhat elaborate explanation of the anthropomorphic language of the Old Testament. 'Iam nunc, ut et cetera compendio absolvam, quaecunque adhuc ut pusilla et infirma et indigna colligitis ad destructionem creatoris, simplici et certa ratione proponam, deum non potuisse humanos congressus inire, nisi humanos et sensus et affectus suscepisset, per quos vim maiestatis suae, intolerabilem utique humanae mediocritati, humilitati temperaret, sibi quidem indigna, homini autem necessaria, et ita iam Deo digna, quia nihil tam dignum Deo quam salus hominis [3].'

Attention has already been called to the fact that Origen met the attack of Celsus upon the Incarnation by referring the whole to a moral motive in God—to love, to a spirit of condescension and sympathy with the infirmities of man. The same principle is at work here on a large scale. The idea of the moral being of God is taken in its fullness with all its consequences, and with a clear knowledge of its difficulties. And it is seen to be necessary to the very foundations of the Christian faith. As such it became the normal assumption

[1] *Adv. Marc.* I. 26. [2] *Ibid.* II. 7. [3] *Ibid.* 27.

of all thinking Christian men. This is a matter of no small importance. For indeed it gives the rational key to the ethical position of Tertullian and of those who held with him. In the days of Tertullian and Cyprian men asked questions, as they ask them now, about the order of the world. Why is there still evil in it? Why has not all war ceased? Why is there persecution, and why is it not right to flee from it? On all these points these authors fall back on the moral order of the world as devised by God, and point to the Incarnation and Death of Christ as facts declaring the love of God to be so far beyond the conception of man, that it becomes possible in the strength of them to face even the evil of the world. The nature of God is the truth which Christ has revealed (Tertullian points out that till Christ came the Fatherhood of God was unknown [1]), and it is the truth which translates itself into the peculiar worship and order of the Christian Church.

The passages here cited and referred to are not isolated or exceptional. But the very fact that the ideas they express are characteristically frequent lends them an additional value. They prove that the African Church had applied the doctrine of the Incarnation, with all that this means, to the interpretation of human life as they knew it. Their experience was made to centre round this fact: they defined themselves as against the world in virtue of their relation to this fact. They had not yet systematized morality anew; the outward conditions were not yet favourable. They dealt with questions as they arose, and their decisions on some points were not finally ratified by the rest of the Church. But the important point is that though they approached the question from a wholly different point of view to the philosophic Alexandrines, and though there is a strange lack of similarity between their writings and those of their philosophical contemporaries, the result of the strivings of both is essentially the same: to seek the interpretation of human life in the Incarnation and at the Cross of Jesus Christ.

[1] *De Orat.* c. 3.

The work of Ambrose, *De Officiis*, is interesting chiefly as being the first treatise on Christian ethics produced in the Church. There is nothing in it of the anxious and eager passion which marks the African writers. The times have changed, open persecution is at an end, the chief foes are within. And Ambrose is a methodical official person who has spent a considerable portion of his life in political business, and has only become a bishop under the strong pressure of his fellow-citizens. His treatise, therefore, keeps steadily on ordinary levels. It is somewhat ill-arranged, and the thoughts are not well connected; though it runs close to the *De Officiis* of Cicero, it fails signally as compared with its model. It represents a different attitude towards pagan thought and speculation. Already the Alexandrines had borrowed honey from the hives of Greek philosophy; and though the regular Latin view had been to regard this as dangerous, Ambrose is strongly under the influence of Alexandrine and other writers, to whom a more liberal view of pagan writings had become natural. His method of interpreting Scripture is clearly borrowed through Origen from Philo, but his attitude towards pagan culture is characteristic rather of the Apologists than of the Alexandrine School. As is naturally to be expected, he finds his chief points of contact with the ancient world in Stoicism; both in regard of the belief in the providence of God, and in the type of virtue which he commends. He fixes on various points in which heathen thinkers have anticipated or are in harmony with Christian truth; but he has no complete scheme or theory of the relations of paganism and Christianity like Clement or Origen. His treatment of the four cardinal virtues has been mentioned already in the Lectures[1], and it is highly characteristic. He has adopted the terminology of virtue from the Stoic philosophers, but he searches for his instances of virtue in the Old Testament history. It had already been argued that the virtues were coherent, and could not be expected to occur alone. Ambrose

[1] Page 138 above.

maintains the same position [1]; but the point of unity between the virtues is different. Abraham, for instance, displayed them all in the sacrifice of Isaac [2]. 'Fuit sapientiae Deo credere, nec filii gratiam anteferre auctoris praecepto; fuit iustitiae acceptum reddere; fuit fortitudinis appetitum ratione cohibere. . . . Accedit et quarta virtus, temperantia. Tenebat iustus et pietatis modum et exsecutionis ordinem. Denique dum sacrificio necessaria vehit, dum ignem adolet, dum filium ligat, dum gladium educit, hoc immolandi ordine meruit ut filium reservaret.' Here the most noticeable change is the reference of prudence or wisdom to God. In a similar way, the other three are shown to cover purely spiritual conditions. Justice, as was said above, is based on faith; that is, it is a bond of social union which holds men together primarily in the State, and, in a higher degree, in the Church, Christ being the foundation-stone of the Church and the object of our faith [3]. Fortitude includes the habit of those who resist flattery and other temptations, on the one hand, and, on the other, stand forth as Christ's athletes and win the crown of martyrdom. The temperate are those who are modest and know their place, as well as those who have their passions well under control [4].

These, especially the first three, introduce us into a Christian atmosphere, however closely the language is modelled on that of Cicero's *De Officiis*; and the effect is intensified when we read in later books of the end of life, or of the virtues of faith and kindliness. It is not that these are wholly absent from the ancient writers, but that they are based upon a new motive. While he accepts Stoic language referring the true end of life to knowledge and virtue, Ambrose explains it to mean life eternal—the knowledge of God and Jesus Christ whom He has sent, and the works which

---

[1] *De Off.* I. xxvii. 126, and other places. It is not always the same virtue that appears at the head of the classification.

[2] *Ibid.* xxv. 119.   [3] *Ibid.* xxix. 142.

[4] Cf. *Comm. in Ev. Luc.* V. §§ 64-68 and following. Ambrose finds the four cardinal virtues in the four beatitudes which St. Luke puts in the Sermon on the Mount.

Christ commands[1]. Faith is the virtue by which we attain this. He accepts the philosophical principle that no man should injure another, or gain by another's loss, but entirely rejects the philosophical restriction of this kindliness to those who are wise[2].

These few instances, and they could be considerably increased in numbers, are sufficient to indicate the relation in which Ambrose stood to the philosophical ethics of his day. In other writings on moral subjects, though he is still under the influence of philosophy, and especially of the philosophy of Cicero, he is dealing more directly with questions arising in Christendom. He is commenting on some books of Holy Scripture, or training up catechumens, or writing letters of advice to meet spiritual difficulties. Hence he is somewhat hampered by the necessities of exegesis, or other like causes. And here there is no question possible as to the drift of his mind. He is the first, as has been said, to attempt to produce a definite system of Christian moral philosophy; and it must be granted that he has not done more than lead the way[3].

One great merit of St. Ambrose is the indirect service he performed by influencing St. Augustine, to whom we now return. When Augustine came in contact with Ambrose he was in the position of an inquirer. He had already passed through various phases of thought, and was learned in Platonism

[1] *De Off.* II. ii. 4-6.

[2] 'Quaerunt aliqui, si sapiens in naufragio positus insipienti naufrago tabulam extorquere possit, utrum debeat ? Mihi quidem, etsi praestabilius communi videatur usui, sapientem de naufragio, quam insipientem evadere, tamen non videtur, quod vir Christianus et iustus et sapiens quaerere sibi vitam aliena morte debeat. . . . Cur enim te potiorem altero iudices, cum viri sit Christiani praeferre sibi alterum . . . ?' *Ibid.* III. iv. 27, 28.

[3] A valuable work, *Saint Ambroise et la morale chrétienne*, by Raymond Thamin, has come into my hands while this note was in proof. If I had seen it sooner, I should, doubtless, have gained more help from it. I am glad, however, to find myself in general agreement with it as to the definitely Christian character of Ambrose's ethical doctrine.

Note to Lectures III and IV

so far as a man with his slight knowledge of Greek could be. And he had been persuaded that in this learning there was much truth; he had never taken the problems of life quite lightly, nor supposed that truth was an indifferent matter. But we may feel thankful that at a time when he was most anxiously searching for his final position, he met with Ambrose rather than with a man such as Tertullian. The cool and receptive attitude of Ambrose towards Greek learning and thought must have given Augustine that sense of unfettered freedom and unbiassed moderation, without which no person who is thinking out his own problems ever attains a final solution of them. Nor was this an accidental result merely. The apparent indifference of Ambrose to the prayers of Monica shows that he saw what Augustine chiefly wanted; not exhortations or arguments, but the sight of the Christian principles in action—the lesson that the difficulty of placing in due order the half-truths of earlier teachers, and of harmonizing the contradictory voices of argument and discussion, is best solved in the regular, unperplexed, straightforward Christian life.

Tertullian had recognized in Greek and popular language, with its tendency towards monotheism, *testimonium animae naturaliter Christianae*[1]. But this does not prevent his being highly suspicious of all attempts to bolster up Christian doctrine with Greek philosophical ideas. 'Nostra institutio de porticu Solomonis est, qui et ipse tradiderat dominum in simplicitate cordis esse quaerendum. Viderint qui Stoicum et Platonicum et dialecticum Christianismum protulerunt. Nobis curiositate opus non est post Christum Iesum, nec inquisitione post evangelium[2].' But things have changed since his day. Augustine is prepared to use Plato to a very considerable extent, and to treat him as making serious contributions to truth. Indeed he goes so far as to discuss a question which had already received much attention, whether Plato may not have heard Jeremiah or read Moses. The first point is set aside on grounds of

[1] *Apol.* c. 17.   [2] *De Praescr. Haer.* c. 7, ad fin.

chronology[1], the other left open; it is possible that in conversation Plato may have acquired possession of scriptural ideas. But Augustine had to deal with a very peculiar and degraded form of Platonism. He is constantly appealing from the Platonists to Plato. In the later stages of Neo-Platonism a doctrine had been developed, according to which there was in existence a large population of malevolent and semi-material demons. These stood between God and the soul, and hindered advancement. They had to be dealt with by magic, and set one against another. To a certain extent countenance had been given to this by the doctrine that the stars and other luminaries were living and conscious beings. But the real source of it was not Plato, but the crowd of Oriental soothsayers and devil-dancers which infested the cities of the Roman world[2]. These degraded the name of the philosopher, whose glory it was that he had rejected all such unworthy conceptions of divine beings.

Hence Augustine's philosophical polemic was largely concerned with the Platonists of his day; though at the same time his teaching was much influenced by Plato and Plotinus, who is the only Platonist whom he thinks worthy of comparison with Plato. To a large extent Augustine's use of Plato consists in the adoption of Platonic ideas which had already become familiar in theological thought. He adopts with some reserve the doctrine of Ideas, emphasizing the position that the mind must be akin to God and advanced in purity and love, before it can attain to the vision of the ideas[3]. He commends Plato for his doctrine of God; for his unswerving belief in His goodness; and for his connexion of man's destiny with the knowledge of God. 'Si ergo Plato Dei huius imitatorem, cognitorem, amatorem

---

[1] St. Augustine had originally held the view that Plato had met Jeremiah, *De Doct. Christ.* II. xxviii. 43; but withdrew it, *De Civ.* VIII. 11, and *Retract.* II. 4. The theory that Plato was influenced by Jewish writings or traditions was common in Alexandrine circles, and is asserted in Justin, *Apol.* I. 59. The same thing is suggested by Philo of Heracleitus, *Quis rer. div.* 43, I. 503 M.

[2] Cf. *De Civ.* VIII. 13.   [3] *De Div. Quaest.* XLVI. 2.

Note to Lectures III and IV

dixit esse sapientem, cuius participatione sit beatus, quid opus est excutere ceteros? Nulli nobis, quam isti, propius accesserunt[1].' He quotes and compares with the Christian doctrine of the Trinity the *principia* of the Platonists. He is puzzled by Porphyry, who seems to have departed from the doctrine of Plotinus[2]; but he does not use any of these doctrines to any large extent as supports to his own. He notes them rather as signs of the presence of the Spirit of God amongst the Gentiles, guiding them by degrees towards the full vision of the Truth.

The decisive line of division between Augustine and the philosophers comes to light over the doctrine of the Incarnation. This they all reject and declare to be unworthy of God and impossible. St. Augustine is inclined to ascribe their rejection of this truth to pride, especially in the case of Porphyry[3]. They will not face the humiliation it implies or the moral sacrifices it involves[4]. Whereas, according to Augustine. this doctrine supplies the key to the whole moral position of man, explaining also all the success of philosophers in attaining truth as to the immaterial nature of God. and the like : yet, while they recognize a kinship between the rational soul and God, they fail under the test of the Incarnation. They leave the body wholly unexplained—as a thing from which all evil comes, and from which they must flee who would achieve happiness. And though they hold that the world is an animal possessed of soul and body and rejoicing in happiness, and that the sun and moon are semi-divine beings, they shrink from the idea of Christ come in the flesh.

Thus the Incarnation, at which the Platonist stumbled, is the pivot on which the whole system of Augustine turns. God had made the world by His changeless wisdom and will. This is a first principle of revealed doctrine which Plato also shared when in the *Timaeus* he ascribed the creation of the world to the ungrudging goodness of God : ' Sive ista legerit, sive ab his qui legerant forte cognoverit : sive acerrimo ingenio

---

[1] *De Civ.* VIII. 5 ; X. 1, 2.   [2] *Ibid.* X. 23.
[3] *Ibid.* 24.   [4] *Ibid.* 29.

invisibilia Dei per ea quae facta sunt intellecta conspexerit, sive ab his qui ista conspexerant ipse didicerit[1]'. The world was made good and the various component parts and characters in it worked together—'tamquam in communem rempublicam conferant[2]'—so that there was no evil present in it at all. Man's will, however, being free, there was an opening to evil, through which opening evil came. It was no inherent mischief in the flesh, but a sinful rebellion that constituted evil. Thus it was that the two rival cities—the city of God and the earthly city—are established in being. Both of them spring from love—the former from love of God, the latter from love of self[3]—and their history runs in parallel lines throughout the whole of past time. Into this parallel development we need not enter.

But the most serious result of the Fall in one way is the permanent disturbance of the balance in man's nature. The will can depart from the good at its own pleasure; but not from the evil[4]. It has bound itself to that which is hurtful to it, and cannot return. Hence arises Augustine's criticism upon the older type of virtue. There were many, he says, in the old time who aimed at the suppression of the lusts of the flesh; the Stoics, for instance, who held that man's highest good lay in the service of the soul—may not these be said to have risen out of the carnal life? Such a commendation of these philosophers may seem tempting, but it cannot be sustained. The carnal life consists not merely in carnal pleasures strictly so called; it covers all the errors and vices of the mind. And more than this, all vice whatever arises from the mind, from the misdirection of the will; it is not merely the inevitable result of the burden of the flesh[5]. This is the cause of the failure of their speculations. They strove to find happiness in many ways. Varro seems to have counted up 288 sects[6]. And even the best of these failed; they never succeeded in concealing or mitigating the miseries of life; even their

---

[1] *De Civ.* XI. 21.   [2] *Ibid.* 22.   [3] *Ibid.* XIV. 28.
[4] *Ibid.* 8, XV. 21; *De Bono Vid.* 17; *Conf.* X. xxix. 40.
[5] *De Civ.* XIV. 2.   [6] *Ibid.* XIX. 1.

Note to Lectures III and IV

four virtues conceal a perpetual strife with sin—a strife which in the ideal life will have no place. Temperance never subdued or extinguished lust; prudence never removed men from the pressure of evil and the liability to mistake; justice never succeeded in imposing rational order on mankind; fortitude is an open declaration that we are in the midst of trouble, which we must do our best to endure[1]. Civil law is, as it were, an external repressive force, which 'in eo defigit imperandi oboediendique concordiam civium, ut sit eis de rebus ad mortalem vitam pertinentibus, humanarum quaedam compositio voluntatum[2].' This is the life of the flesh in the true sense; the life which is under the ruin of the Fall; the life from which God is left out, which is not ordered so as to include the spiritual world. It is not true that it is absolutely evil, or that all the efforts of these many philosophers have come to nothing. This would contradict the position on which we have already laid stress, namely, that much may be gained from the works of pagan thinkers. It simply means that human life has been under a cloud—has been working on false principles and with impaired powers, and therefore has missed its aim. Its work is good so far as it goes; but it is insufficient. Even now, as the end is not yet, the city of God, so far as its earthly position is concerned, will use the good that is in the earthly order. 'Civitas caelestis, vel potius pars eius, quae in hac mortalitate peregrinatur, et vivit ex fide, etiam ista pace necesse est utatur, donec ipsa, cui talis pax necessaria est, mortalitas transeat[3].' Moreover, there is no need for an absolute breach with all human life. The philosophers who have joined the Church have not changed their dress or pursuits. The three types of life of which so much has been said— 'otiosus, actuosus, et ex utroque compositus'—are before the Christian for his choice. He must not be selfish in his leisure, or forgetful of God if he is busy. His life will differ from that of others in its motive. ' Otium sanctum quaerit caritas veritatis; negotium iustum suscipit necessitas caritatis[4].' The

---

[1] *De Civ.* XIX. 4.   [2] *Ibid.* 17.   [3] *Ibid.*   [4] *Ibid.* 18.

Christian motive will redeem the life from its doom of failure[1].

The true source of all this trouble is the fault in the will, as has been already said; and therefore the true remedy must restore the will. This restoration can only be effected by the Creator of the will Himself. Hence the whole process of redemption and restoration depends upon the Incarnation and the Sacrifice of Christ. This is the way of purification which the Platonist sought in vain. He, the Word, by living the life of obedience in the flesh, showed that the flesh was not the source of evil; that even death itself, though it was the penalty of sin, could be endured without sin. 'Ideo solvere potuit moriendo peccata, quia et mortuus est, et non pro suo peccato[2].' We are not concerned with the way in which the Incarnation and Sacrifice of Christ are applied to the restoration of the will. The question would lead us into some of the most perplexed regions of Augustine's theology—the doctrines of grace and predestination. But it is necessary to complete the statement of the effect of this restoration upon life.

Life, as we have already seen, enters upon a new stage in consequence of the coming of Christ; one that ends in success and not in failure. Augustine institutes several comparisons between the old methods and the new. In a sense, he urges, the life of philosophical effort, such as Plato set up as an ideal, is parallel with the life under grace. Plato and his followers all agree that man cannot in his own strength attain to the fullness of knowledge, and that the true spirit of philosophy is granted but to few. 'Videtis utcumque, etsi de longinquo, etsi acie caligante, patriam in qua manendum est, sed viam qua eundum est non tenetis[3].' They had realized their need vaguely and incompletely, but had fallen on the wrong road. 'O si cognovisses' (he goes on, apostrophizing Plato), 'Dei gratiam per Iesum Christum Dominum nostrum, ipsamque eius Incarnationem qua hominis animam corpusque suscepit, summum esse exemplum gratiae videre potuisses.' The Incarnation was not a strange and alarming novelty,

[1] Cf. *Ep. ad Diogn.* c. 5.   [2] *De Civ.* X. 24.   [3] *Ibid.* 29.

it was the satisfaction of the needs which men had felt before. So, again, he compares the life of virtue under the old conditions with that under the new. The philosophers who loved virtue drew a gloomy picture of the Epicurean conception of life, in which the four virtues were all the handmaids of pleasure, while pleasure ruled over them as a queen[1]. And to correct this misapprehension they themselves either adopted virtue as an end in itself, or made it a means to the glory of man. This charge lies as well against those who used the virtues as a means of acquiring reputation, as against their rivals who despised the opinions of men and congratulated themselves on their wisdom. Their end was inadequate. It required to be enlarged by 'vera pietas in Deum,' whom the virtuous man 'diligit, credit et sperat.' In the strength of this union with God he will subordinate all his interests and pleasures to the one end of pleasing God; he will attain where others only strove[2]. These three movements of the soul towards God are discussed in the *Enchiridion*. In this work *fides* is somewhat narrowly restricted to the tenacious profession of the whole creed; but the more definitely moral use of the word, by which faith means an unswerving trust in the goodness of God, is common enough. 'Fides credit: spes et caritas orant[3].' That is, hope and love represent the atmosphere of close communion with God in which the soul lives. And these habits are therefore the true expression of the Christian life[4], forming the basis of all social action. For, as we have seen, the Christian is not wholly separate from all the world; he lives and moves there like any one else, only he acts upon a deeper motive. Hence the old four virtues, which represented the demand of society upon the will in pre-Christian days, are modified in character. They centre round, and are manifestations of, love[5].

[1] *Cf.* Cic. *De Fin.* II. 21, 69.
[2] *De Civ.* V. 20; cf. XIX. 24; *De Trin.* XIII. 19, XIV. 1.
[3] *Ench.* c. 7.   [4] Cf. *De Agone Christ.* 13, 14.
[5] See above in Lecture IV. In *De Div. Quaest.* XXXI, Augustine repeats, practically without comment, the ordinary statement about the cardinal virtues (cf. Cic. *De Inv.* II. 53, 54, §§ 159-166).

The presence of the Church in the world is still incomplete; the full effect of the will of God is not as yet seen. And in the Church as at present constituted there is grave need of discipline. Thus we hear of the wrong involved in attending the theatres; we have extensive discussions of the relative merits of the married or the single state; rules laid down about divorce, and other questions of conduct. In matters of discipline there is less said of the dangers of pure Paganism than we found in Tertullian and Cyprian, and a more liberal attitude towards the world. Thus, for instance, Augustine mentions the fact that many actors have approved themselves not only in temperance and patience, but also in faith, hope, and love[1]. But there are two excesses in the way of discipline of which Augustine has much to say. One is the belief that for those who have faith, works are wholly unimportant; the other is the denial of all absolving power in the Church. Both of these are grievous errors; the one absolutely relaxing all moral claims whatever: the other rejecting the divine commission of the Church[2].

With St. Augustine a turning-point is reached in the history of the Church; its first period of open conflict with Paganism is at an end, for, indeed, Paganism itself had been tried and found wanting. For the future its traces would be found, if at all, in holes and corners; in indirect influences upon life and thought; in quaint ritual survivals, or among belated philosophers. Its most brilliant and most successful effort to solve the problem of the Universe, the philosophy of Plato, was drifting into the dull routine of the school of Athens or the wild imaginings of the Syrian magicians. Augustine has already seen this coming; he laughs at the magic, and he shows no sense of terror of the philosophy. He has learnt much himself from the philosophers, and he is prepared to recommend their use to others. Thus with him pagan philosophy has found its place; it is not any longer an uncertain factor, extravagantly praised by some, by others

[1] *Ad Simpl.* I. ii. 22.
[2] *De Fide et Operibus*, c. 25 and following; *De Agone Christ.* c. 31.

Note to Lectures III and IV

extravagantly denounced. As the Alexandrines had met and triumphed over pagan philosophy while it was still in the ascendant, Augustine has to deal with it when it is on its decline. It enters into his thought and affects many of his ideas; but it is assimilated; and for this, among other reasons, the Western Church is content for a long period to draw its knowledge of Greek philosophy from St. Augustine. This could not have happened if philosophy had been still a potent force with which every person, who thought at all, had to reckon. If it had been alive, continually producing books, throwing new lights on life, and raising new questions, St. Augustine's presentation of it must have become sensibly obsolete. As it did little or nothing for itself, and Augustine had, so to speak, marked the useful passages in its books, it was sufficient to read these, to pick up the useful principles or formulae or arguments, and for the rest to leave it alone. So St. Augustine stands at the beginning of an age from which original speculative philosophy was to be left out.

The disappearance from the field of the original antagonist of the Christian faith involves, of course, changes in its point of view. Throughout the early years of its career, the Church was struggling for bare existence. It is actuated throughout the contest by certain leading ideas, the play of which we have been considering in the one field of Ethics. These are brought into full consciousness in the works of St. Augustine.

From the first the Church had found in the Person of Christ the solution of the difficulties and perplexities of life. Whatever be the date of the Acts, the speeches recorded there are essentially in harmony with the whole history of Christian thought. St. Peter and St. Paul alike promise deliverance from the bands of sin, and immortality in communion with God, through the name of Jesus the Lord. It may not have been fully clear what were the inferences which this admission carried with it; these were brought into light by the processes of history. But the central conviction was never held doubtfully or changed by the Catholic Church. The rise of various interpretations of it served to bring out more and more decisively the traditional belief, and were the means by which the Church adjusted its relations to prevalent modes of thought.

Again : from the first the Church realized itself as a society. The belief in Jesus as Lord was an individual act, involving individual relations with God. But the acceptance of this faith was not a pious opinion merely ; it was accompanied by admission into the society of believers ; it involved a change of status through the sacrament of admission : those who held it were 'in the Lord.' And the society from the first had rules and ideas of its own. It was, from the moment of the admission of the Gentiles, independent of the old geographical and racial distinctions ; it was both wider and narrower than they. It aimed at producing a moral life which, though akin to that already recognized as desirable, was loftier and more severe. Over all this ground, as over the region of doctrine, the Church had to feel its way, and to define its position by degrees. As people from time to time, through actual ignorance of the faith, or through lack of clearness in thought, or through positive distaste for the doctrines, devised phrases which fell short of the fulness of the creed, so from time to time men indulged themselves in practices which were really incompatible with the demands of the faith. As the intellectual limits of the freedom of speculation were gradually defined by reference to the test of the Incarnation, so the limits of moral or immoral enterprise were similarly fixed by degrees, and by reference to the same test. It was the belief in the Incarnation that was the link between the moral and the intellectual life, a belief which was held by faith and verified in experience.

We have seen in Lectures III-IV, and in the course of this note, some of the stages by which this process was carried out. St. Augustine's work represents a turning-point or epoch in it. By his day the time when questions were determined as they arose was past. The conditions requiring something like a definite code of moral rules were at hand. St. Augustine belongs partly to the old order and partly to the new. He writes treatises, like Tertullian or Cyprian, on definite moral or disciplinary questions, such as the relative importance of marriage or celibacy; and these have been manifestly called forth by actual discussions. But at the same time his principles and technical terms are more fully developed; the materials are to be found in his work for a precise treatment of moral questions. An illustration of the use of St. Augustine's writings for these purposes is supplied by many of the works printed in the appendix as being spurious. In many cases they consist of excerpts from the genuine works strung together so as to bear on some special point or to form manuals of instruction. And the most cursory glance at a work on Canon Law will show how sentences from St. Augustine were used as decisive authority upon matters of ethics or discipline.

It would take us beyond the limits of this note to work out in detail the influence of Augustine, in the region of ethics. But a few words may be said upon his relation to his contemporaries and to certain of the more important of those who followed him.

There is indeed comparatively little to be said, even of the more distinguished of those who flourished at or about the time of St. Augustine, with reference to our special subject. The name of Jerome stands high in the roll of scholars and commentators, but it has no title to fame in the history of moral speculation. Jerome added nothing new to the traditional way of conceiving Christian virtue. He uses the phraseology to which we are accustomed, and is quite prepared to give a Christian bearing to the current ideas of virtue. But the terms he uses appear most commonly as illustrations of some general principle, or as a means of applying some text; there is not in Jerome, as there is in Augustine, a continual reference to a system, more or less complete, of moral ideas. One passage, however, is worth mentioning, in which Jerome gives clear utterance to the principle that Christ is the true source of all virtue. It comes in the Commentary on the Ephesians, after a long passage in which Christ has been set forth as our means of access to the Father[1]. Then he says, 'Qui igitur omnia ratione et ordine facit, iste credit in Christum sermonem atque rationem: qui sapientiam potuerit comprehendere, credit in Christum sapientiam: qui intellexerit veritatem, credit in Christum veritatem: qui iuste vixerit, credit in eum iustitiam.' This passage is important in that it definitely declares Jerome's views on the ultimate source and sanction of virtue. But Jerome's interest in ethical matters is influenced by one very powerful prejudice or conviction. He is strongly under the sway of the desire for monastic life. His letters of spiritual advice are largely concerned with this question, and his view of the nature of virtue and of the demands made by the Law of Christ is formed under this prepossession. Moreover, there was a vehemence about Jerome's own character which makes his evidence of less value as to the general course of human life. It would not be true to say that he ignores the need of vocation for the ascetic life; and it must always be remembered that he interposed at times to prevent excesses of rigour in the self-discipline of those who consulted him; but still the aspect which human life bore to him was severer and less natural than that which is found in the writing of Augustine[2].

The next writer of whom it will be well to speak is Gregory, the great pope. By his time the Augustinian principle of the unity of all virtues in love was firmly established. It reappears, of course, in Gregory. And the opening given by previous thought for the development of scientific system is, as has been mentioned in Lecture IV, beginning to be used. There are few writers, perhaps, who present such a puzzling aspect to the modern eye as Gregory

---

[1] *In Eph.* II. iii. 12.
[2] In the Epistle to Pammachius, No. 66, § 3, we find the cardinal virtues pressed into the service of the monastic life. The practical meaning of prudence is the choice of the things heavenly in preference to the ordinary social life of men.

Note to Lectures III and IV

the Great. It is impossible to read him without feeling that he profoundly deserved his title, the Great. The history of his life shows him to have been a far-seeing and wise ruler, whose bent was practical rather than speculative, and who could be trusted to take a sane and reasonable view of any question that might be brought before him. So again throughout a large portion of his writings the quality which is most impressive is straightforwardness and directness of insight in spiritual matters. On every page there are indications of his power and certainty in reading the human heart. But yet he is entirely bound by the eccentric method of Scriptural interpretation which prevailed in his day, and his efforts at systematizing his ethical ideas depend in large measure on his exegesis. It is not, of course, a ground for surprise in any real sense that this should be so; it was not Gregory's mission to initiate critical science, and he accepts, therefore, the methods which prevail. But in a man so great as Gregory, the contrast is more startling between the depth of his moral perception and, as it seems to us, the astonishing futility of the reasonings by which his moral utterances are supported.

It has been necessary to make these remarks at this point because to a large extent the growth in systematic completeness, which owed so much to Gregory's writings, depends on the method of interpretation he employed. He starts with much the same ideas as to virtue which we have found in Augustine, but he satisfies his desire for system by seeing types or suggestions of the three theological and four cardinal virtues in various passages of the Bible where an ingenious use of allegory can extract them from the written word. Thus, to take one instance only out of many, the three theological virtues are symbolized by the three daughters of Job[1]; the four corners of the house overthrown by the wind are the four cardinal virtues, shaken by sudden temptation[2]. So Gregory dwells on the seven gifts of the Spirit, Job's seven sons, and explains that these can never be brought to

[1] *Mor. in Job.* I. xxvii. 38. [2] *Ibid.* II. xlix. 77.

perfection without the three theological virtues, the number of perfection being ten.

In all this Gregory is simply applying on a grand scale and with special reference to practical life a method that had been used many times before since the days of Philo. But the spiritual value of the remarks he makes has helped to give currency to the system which is based on this allegorical method of interpretation. His works continued to be read for the sake of their own beauty. The use made of Scripture seemed natural enough; and thus the lines were laid down within which Christian ethical teaching was to move [1].

The conception of Christian virtue developed by Augustine and Gregory rules the moral ideas of all the writers in the West till the time of the greater schoolmen. The Second and Third Books of *Sententiae* by Isidorus Hispalensis are closely connected with Gregory's Morals on Job, and contain the traditional theories of virtue. At a still later date Alcuin reproduces the same point of view in the treatise *De Virtutibus et Vitiis*. Thus so far as the West is concerned the doctrine already described prevails all through the early Middle Ages, and forms the starting-point for the scholastic discussions. The characteristic feature of scholasticism is, of course, its elaboration of systematic classification. The connexion between the theological and cardinal virtues was drawn closer; a variety of virtuous and other conditions, which had hitherto occupied an uncertain position round the seven virtuous states, have their place in the moral system

---

[1] It is noticeable that there is much less tendency to hard and fast divisions in the *Regula Pastoralis* than in the exegetical works. Where Scripture is quoted, it is interpreted on the same principles as in the Homilies or the Morals on Job. But the desire for system is less apparent. The virtues and vices are discussed singly, as representing various characters, a virtuous and vicious character being frequently contrasted, with a view of illustrating the method in which the priest will deal with various types of men. It is possible, therefore, that the classification of which we have spoken above was attractive by reason of its convenience and value in preaching.

Note to Lectures III and IV

decided and their definitions made precise. It has been shown in Lecture IV that St. Thomas, in whose *Summa* scholasticism obtained its most effective expression, used the Aristotelian definitions of the cardinal virtues, reading them in the light of St. Augustine. It will not be necessary to dwell at length on the smaller changes of meaning which this or that virtue acquired under the influence of scholastic treatment. The chief interest of the schoolmen from our point of view consists in their attitude towards the relation of the moral law to the Reason and Will of God. This point will be considered in a note to Lecture VI.

It is not easy to find signs of a growing system of ethics in the great Greek Fathers after Origen. It seems as if the formulation of ethical ideas belonged more naturally to the Western mind, while the Easterns occupied themselves most prominently with the definition of the speculative elements of the Creed. It is not that there is in them any essentially different way of conceiving the effect of Christianity on life, but rather that they treat it incidentally, and the need of a precise scheme of moral ideas is not apparent to them. Chrysostom, for instance, asserts that love is the cause and centre of all virtues, as Augustine might have done[1]; he enters into the question of the presence of virtue in the days before Christ, and remarks upon the vast difficulty of it under those conditions[2]; he speaks of the work of Christ in Redemption and the closeness of the bond of the Christian society. He connects humility with σωφροσύνη[3], declaring that St. Paul distinguishes it from τὴν ἀντιδιαστελλομένην τῇ ἀσελγείᾳ ἀρετήν, and identifies it with τὸ νήφειν καὶ ὑγιαίνειν τὴν διάνοιαν. Other virtues are mentioned and commended on almost every page. But it remains that Chrysostom is primarily the preacher. He draws lifelike pictures of the society of his day, and applies to them with telling force the words of Scripture; but his ethical references are occasional

[1] *De Sacerdotio*, VI. viii. § 588.
[2] *In Joh. Ev. Hom.* LXXI. p. 420 D, ed. Bened.
[3] *Hom. in Rom.* XIII. p. 567 B, XXI. p. 660 E, ed. Bened.

and not systematic. They rise, most commonly, out of the immediate circumstances before him, and, though they naturally rest on the same assumptions in every case, they do not suggest anything like a formal classification.

One special point however must be mentioned in connexion with Chrysostom's name, and that is his attitude towards Monasticism. He had himself in early life desired to bind himself with monastic vows, and had lived for some time in a highly ascetic manner. But, though he feels strongly the glory of this life of self-dedication, we find him maintaining in the most decided terms the true Christian value of the secular life. Its very temptations and difficulties are, he argues, true proofs of its loftiness[1]. 'The struggle of monks is great,' he says, 'and their toil heavy; but if any one compares the sweat of their life with the priesthood rightly administered, he will find the difference as great as that between a private person and a king[2]. This attitude, which carries with it a disposition to regard the life of the ordinary layman as a Christian vocation, is a very important note in Chrysostom's thought. It means that for him Christianity is definitely regarded as leavening ordinary life, and not as involving the total destruction of all social order.

Basil the Great shares some of the characteristics of his friend Chrysostom, but with great differences. Like other Greek Fathers of this age, his interests are largely dogmatic. But there are among his works treatises of a definitely ethical kind. One is a body of detached statements on moral questions. Another, the canonical letter to Amphilochius, contains a number of decisions on various ethical points, chiefly of a disciplinary character. Another deals with the questions arising in connexion with the monastic life. On the positive side of moral exhortation there is little that is new to us in the conception of virtue; on the side of penitential rules and casuistry Basil has much to say, but of this we must defer giving any account till the note on the next Lecture. On the whole, Basil is much less a man of the

---

[1] *De Sacerdotio*, VI. i-viii.　　[2] *Ibid.* c. v.

Note to Lectures III and IV 205

world than Chrysostom. He has a much stronger desire for the monastic life than his friend, and though he rises to the demands of the episcopal office, his heart yearns for peace. He deals firmly and successfully with the questions brought before him because he must, not because he likes doing so; and it would seem as if his ideal of the Christian life were a complete ascetic separation from the world.

This very fragmentary sketch of the progress of ethical thought within the Christian Church will, it is hoped, be sufficient to make clear the positions asserted in Lectures III and IV. In the ethics of the Christian Church the two streams of ethical thought which belonged to the past are brought together—the Jewish morality, which was largely religious, and the Greek, which was chiefly secular. Until this fusion was effected there was a hiatus in the life of man; it did not yet fall under the rule of any one principle. The nearest approach to such a fusion in the Gentile world was probably the doctrine of Providence, which implied some interest in man on the part of the gods. But the connexion thus established is weak and vague; it required something much more definite and detailed to introduce unity into life. Christianity performs this function necessarily, in virtue of the Incarnation. For through that event the divine is mingled with the human in a way which cannot but force itself on the attention. We have seen how this took shape in the idea of a complete and perfect human nature, and a spiritual society in which men dwelt by virtue of their relation to God. But it was not enough that these conceptions should be displayed to the world; they had also to discover and make their own those elements in ancient thought which had closest affinity with the new truths. Philo had tried, but without decisive effect, to weld together the Jewish religion with the essentially secular philosophy of Greece. His effort is important and of permanent interest, but still it was premature. The Judaism of his experience had not in it the capacity of assimilation; it could only be forced into agreement with the philosophy of Plato or the Stoics by the free use of allegory. And the philosophy which he followed had not the final word on the problems of human life. Moreover, Philo himself was not the man to effect so great a fusion.

The problem he left unsolved was taken up by the Christian Church. And the Church begins at the opposite end of the process; it is first practical and only secondarily theoretical. Men find by the sure road of experience that the example of Christ, interpreted by the Spirit, enables them to achieve success in the moral world. In this the school of Christ triumphs over the schools of the philosophers; Christ's followers had to deal theoretically with a moral experience as well as a moral ideal. Various plans, of which something has been said in this note, were adopted for this purpose, which contact with Gentile thought made necessary. There were those, like Tertullian, who would have nothing to say to pagan literature, however high its aim. There were those, like Justin or Lactantius on a very small scale, like Clement and Origen on the highest scale, who did their best to meet halfway the moral impulses of those who were still outside the Church. And the principles they adopted, owing especially to the genius of Origen, ruled the ultimate decision of the Church. The Western facility for organization led Augustine and Gregory to formulate into a definite scheme the morality which prevailed in the Church. But throughout the whole process the essential Christian features were never neglected. It was never forgotten that the power of holiness depends on union with Christ, and that the sphere of holiness is the Church, which is His Body.

LECTURE V.

'If any man see his brother sinning a sin not unto death, he shall ask, and God will give him life for them that sin not unto death. There is a sin unto death: not concerning this do I say that he should make request. All unrighteousness is sin : and there is a sin not unto death.'
1 JOHN v. 16, 17 (R.V.).

THE most decisive test of the character and value of any ethical system is its treatment of the fact of evil and the tendency to sin. This is the most real and most perplexing of all the problems which beset life. Nothing brings us so directly into contact with hard and grim fact, and nothing complicates so mysteriously and disappoints so dishearteningly our calculations and our hopes. However fully we may recognize sin's power and prevalence, it always interferes somewhat unexpectedly. There are strange possibilities of sinfulness in the best and most steady of men: the most regular and orderly life conceals tendencies which some unforeseen occasion may bring to light: the most candid and frank of mankind have reserves in their lives which would probably astonish those who know them best. And yet though we know all this, the most cynical of men hesitate to anticipate evil in others; or, at least, the worst forms of evil :

a suspicious temper is oftener the result of sin than of experience of others' wrong-doing, so deeply is the conviction rooted that sin is an abnormality, a breach of natural order, a departure from the true rule of human life.

The presence of this disturbing element has been recognized, as indeed could hardly have been avoided, by almost all thinkers in the ethical region. But the consequences of the admission have by no means been identical. All agree that evil does constantly occur, but they diverge when they attempt to explain the reason; and yet though the results of inquiry have differed, the point at which the investigation has been taken up has been generally the same. It has always seemed a marvel that men should not be able to avoid sin in practice, however heartily they may disapprove of it in theory. This is one of the salient characteristics of evil, that men produce it themselves. Not merely are they always apt to be involved in evil through the malpractices of others and the incomplete adjustment of the world, but also they themselves constantly do acts which they regret sooner or later, and which they see should have been left undone or done otherwise. The disorder affects their own wills, their own designs, their own contribution to the course of human history: they experience failure to which they themselves have given occasion.

It is clear that the method by which so peculiar a fact as this is brought within the compass of an ethical system, will have a large influence in determining the character of the system as a whole.

Systems will differ, in other words, according as the evil of the world is regarded as a necessary outcome of the finite position of man, or as an abnormality which has no right to exist even in the limited lives of finite creatures. The former point of view rules for the most part in all metaphysical systems of ethics. Wherever the interest of the speculation consists in finding an explanatory formula of the mere facts, in co-ordinating phenomena and reducing them to general laws, such an explanation of evil seems sufficient. For the purposes of such a method as this the obvious truth, that there is often a soul of goodness in things evil, suggests a principle by which such facts may be classified. Such a point of view betrays itself in the emphasis laid upon the question both in ancient and modern times, Is virtue knowledge? So long as this question is answered in the affirmative, there is a bias in favour of regarding the limiting force of circumstances as the true cause of evil. For if virtue is to vary directly with knowledge, and if evil is to be always the result of mere lack of knowledge—if it may be assumed that the will always follows the lead of knowledge—it must follow that the will of man is not only theoretically but practically on the side of good, and fails to attain it through no fault of its own, but through the delusion which lack of knowledge engenders. Knowledge that is complete and therefore sufficient to inform unerringly the practical principle in human action is necessarily out of reach, and from this misfortune all the trouble flows. No person can be supposed to sin willingly; all alike wish to do well, but fail to attain their desire through lack of information as to the proper course to take.

In such theories as this moral evil is the result of intellectual error, which again flows from our necessarily limited knowledge; but, strictly speaking, the cause of the intellectual error matters for our purpose but little: the important point is that evil is ascribed to some general feature of man's life rather than to any personal decision of his own. To some, for instance, it has seemed that the burial of the spirit of man in matter is the real cause both of the limitation of his knowledge and of evil; but this does not affect the general aspect of the theory. Its moral importance depends entirely upon the fact that on some ground or another man is seen to be confined within certain limits, and that the existence of these produces evil quite irrespective of the individual man's will. It is manifest that an attitude such as this towards evil must necessarily colour the whole conception of moral life.

Systems which contain this theory of evil tend to be, on their practical side, political rather than strictly ethical systems. They start, as I have said, by viewing evil externally as a part of the general conditions of human life: the science of life must include that particular class of facts in its enunciation of uniformities in the moral world. For if it can be shown that evil is inevitable, depending on the actual conditions in which man's life is cast, no further explanation is required: it is only necessary that evil should be put in its proper place, and allowed its due proportion of significance in the systematic statement of moral facts. The practical philosopher will deplore it, discourage it, indicate the ruinous waste and mischief of it, endeavour to mitigate its effects. But the most that he can say of it is that it is there and is inevitable. Further, evil will necessarily be to such a thinker very much a matter of external action. It will be the result of the will of man baulked and misdirected by his limiting surroundings. The moral condition of the will must be a secondary consideration at the best; and it will tend to become increasingly unimportant, the more unreservedly it is assumed that the will of man always wishes for that which is right. That is, of course, an obvious result. The more safely one can trust the will of man to take the right initiative, the less necessary it is to investigate its actual attitude minutely. I am not, of course, attempting to maintain that there is no interest in the condition of the individual will to be found, for instance, among ancient classical writers on ethics. The history of the gradual degradation of the ideal man in Plato, the emphasis laid on the habitual condition of the soul by Aristotle, the indifference to external circumstances among the Stoics, if the will itself is virtuous, would each and all of them give the lie to such a sweeping generalization. At the same time, wherever evil is traced primarily to some changeless inevitable condition of life, such an interest is somewhat of an unexplained mercy; it lacks logical justification in a system which ascribes evil entirely to external conditions and limitations, and treats the state of the will as a secondary factor affecting in some degree the character of the acts produced. For instance, a passionate and ill-regulated state of temper may tend to give rise to acts of violence which are contrary to the interest of a well-ordered state: and, on the other hand, the cultivation of self-control and orderly thinking will make for peace in any society. No ethical system can afford to ignore such facts as these; every ethical system must encourage self-control and discourage ungovernable temper. But so long as the real cause of the evil is found in the lack of knowledge of the full danger of such temper, or in the limiting conditions of matter which prevent such knowledge being easily attained, the study of the individual will and its states is not undertaken for its own sake, but rather as a means of supplying the need of full knowledge, and so enabling the will to act rightly. It may be worth while to show that this or that feeling of resentment or annoyance may take effect in one particular direction, in acts that every one condemns; but it does not follow that such analysis really carries with it a keen sense of personal wrong-doing, and its aim may be rather to clear up the intellect and direct the choice than to estimate moral guilt.

In strong contrast with this point of view stands another to which all evil is, in its final character, rebellion. That is to say, to this point of view no evil anywhere is ideally inevitable: it falls outside the ideal order of the world: some one is responsible for it wherever it occurs: there is no evil that is not ultimately sin. This theory, which seems to underlie the simplest moral conceptions of men in various parts of the world, is developed to its highest point by Christianity; and it is, of course, with this higher development of it that we are chiefly concerned. It is, however, necessary to point out that the view of sin which belongs to Christianity was in large measure an inheritance from the earlier faith of the Jewish nation. The Christian conception is ruled by three chief ideas —the notion of man's true relation to God, the sense that he is free and responsible, and the notion of the true social relations of mankind. Of these, it is the former which goes back furthest into the heart of Judaism. For the governing idea of Jewish moral life, appearing in the prophets, psalmists, and some large tracts of the Law, was the holiness of God; an attribute which laid heavy claims upon man's life, which he was bound in his degree to imitate, which he had it in his power to outrage by his sin. I will dwell at some length upon these primary ideas in the Christian view of sin.

I. *Man's true relation to God.* Under the old covenant there is a curious combination of joy and fear in the attitude of man towards Jehovah. The national pride at the uniqueness of God's dealings with His chosen people is crossed by a fear born of the danger of using the privilege of intercourse with God unworthily. In this respect the story of the revelation at Sinai, whatever may be its date, embodies the regular Jewish attitude towards God. They fear to approach the Mount, while, at the same time, they recognize the fact that God is wishing to communicate with them. Even Moses exceedingly fears and quakes. And it is the same with a prophet like Isaiah, who, at the very moment of his supreme vision and call to the prophet's work, is reminded of his moral unfitness to stand forth as the spokesman of God.

The cause of this mixed feeling (of which other instances will readily occur to the mind) is not merely fear of the *power* of God—that would not account for the attractive force of the presence of God—but depends upon a sense that the holiness of God is in some way a law to men, and that they fall short of their ideal. It is this idea which, I think, is the most distinctive feature of Jewish morality, that the goodness and holiness and, in another connexion, the wisdom of God are to be the types of such attributes in men. The Jews seemed to have reversed the order so often followed in religious speculation; they have not built their notion of God out of their experience of man, but rather they start in their moral thinking from the nature of God as an ideal, and proceed to test the life and character of man by relation to it. It is unimportant for our present purpose to inquire by what process of inspiration or reasoning, or, as perhaps we ought rather to say, of inspired reasoning, the Jewish thinkers attained this result; but it is of the highest importance to insist that the typical idea in Jewish ethics is of a God Whose own Being forms the rule of man's life, from Whom the moral law has come, Whose supreme rights are infringed by sin. The sense of sin, of course, grew with the growth of the people, and the particular contents of the idea must have varied greatly in different individuals; but throughout the whole history the nature of God formed the moral ideal, and departure from this ideal was not merely mistake or inevitable evil; it was rebellion, it was sin. This characteristic use of the moral being of God reappears and is developed in Christianity. It underlies the promise of Christ in the Sermon on the Mount that we shall be perfect as the Father is perfect; and it is carried to the highest point of all when the unity and love of the Divine Persons is held out as the type of the unity and love of the Church.

Thus the genius of Judaism in the moral region was largely occupied with this one part of the whole matter, the moral nature of God. On this head, however variously the duty of man was conceived or interpreted, there was never any doubt as to the holiness of God and the commanding claim of His holiness upon men. It was well that this was so. It was well that the minds of those who lived the highest life under the Old Covenant should rest in the thought of God and His perfection, rather than perplex themselves with minute analysis of man's nature and his failings and their causes. It was also well that their sense of sin should grow as they came to know more of God. For it is difficult to conceive how life could have been possible under the old conditions, if all the meaning and all the cost of sin had been understood before its power was destroyed by the Death and Resurrection of Christ. Those who lived nearest to God knew most about its deadly meaning, even as it was. We read and enter into, as best we may, the passionate penitence of psalmist and prophet: we understand their hopelessness, and the intensity of the longing which sounds in their words; but it may be questioned whether we do not carry back into our interpretation of their words some of the fuller knowledge of man and his possibilities and his perils which is derived from the teaching of St. Peter or St. Paul. Their hatred and terror of sin was touched with comfort by the thought of the choice of God resting upon His people: the Cross of Christ was yet to lend to man's estimate of evil a shade of blacker gloom than any of which psalmist or prophet had experience.

At first sight, no doubt, the opposite effect is the result of passing from the Old Testament to the New. To contrast, for instance, the furious hatred of evil which breathes in some psalms and in some of the writings of Isaiah, with the almost matter-of-fact way in which St. Peter in his early speeches describes the message he has to deliver, might seem to justify the most lighthearted modern methods of explaining away sin. It has been, says St. Peter: a conspicuous case has occurred in the crucifixion by wicked hands of that Just One. But this was an act of ignorance on the part both of people and rulers, and the time has come now for repentance, by which, with baptism, the old misery will be done away. But this impression does not remain. The whole treatment of sin in the New Testament is cooler, but it is no less severe than that in the Old. It is cooler because it is more certain of itself. There is less of the tone of panic in it, because the nature of sin is more clearly revealed, because it is no longer a haunting fear against which it is impossible to provide, because, in other words, the separation between man and God is at an end; the divine ideal is no longer a remote and unattainable ideal: the divine Life has been lived on earth, and the whole nature of man has been raised up into relation with a spiritual order. In the light of the Life and Death of Christ the true spiritual meaning of moral life is revealed; it is seen what God thinks of sin, and what He is prepared to do to overcome it. Hence we have to notice not merely a change in the conception of the divine nature, but also a far more elaborate analysis of man and his nature, which is expressed, as the Church lives on, in a profound and searching analysis of sin. It is here that the other two fundamental ideas already mentioned come up for consideration.

II. The freedom of man. The question of freedom is a perpetual source of trouble to the philosopher, owing to the obvious difficulty of reconciling it with any full and consistent view of the world. Fortunately we are not immediately concerned with the metaphysical difficulties that surround it: they are not discussed, nor is there any sign of any consciousness of their existence in the New Testament: we are only bound to consider the question from the ethical point of view. In ancient days under the old law men had felt themselves responsible for their acts, and not merely for their overt acts, but also for the tendency and condition of their wills. From the days of Samuel onwards there were some who knew that to obey was better than to sacrifice, and that the one thing needful was that the heart should be right with God. Even the penetrating interpretations of the old Law in the Sermon on the Mount should hardly have lighted upon wholly unprepared and astonished minds. The imperative need of spiritual harmony with God, however, is developed and absorbed in the tremendous idea of judgement which is characteristic of St. John. I do not, of course, allude to the stern but comparatively comprehensible notion which associates judgement merely with a great Day of Assize, on which, somewhat after our human manner, accusations are made and absolutely true verdicts given. But I refer to that far more stern and relentless conception of judgement, according to which the facts of a life simply register its inner character—its actual relation of allegiance to or rebellion against God. This has all the slow inevitableness about it which belongs to the law of habit, and all the unerring certainty which is connected with the idea of an omniscient judge. But it takes its peculiar character from the fact that by it man is seen to be acting in a spiritual order, in which every motion of the spirit is a register of a spiritual choice. Every act is a spiritual event, bearing a spiritual meaning; it is the answer of the individual soul to the appeal which outward circumstances convey. And for such a view as this, it is not enough to say that the will is free enough to make the man responsible. Butler's answer to the Necessitarians, that if the act is under compulsion, the punishment which follows is inflicted under compulsion too, is not sufficient. That belongs to another sphere altogether —the sphere of law administered in a civil state. The Johannine idea of judgement means that the man has a power of declaring himself—of taking up a ground in opposition to God: and the judgement is just the bare statement of the fact that he has done so. " This is the judgement, that the light was manifested, and men loved darkness better." They, in their inward selves, rose up and forsook the way of God, turned their backs upon His manifested light, as truly as a child might rise up and leave his father's house. As the child has command over his body, whatever forces may surround and condition it, so the soul has such command over itself. In this sense the belief in freedom is necessary to the Christian view of life. I need not dwell upon the further results of this assumption, nor inquire whether there is room in the idea for such a declaration against God as is final, past all recovery: whether, in other words, the separation which the soul has chosen may be maintained for ever; nor need I consider how this doctrine of judgement bears on the day of reckoning at the Parousia. But I must try to show how this view of freedom gives a peculiar significance to sin.

If the meaning of sin is that the soul in the very core of its being breaks off from God and declares itself in opposition to Him, then it is plain that the range and character of the idea must take a particular form. Sin will be possible at every point at which the soul may either be in contact with God, or may by its own act create a breach. And the character of the sin will depend not upon any social result it may have, but upon the relation between the soul and God, out of which it arises. Thus, for instance, a particular set of erroneous opinions, a particular refusal of belief in God or in Christ, may be not merely a regrettable departure from conventional convictions, but a moral outrage—morally comparable not with a physical stumble over some hidden obstacle, but with murder or adultery or any other crime, the recognition of which is forced on the state by its ruinous effects. I say this may be in particular cases; but this is hardly adequate. It *must* be whenever the will has entered into and coloured the result. In many cases, such, for instance, as those of the heathen, the difference between their beliefs and the highest possible knowledge of God is not one, from the very nature of the case, in which the will has determined the result. And doubtless there are many other cases morally on a level with these. It may possibly be true also that whenever intellectual error is morally deserving of condemnation, it has arisen as a consequence of some moral depravity. These are questions which may modify the particular estimate of particular cases. They do not affect the general truth, that unless the intellect is of necessity incapable of being in contact with God altogether, a wilful breach of contact with God must be possible in the intellectual region, and that when it occurs it is sin. It is concerning sin that the Spirit convicts the world, because they believe not on Christ. It may be that this moral aspect of intellectual error, for various reasons, sounds especially hard to modern ears. If we do not formally maintain that virtue is the same thing as knowledge, we do not readily allow that it is possible and even easy to use knowledge for the purpose of sin, as a deliberately chosen rival to the true desire for God. But this seems to be necessarily involved in the Christian idea of sin.

Again, there are certain subtle moral conditions, besides those concerned with the intellect, which an external moral system could not take into account, but which this view of the moral bearing of spiritual action must treat as sinful. St. James condemns severely the double-souled man, δίψυχος: and his condemnation is echoed by the Shepherd of Hermas. And why? Not merely because this temper tends to prevent decisive action; as such it would be condemned by any ethical system; but because it destroys the meaning of prayer; it is a sign of impurity of heart; it is a lack of complete sincerity of allegiance—a real sign of detachment from God. Temper, emotion, the general set of the mind, are under this new point of view brought within the range of the moral law. Even social life takes on a different aspect. The failures to do what the conditions of society demand, failures, still more, to answer to the claims of the spiritual society, are not only misfortunes and injuries to the fabric of society, they are sins against God. The delay, for instance, on the part of an employer to pay his just debts is said to cry to the Lord, and the cries of those that laboured to no purpose are said to enter into the ears of the Lord of Hosts[1]—phrases used elsewhere

[1] St. James v. 4.

only of the sin of Cain and the sin of Sodom. And
again the obedience of servants is inculcated in the
name of the Lord. In all these and similar cases
the close connexion in which God stands to the spiritual
order—the true home of man's moral life—gives the
force of sin, of deliberate rebellion against God, to
wrongs which the instinct of a state towards self-
preservation and freedom of life would lead it to
condemn. And all through, the essential point in the
whole matter is that the act is due to the man himself.
It is he—the finite spirit—who, in the presence of
a definite and real alternative, throws his weight into
the scale against God.

III. Freedom then is necessary to the Christian
conception of sin, but it is crossed by another conception no less necessary and important—I mean, of
course, the idea of the unity and solidarity of mankind.
This idea, which was foreshadowed in the Old Testament, comes out into clear prominence in the New, for
it belongs essentially to the mode in which the Sacrifice
and Death of Christ are presented to us. If there were
nothing to be said about man but that he is free to
forsake God, then it would seem as if nothing were
required to bring him back again but added knowledge,
or a more moving example than had been before him
in the past. But this simple version of the case is too
simple even for the simplicity of the Gospel. The
tenacious hold which sin has upon the will of men—
upon their will, as St. Paul found, even if they agreed
with the Law in their minds—points to a hereditary
taint of disease pervading the whole man and limiting

his power of obedience to God. It is this inexorable fact, a condition of life, to all appearance, as impossible to be removed as any other of the accidents of birth, which explains in part the action of God in the Incarnation and Passion. These justify the ways of God to man, even if he only in part understands them; not merely because the threatened penalty on sin is exacted to the full, but because the evil thing is removed from which the trouble sprang. The yearnings of penitent souls which never did and never could save them so long as the inherent fault remained, were shown by Christ to be rational, they ceased to be idle hopes that could not be realized. Repentance was made, as it were, worth while; the hatred of the past changed into a resurrection from a dead self; forgiveness and even union with God became possible to the human will. It became possible through union with Christ to carry out a real dissociation of oneself from one's own past: to begin anew on a new basis, which mere repentance could not do, but of which mere repentance was a figure. And let us notice that salvation, as it is put forward in the New Testament, depends for its method and principle absolutely on the truth of the ultimate unity of mankind. If each man had been considered merely as a single atom, who in his own unmodified independence and freedom rebels, then the whole moral attitude of the Church must have been different. The language of St. Paul would be proved to be exaggerated; all men would have started with a fair prospect; there would have been no hereditary impediment to a complete return to God. It would have been an exaggeration to speak of Christ's death as a sacrifice; and, indeed, such a phrase could hardly have had a meaning in days when sacrifice was familiar as a practice, and when its ancient meaning as a restoration of communion between God and man had not yet been lost. In the sense that Christ by dying accepted unpleasant consequences or resigned pleasant things rather than forego what He held to be true, it might have been possible, of course, to speak of His death as a sacrifice; but this, as we have now learnt, is a late notion of sacrifice, and one which is conspicuously absent in the apostolic writings in the passages dealing with the sacrifice of Christ. The idea of an act of mere self-renunciation, which should appeal by its own inherent beauty to the minds of men, is not forcible enough to fill the apostolic language: they spoke as they did because, though they held unquestioningly, possibly even uncritically, the belief in the freedom of man, their faith in the efficacy of Christ's sacrifice involved the idea of solidarity. Hence their view of sin and its consequences and its remedy was determined by these presuppositions, the freedom and the solidarity of man. Sin was a deliberate breach of union with God, carried out by the individual will; and the constitution of man was such that the original departure from God and the restoration of communion were effected by individual but pregnant acts in which the whole race was involved.

Such a view of sin as this could not possibly exist in any body of men without affecting their action very seriously. It would not be possible to ignore the meaning of any sinful act, if it were a free act of open rebellion. And the significance of sin would be still further enhanced if it occurred in a society, of which purity from all sin was the law, and which was itself the outcome of those acts by which the hold of sin upon the race was relaxed. Hence it is that from the apostolic times onwards, a discipline was exercised in the Church over individual members—throughout the whole Church without exception until the Reformation, and in the larger portion of it until the present day. This was necessary from the nature of the case. So long as the idea ruled the thoughts of men that Christians were one Body, living one life in one Spirit, it was not possible that individuals could be left to themselves to act or not act up to the standard of the faith. The fortunes, the character of the Church as a whole were involved. The sin of one was not merely that one's own concern: he was not merely misusing to his own loss the freedom which he had, but dealing a blow at the life of the Church—a traitor's blow from within. And here again the fuller content of the idea of sin would enter from a new point of view. Sin does not consist to the eye of a Christian merely in the overt act: it occurs, as we have seen, at any point where the soul breaks away from its proper union with God. And therefore the Church's discipline deals not merely with the open and declared acts of wrong like any ordinary type of law, but with the motive that produced them. I do not mean only that in preaching and exhortations it was said, 'See to your motives and the acts will follow suit.' It was not that the motives were treated as a recognized source of action and no more; but it was these thoughts of the heart—acts as they really were in a spiritual order of things—that formed the subject of external discipline. This begins from the very first. It was not for producing less than the whole price of their property that Ananias and Sapphira were condemned; there was no obligation upon them to produce all or any part of it. It was the thought in their hearts, the desire and the conspiracy to deceive, that St. Peter denounced. That was the breach of the social order in the new society, with which, as such, no civil law would concern itself. Though it might punish an act which was against the public peace, and had sprung from such a motive, the motive alone would not be the subject of its condemnation. It could not be so with the Church. For the Church, as I have said, was always a spiritual order; however manifested upon the earth in visible form, it was not earth-bound. It passed beyond the bounds of time, and covered under its shadow living men and men who had passed into the unseen. It was this spiritual order in which the individuals lived, and it was by its canons that actions were judged. Wherever there was room for the new life to express itself in action, whatever region of life the new spiritual forces could touch and illumine, there was room enough for sin. And it was sin, rebellion against God, spiritual misdemeanour, with which the Church was really concerned.

The exercise of discipline has been one of the most perplexing and difficult problems in the whole history of the Church. It was, indeed, a matter for deep disappointment that it was required; that the first vigour of the new zeal lasted so short a while, and that so soon the forces of the world made themselves felt within the bounds of the Kingdom of Christ. The ideal before men's eyes was always that of the stainless Bride of Christ, the new Jerusalem, from the walls of which every evil thing was carefully excluded. And from very early days there were some who feared to face the problem of dealing with sin within the Church's bounds: men, like the Montanists and Donatists and Novatianists, who hoped to secure even in the conditions of this life an absolutely perfect Church. It was a brave hope, natural to men who were full of the vision of the city of God; but it has never yet been realized, and when it has been assumed as an immediate practical possibility, it has revealed the presence of certain dangers. It has tended at times to diminish the power of the conscience, and to produce either an elastic and easy-going, or a narrow and limited view of sin. It has rarely, if ever, happened that those who have maintained their own freedom from sin, or secluded themselves from the Church in some narrow sect based on severer principles, have tested themselves by a very exacting code. There is a lack of proportion in such efforts which always avenges itself in some form or another. The stainless purity of the Bride of Christ is indeed the prayer of all Christian men: for the sake of this no separation from the world is too stern for us to face: but still the attainment of this ideal is not in the hands of man, nor is separation the highest hope of the Church for the world. If it must be, it separates itself; if it may be, it includes and subdues the world.

On the other hand, the central body of Christians, the Catholic Church, has never adopted this impossible rule. It has treated sin always as a mournful fact, and has always held that a state of sin excludes men, while they are in it, from the privileges of Church communion. And in this connexion it has elaborated a complex system of penitential rules, by which the internal order of the Church has been regulated. It has erected a distinction between two kinds of sins—mortal and venial. This distinction runs back upon the words of St. John's First Epistle which I have chosen for my text. There can be no doubt that the language of St. John had to be strained before it would bear the later technical meaning; though it is clear that he recognizes in his phrase a distinction of character in sins. In the later usage of the Church the distinction was a moral rather than an external one. It meant that certain sins involved a moral attitude towards God which others did not; the one class implying that God and the things of God were deliberately rejected in favour of the things of this world; the other class not conveying this implication[1]. A particular act might fall under one or the other head according to the moral circumstances of its production. And further, not only was there this broad line between classes of sins, but there was also a classification inside the class of deadly sins. The history of this classification is some-

[1] Cf. S. Thom. Aq. *Summa*, Prima in corp. art. Sec. Q. lxxii. art. 5.

what obscure[1]. In the letter from the apostolic council to the Gentile Churches given in Acts xv, four things are forbidden. They are warned to abstain from things offered to idols, from fornication, from things strangled and from blood. Codex Bezae, and a certain number of Latin authorities, omit the words τῶν πνικτῶν. The three remaining prohibitions (that of *blood* being interpreted as a command to abstain from murder), appear constantly as the outline, as it were, of a scheme of heinous sins—sins that are serious enough to exclude the sinner from communion. They appear thus in Tertullian and in various other writers down to the time of the mediaeval Penitentials: usually separate, but at length in combination with the scheme of the seven deadly sins. In Cassian's ascetic writings we read of eight principalia vitia. Augustine (an earlier contemporary of Cassian), though he recognizes the fact of mortal sins, has no fixed scheme of them. But after Augustine the number is usually seven, and the sins catalogued in the classification are mostly the same. It is somewhat hard to say on what principle the classification was made, and it is difficult not to feel that it might have been improved. It is strange, for instance, to find that luxury and gluttony are classed as co-ordinate vices, and at the same time that untruthfulness has no place in the list at all. For however clear it may be that untruthfulness arises from more than one of those vices which are named, it seems to be a distinctive type of evil, more widely separate from the others than luxury is from gluttony, or envy from

[1] See note to this Lecture, pp. 259 and following.

avarice. The truth is, no doubt, that the desire for the mystic number of seven and such other comparatively accidental considerations determined the order and contents of the classification.

It would be wrong to suppose that these seven in themselves were supposed to exhaust the possibilities of evil. The four cardinal virtues, for instance, have their accompanying vices in ecclesiastical writers as they have in Aristotle. And these do not always fall naturally and without pressure under the head of any one of the seven sins. But what may be said safely of the larger portion of the writings on these questions, is that though the classification seems often artificial, it is the classification that is so, and not the moral judgement which it implies. In that the acute analysis of moral conditions, which the Christian theory of sin leads one to expect, is well sustained. Time would fail me to illustrate such a point as copiously as might be. I will only here take two instances, which I choose as they take us back into the earliest days of the Church[1].

In St. Thomas Aquinas the reader will find *timor* or fear mentioned as the defect of the cardinal virtue of courage. What was said of this virtue in the last lecture will have prepared for the Christian treatment of *timor*. It implies a lack of faithfulness, a desire for ease and peace in preference to the hard and laborious effort necessary for the due defence of the cause of God. It is of course obvious that such a lack of vigour is troublesome and dangerous; still one's disposition is to regard it as partly physical, dependent

[1] See further instances in the note at the end of this Lecture.

in very large degree upon nervous conditions. But cowardice has a bad name in Christian ethics. The fearful—δειλοί—head the list of those in Rev. xxi. 8, who have finally rejected God and have no share in His redemption. Fear is not merely an unfortunate emotion; it is a sin.

The other case I will mention is that of sloth (ἀκηδία). This is the thankless distaste for all that goes on in the world; the feeling of angry annoyance at all the world which often attends upon ill-health. More even than cowardice, this seems a strange thing to regard as a sin; still more, a sin so grave as to separate the sinner from God. And yet it is no mediaeval or monastic invention, as is often supposed. It goes back at least as far as the day when the *Shepherd of Hermas* was written. Already by that time men had found out the sinfulness of this state of mind, and one of the Mandata is directed specially against it [1]. In both these cases the Church has taken, if I may say so, an unpopular line. It has condemned a thing which it might seem easy to excuse. But the explanation is the same in both cases. In both, the source of error is in the remotest centre of man's being. In both, acts which, as I have said, seem easy to excuse, quiet and unobtrusive withdrawal from trial, or unreasoning ill temper in the world God has made, are seen to rise out of a spring of selfishness, the presence of which implies that the heart is not right with God.

I have said that a system of ethics is stamped

[1] Herm. *Past. Mand.* c. x.; cf. also Paget, *The Spirit of Discipline.*

according to its treatment of the question of evil. What I have since said is enough to show that the view of it taken by the Church of Christ is a sufficiently grave one. Indeed, the world has persistently maintained that it is harsh and exaggerated beyond all the bounds of reason. And it is natural that this should be so. For it seems as if the world were roused into condemnation of evil chiefly when an overt act is discovered : it cares little enough for men's moral state provided their actions are hidden, or their base impulses restrained within the limits of decency. That application of the moral law we find all around us. But the question is after all whether the severer rule is not the truest to fact; whether the pressing of evil home to the centre of the will and judging it there, does not correspond best to the real nature of man. If it does, it may be worth considering whether it would not be to our advantage to bring our lives relentlessly before such a standard as this ; lest we find ourselves judged of the Lord by rules which we have refused to apply to ourselves.

NOTE TO LECTURE V.

THE question of sin is forced upon the Church by the failure of its members to attain its moral ideal. The consideration of it is, therefore, largely disciplinary. An attempt has been made in the note to Lectures III and IV to illustrate the effect of Christian ideas upon the theory of virtue. The idea of sin belongs more closely to the circle of ideas out of which the Church arose than to those of philosophy. Hence we need chiefly to illustrate the various assertions that have been made in the Lecture. In the Lecture it has been maintained that the Christians, following on the lines of the ancient Jewish faith, regarded sin as a definite act of rebellion, springing from a free will; and hence, though sin at the same time affects the lives of others besides the agent himself, the acts which were included in the category of sin were often different to those of which the ordinary social morality took cognizance.

By way of preface it will be necessary to call attention to some points in the moral theory of the philosophers, especially Philo and the Neoplatonists. From what has been already said of Philo under the other head it will be manifest that he can have but a meagre theory of sin. To his eyes the one thing needful was to separate oneself from all the physical and sensuous life, and rise by a process of gradual knowledge to the vision or fruition of God. He speaks of certain vices which are the opposites of the virtues; but the practical life of ordinary virtue is a low one in his scheme. Hence sin is rather a failure than an act of wrong. The true glory of human life is never to do wrong: but this is ἴδιον Θεοῦ, τάχα δὲ καὶ θείου ἀνδρός. Penitence is a secondary good—the remedy for almost inevitable failure[1]. The elementary form of moral

---
[1] *De Poen.* c. 1, II. 406, ed. Mang.

development is to surrender polytheism for monotheism καθά-
περ ἂν εἰ καὶ τυφλοὶ πρότερον ὄντες ἀνέβλεψαν ἐκ βαθυτάτου
σκότους αὐγοειδέστατον φῶς ἰδόντες[1]. But there are other forms
of it: when a man awakes 'from folly to wisdom, from incon-
tinence to continence, from injustice to justice, from cowardli-
ness to courage[2].' The process consists in the drawing near
to God: 'when the man hastens to serve God, and God
without delay hastens to make His own the suppliant, and to
meet beforehand the will of one who truly and without pretence
comes to serve Him[3].' The case of Enoch[4] shows that the
method of this approach to God is ἀποικία and μόνωσις: to
desert the haunts of men and to draw in upon oneself,
and live ἀπραγμόνως, practising the virtues and learning
wisdom[5].

So also, freedom is not considered from the point of view
of psychology, still less from that of the order of nature. It
too consists in independence, in separation from the various
interests and enjoyments which hinder the ordinary soul from
getting to God[6]. Distraction is of the essence of the Fall.
Adam was doomed when Eve appeared. Change was his
portion as a created thing. His false step consisted in
his losing the unity which he had when he was alone. The
desire and the love of these two 'begat bodily pleasure,
which is the origin of wrong and transgression, by which men
acquire the mortal ill-starred life in exchange for the happy
and immortal one[7].' Consistently with this view of freedom,
the ordinary life of man can never be really free, because in
ordinary life a man is necessarily impeded by various entice-

[1] *De Poen.* c. 1. [2] *Ibid.* c. 2. [3] *Ibid.*
[4] *De Praem.* c. 3, II. 401 M; *De Abr.* c. 4, II. 4, 5 M.
[5] For the position and value of the virtues see above, p. 156. On Philo's moral theory see Zeller, *Griech. Phil.* Bd. v.; also Siegfried, *Philo*, p. 249 and following.
[6] *Quod Omnis Probus Liber.* c. 3, II. 448 M.
[7] *De Mundi Opif.* c. 53, I. 36 M. In *Leg. Alleg.* II. cc. 1-3, Philo explains that for man to be alone would have been an infringement of the prerogative of God; hence he receives from God the woman, who symbolizes the irrational part of his soul.

Note to Lecture V

ments and desires, and is excluded from the possibility of isolation [1].

In the same way Plotinus regards the separation from all earthly entanglements as the essence of good [2]. The soul, having left the position it once held, has come down to earth [3] and occupies a body. On the whole it gains by this, for the knowledge of evil which it thus acquires tends to increase its appreciation of the good [4]. So long as the soul is asleep, i.e. insensible to the presence and claims of the One, it is the subject of vice. Freedom consists in the longing to regain communion with the One; virtue, in the ordinary meaning of the term, is the earliest way of awakening the soul: ecstasy is the climax of its effort.

In these metaphysical and intellectual schemes there was nothing that could be called an essentially new departure. Philo has none of the stern feeling against moral evil as such that pervades the prophets; he is attracted by the Law, and spends his time in interpreting it in terms of philosophy instead of using the interpretation which the prophets provided. Hence, as in the case of virtue, he falls into line with the succession of Greek philosophers; his affinities are with Plato and Plotinus, and not with St. Paul or St. John. And Plotinus carries out to their extreme development the conceptions which he had inherited from his master Plato.

We must now return to the history of Christian ideas. The conception of sin, which was inherited by the Church from the Jews, implied rebellion; it was the deliberate departure from the better course. The Will of God, the Law of God, con-

[1] Cf. Ar. *Met.* XII. x. 4, p. 1075 a. 20, where he says that the highest life is probably the most narrowly limited; as in a great house the subordinates and servants can do many things which the master may not.

[2] Plot. *Enn.* I. viii. 7.

[3] This descent is the soul's own act; and it is in this sense that Plotinus speaks of the origin of evil as $αὐτεξουσιότης$, i.e. self-will, *ibid.* V. i. 1. His position in this whole matter is uncertain and vacillating. As stated above, he is inclined to defend the action of the soul in coming; yet, at the same time, the descent did involve departure from the unity which it is the man's whole aim to restore.

[4] *Ibid.* IV. viii. 7. On the nature and origin of evil, cf. *ibid.* I. viii. 3.

stituted the test to which action was to conform. It was a matter of obedience or refusal to obey. The sanction for the Law is found not primarily in its expediency or its superior wisdom, but in the fact that it figures forth the holiness of God. This, as has been shown in Lecture V, is the starting-point of the Christian view of sin. It need hardly be said that very serious problems are wrapped up in this naïve and simple theory. The will of man belongs to him as a created being. It is part of the equipment he has for dealing with the world. It is not original, independent force; it is created, set in motion in its own peculiar fashion by the Maker of all. Thus its independence, its limits, and its responsibility in view of these limits require to be considered [1].

From another side, also, various questions are involved in a theory of sin. The command of God, the capacity to respond to it, the interference and counterclaim of the devil, the need of God's help, are all necessary factors. But it is some time before the discussion appears in its complete form. There are various causes which brought it up. In the first place, there is the very strong language of St. Paul on the subject of predestination; secondly, there are the arguments of philosophers to be met; and lastly, in the West, the heresy of Pelagius left the Church no alternative but to define its meaning on the subject of freedom.

Hermas is, perhaps, the first writer after St. Paul who shows consciousness of difficulties of this nature. After a recital of the various commandments imposed upon him by the Shepherd, Hermas raises the question whether they are within the capacity of a human being to keep. The Shepherd replies in great anger that it is merely a matter of will. Ἐὰν σὺ σεαυτῷ προθῇς ὅτι δύνανται φυλαχθῆναι, εὐκόπως αὐτὰς φυλάξεις,

---

[1] It will not be necessary to prove at length that the old simple language of rebellion was common in the Church in the earliest days. Instances of such phraseology are not difficult to find. In Clement of Rome, for instance (1 *Ep.* xii. 4), lapse from holiness is spoken of in the phrase λειποτακτεῖν ἀπὸ τοῦ θελήματος αὐτοῦ (i.e. of God). And in like manner St. Ignatius speaks of sin as desertion: μήτις ὑμῶν δεσέρτωρ εὑρεθῇ. *Ep. ad Polyc.* vi. These are Roman versions of the old idea.

Note to Lecture V 237

καὶ οὐκ σονται σκληραί. Then, seeing the confusion of Hermas, he speaks more gently, and explains that man's power to keep the moral law depends upon, and is illustrated by, his supremacy over all nature. The one thing needful is to hold the Lord in the heart, and have no fear of the devil. Hermas in the end professes himself comforted, and hopes that he will be strengthened to keep the commandments of God. ἐλπίζω, κύριε, δύνασθαί με τὰς ἐντολὰς ταύτας ἃς ἐντέταλσαι, τοῦ κυρίου ἐνδυναμοῦντος, φυλάξαι[1].

The great Alexandrines were, in this as in other regards, called upon to face and attempt to solve the questions arising between the prevalent philosophies and religion. Clement, as has already been said, was avowedly an eclectic in philosophy. And this seems to have meant more than that he simply adopted isolated opinions from various thinkers; it means also that he avoided seizing the general bearing of the problems in which he was interested. He dealt with various elements in them, but did not bring them to a combined and consistent result.

There is no question as to his belief in the need and the reality of the salvation offered by Christ. This is plain from his account of Baptism[2], and from the very grave view he takes of sin after Baptism. Baptism has freed men from the toils of sin, and if they take to it again, after having been thus freed from it, there is no more sacrifice for sin (Heb. x. 26). Clement seems to follow the Shepherd of Hermas, whom he quotes, in allowing that God does allow a second repentance to those who have fallen into sin after Baptism; but he adds that 'constant and repeated repentances are in no way different from (the state of) those who have never believed at all, unless in the fact that they recognize that they are sinning:

---

[1] *Mand.* XII. 4-7.
[2] *Paed.* I. vi. 26. Comparing the Sacrament of Baptism with that of Christ, Clement says: καλεῖται δὲ πολλαχῶς τὸ ἔργον τοῦτο χάρισμα καὶ φώτισμα καὶ τέλειον καὶ λουτρόν· λουτρὸν μὲν δι' οὗ τὰς ἁμαρτίας ἀπορρυπτόμεθα, χάρισμα δὲ ᾧ τὰ ἐπὶ τοῖς ἁμαρτήμασιν ἐπιτίμια ἀνεῖται, φώτισμα δὲ δι' οὗ τὸ ἅγιον ἐκεῖνο φῶς τὸ σωτήριον ἐποπτεύεται, τοῦτ' ἔστιν δι' οὗ τὸ θεῖον ὀξυωποῦμεν, τέλειον δὲ τὸ ἀπροσδεὲς φαμέν.

and I do not know which characteristic of them is the worst, that they sin consciously, or that having repented of their sins they go wrong again[1].'

Further, Clement insists upon freedom of will as a condition preliminary to the imputing of sin. He gives a careful but somewhat confused account of the distinction between the voluntary and involuntary, in which he follows very closely the lines laid down by Aristotle[2]. That is, he dwells on the various conditions which may affect the character of an action, and distinguishes the cases in which a man is responsible entirely or in part for the action done[3]. This style of treatment as applied to the will is rather political than ethical, and does not reach the full depth of the question suggested by the fact of sin. And the lack of completeness is further emphasized by Clement's insistence on the doctrine of grace. He affirms that both virtue and faith are a gift of God, and are impossible to man without divine aid[4]. He has therefore dealt only with a part of the subject, and has not realized the difficulty of combining the Christian doctrine on this head with the current philosophical views.

In close connexion with this doctrine of responsibility stands the discussion concerning punishment. Clement defends the combination in God of the attributes of justice and goodness, and gives a long list of the various ways in which

---

[1] *Strom*. II. xiii. 57. It is possible that Clement thought a higher degree of freedom from sin possible to the baptized than is usually attained; he speaks of four conditions as regards sin (*Paed*. I. ii. 4): (1) Never to sin at all, which is the prerogative of God; (2) never to give way to any of the wrong-doings in the intellectual region, which belong to a wise man; (3) to fall into as few as possible involuntary errors; (4) to live in sin as short a time as possible.

[2] *Strom*. II. xiv, xv; cf. Ar. *Eth. N*. III. i.

[3] A very curious distinction is named in the passage bearing on the question. ἀτύχημα δέ νοῦ παράλογος ἐστίν ἁμαρτία, ἡ δέ ἁμαρτία ἑκούσιος ἀδικία, ἀδικία δέ ἑκουσίως κακία. *Strom*. II. xv. 64. In a previous paragraph (§ 62) these three types of action, ἁμάρτημα, ἀτύχημα, ἀδίκημα, are said to correspond to the three forms of voluntary action, τὸ κατ᾽ ὄρεξιν, τὸ κατὰ προαίρεσιν, τὸ κατὰ διάνοιαν.

[4] *Ibid*. iv. 14; III. vii. 57; cf. *Paed*. I. ii. 6.

the Paedagogus disciplines men[1]. But the final explanation of pain as well as of punishment is that it is remedial, and remedial only[2]. This conclusion is, of course, closely in agreement with the highly metaphysical theory of the Being of God which Clement adopts from the philosophers. And it is natural to one who requires an easy and general account of the world as a whole. It is not fully reconcilable with the strong doctrine of Baptism maintained by Clement. For this implies a view of evil as affecting the individual life which is not in harmony with a purely disciplinary theory of it. There is a lack of systematic completeness in his ideas. His doctrine of Baptism depends on a view of evil, different to that involved in the account of evil adopted by him.

The language of St. Paul formed a serious stumbling-block to the mind of Origen. He was convinced beyond all reasonable doubt that the will was free: that it had the power to rise up against God and do the thing which God forbade. Freedom, according to Origen[3], consists in the power of reviewing and deciding upon the suggestions which reach us from without. We cannot regulate the impressions made upon us, but we can decide which of them we follow. Hence no man has a right to accuse external circumstances if he acts wrongly; and God, in full knowledge of this, requires of man obedience to His law — action leading towards man's true end. In the *De Principiis* Origen discusses the Platonic doctrine of a tripartite soul, as well as two other accounts of its composite nature[4]; but none of these theories affects the responsibility of the agent. However the matter is explained psychologically, it remains true that the soul when it sins makes a deliberate choice of wrong instead of right. In some sense it sins freely.

But then, in face of all this, comes the language of St. Paul. Pharaoh is spoken of as one who was compelled to act a certain part without any chance of protest or opportunity of choice. Even the will to do good is in other places

---

[1] *Paed.* I. i.   [2] *Strom.* VI. xii. 99; VII. iii. 17.
[3] *De Princ.* III. i. 3, 4.   [4] *Ibid.* III. v.

referred to the gift of God. What is to be made of such words as these? The answer made by Origen brings out more clearly than before his conception of the meaning of evil. In regard to Pharaoh the precise force of the language is explained away. God is said to harden by a kind of transference or metaphor. The action of God is one, and always for good. But it comes in contact with souls of different kinds; they correspond or fail to correspond with its leading, and the result is accordingly different. Then, the whole action being referred to God, He is said to harden. In like manner the other difficulties are met. The delay of conversion is explained as the expedient of a cunning physician, who, to ensure a more complete cure, takes measures at first that aggravate the disease. God disciplines and proves the soul ἵνα τὸ ἐφ' ἡμῖν ἐξετασθῇ, and in order to produce the highest range of virtue. So God gives us the power to will; we apply it to the particular objects which our character leads us to desire. He makes us and places us in the world; we use the power He has given us, and so become vessels either to honour or dishonour. ποιεῖ μὲν γὰρ ὁ δημιουργὸς σκεύη τιμῆς καὶ σκεύη ἀτιμίας, οὐκ ἀρχῆθεν κατὰ τὴν πρόγνωσιν, ἐπεὶ μὴ καὶ αὐτὴν προκατακρίνει, ἢ προδικαιοῖ· ἀλλὰ σκεύη τιμῆς τοὺς ἐκκαθάραντας ἑαυτοὺς καὶ σκεύη ἀτιμίας ἀπερικαθάρτους ἑαυτοὺς περιϊδόντας[1]. God Himself never forms man to one end or the other, ἐὰν μὴ ὕλην τινὰ διαφορᾶς σχῇ τὴν ἡμετέραν προαίρεσιν, κλίνουσαν ἐπὶ τὰ χείρονα, ἢ ἐπὶ τὰ κρείττονα[2].

Such passages show that Origen found himself in a difficulty. He was firmly persuaded of the necessity of real freedom to the true explanation of sin; but he is startled at the force with which the agency of God is asserted in the connexion with evil. And he is weighted with a difficulty which he inherits from his philosophical predecessors. Though he has completely emancipated himself from the view that evil is necessary, yet to his mind, as to Plato's, evil can only be remedial or corrective. It is there simply and solely to bid the soul 'nor sit nor stand, but go': to

[1] *De Princ.* III. i. 20. [2] *Ibid.* c. 22.

teach it, and awaken it, and raise it from the pleasures of this world to some higher and purer object of search. But St. Paul's language seems to conflict with all this. It implies the presence of evil on a far larger scale than is necessary to satisfy the demands of discipline. The race as a whole is involved in the curse: the evil of one has affected all. It must be confessed that Origen fails to satisfy this language. Perhaps he would hardly claim to have done so. For his scheme of ante-natal experiences is partly required to account for the evil which otherwise remains unexplained. This theory is really fatalistic as regards the origin of evil, and deals only with its effect on individual life, forgetting the truth that the individual life is not the sole element in the problem, seeing that the individual never stands alone. With all his feeling of the organic character of the state Plato never learnt this. And Origen, in spite of the closeness with which he adheres to the words of Scripture, is here affected by his Platonic predilections. It is true, as will be indicated later, that the whole idea of the will was as yet undefined, and therefore it is not to the discredit of Origen that he failed in this point. But it was a real failure[1].

The great African theologians, Tertullian and Cyprian, whom we have to consider next, were not troubled with metaphysical questionings, but they felt very strongly the practical bearing of the Christian creed. And their account of sin is dependent upon this conviction. Both alike assert the freedom of the will in the matter, and explain, by means of this power of the soul, the gravity of the judgements which fall on sin[2]. Both alike are sensible of prevalence of sin[3], and of the immense consequences it bears in regard to Christians,

---

[1] In actual practice, however, Origen speaks with no uncertain voice. He puts forward a severe theory of penance, and his own severity with himself, together with the practical exhortations in his writings, show how little his speculations as to the origin of evil affected his moral judgement. The Church has not accepted his speculations, but there can be no doubt that he had caught its spirit in regard to the spiritual meaning of sin.

[2] Tert. see reff. p. 240; Cypr. *Ep.* 58, c. 7.

[3] Tert. *De Pudic.* c. 29; Cypr. *De Dom. Or.* 12, 22.

encouraging their pagan neighbours to pour scorn on them and delaying the work of converting the world. But though both alike are persuaded that the sin of Adam is the source of all the mischief, and that Christ has come as the second Adam to restore the race, there is very little in either about the nature of grace, or the problems of predestination which Origen found so hard. In Tertullian only is there a somewhat elaborate attempt to produce a psychology of will, and this is in large measure due to his controversy with Marcion and with certain philosophers of the time. It will not be worth while to dwell at length upon this subject; we need only call attention to some few points. In the first place, Tertullian[1] clearly faces the fact that sin comes not from the flesh, but from the mind. It is not the subjection of the virtuous soul to an alien force that produces sin; the guilt of the soul, the choice of the evil, comes first[2]. Further, sin is really against God: 'Qui damni impatientia concitatur terrena coelestibus anteponendo, de proximo in Deum peccat. Spiritum enim, quem a Domino sumpsit, saecularis rei gratia concutit.' From this sin all the others follow. Again, every one is responsible for his own sin. It is not true even to ascribe all our falls to the agency of the devil. Although he aims at producing the opposite of the will of God, 'non tamen facit ut et velis[3].' This gift of freedom is absolutely necessary, so far as we can see, to the perfection of manhood: without it man could hardly have been in the remotest sense worthy of the blessing of communion with God. And God would not have given the first law to Adam, with its sanction, the threat of death, unless He had foreseen the possibilities of freedom in the way of sin[4]. Lastly, the soul, according to Tertullian, seems to be transferred from father to son, as an incident or inseparable part of the physical process of generation[5]. This would have had an important bearing on the question of original sin, if that had been one of Tertullian's problems.

---

[1] Cf. Herm. *Sim.* V. vii. 4. [2] *Adv. Marc.* I. 24.
[3] *De Exhort. Cast.* c. 2. [4] *Adv. Marc.* II. 5-9.
[5] *De Res. Carn.* c. 45; *De An.* 27.

Note to Lecture V

These few notes show plainly enough how Tertullian and Cyprian conceived of sin. It is clear that their relation to the question was chiefly a practical one; they had to deal with cases and arguments brought under their notice, and they applied to the purpose, without careful criticism, the theory which they had received. But these cases and questions were not as yet of a kind to draw out the deepest problems of the will. They were largely the excesses of men who wished to sin, or the survivals in the minds of some Churchmen of inconsistent philosophical doctrines, or definite assaults upon the doctrine of the Church from the side of philosophy. It is only when the Pelagian question arose that the Church was forced to examine the doctrine it had maintained in quiet for so long, and decide whether it was to be retained or modified. In this discussion there are really two interests: (1) to determine the relation of an individual to his environment in the widest sense; (2) to adjust to the newly defined conceptions of the individual the old language of responsibility. The first of these was really a new element in the history of thought. Those who thought philosophically in ancient days looked at the world and at man from without. They endeavoured to trace causes and principles in the working of things, and to connect all that happened by means of universal laws. Hence it was the universal aspect which caught their attention; the individual was most frequently regarded as a falling-off from the purity of the universal. Even the individualism of the Stoic by a kind of paradox consisted in the suppression of all individual interests and pleasures; the ideal Stoic was to pass beyond the world of ordinary cares and excitements, to satisfy himself with bare necessities, and, if these failed, to be content. He hardly existed as a distinct being; he was an offshoot from the substance of God, a part of the general drift of things. He asserted his individuality to its own abolition; his life answered to Schopenhauer's definition of suicide[1]. And what is here said of the Stoic

---

[1] Schopenhauer, *Welt als Wille und Vorstellung*, bk. IV, § 69 : ' Eben weil der Selbstmörder nicht aufhören kann zu wollen, hört er auf zu

applies with even greater force to other systems of philosophy.

It is plain that such a position as this must have a considerable effect on ethical theory. Wherever the individual is treated merely as one among the forces which are active in the world, his actions rather than himself will attract the chief interest. It may be necessary to distinguish the occasions when the individual rather than some other element is to be charged with the production of events. This raises the question of the voluntary and involuntary. And this may be discussed with more or less insight. But ethics will form a branch of natural history—a district of the science of observation, dealing with the actual phenomena of human life. The proceedings of men in society will be observed, registered, and classified; the influence of the individual items in the corporate body will be considered and estimated; but apart from such association it will be hard to know what to say of an individual man. He is ἀφρήτωρ, ἄπολις, θηρίον ἢ θεός.

Christianity crosses all this directly. It introduces a new factor into the problem—the providence of God; and it construes quite differently the relations of man to man. (1) It is the former of these innovations which causes most difficulty. The different view of society could have been arranged without any revolutionary disturbance; but the Christian view of the providence of God involved changes of a very serious kind. It gave with one hand a new intensity and significance to individual life; each individual was the object of the divine foreknowledge and love. But it seemed to take it away again with the other, for each individual was wholly in the hands of God. And this relation to God was not merely an added element to the moral or social environment. Man is, of necessity, absolutely in the hands of God; God made him, gave him life—he knows not how—and sustains him in existence at His good pleasure. All this follows simply from the Christian view of God. (2) Further difficulties arise when

leben, und der Wille bejaht sich hier eben durch die Aufhebung seiner Erscheinung, weil er sich anders nicht mehr bejahen kann.'

the Christian scheme of things is taken into account. For then a new link of connexion is asserted between man and man. No one stands alone. However anxiously men strive to separate themselves one from the other, it remains that they are really part of one family, and that they cannot safely affirm that they are uninfluenced even by persons with whom they seem to have nothing to do. And what is more, the mutual influence is not merely social; it affects the physical and even the moral nature. It is not merely that a man should not desire in any way

> To vary from the kindly race of men.

However earnestly he desires it, he cannot. He starts with a past behind him which is effective in his life; and this is not merely a physical but a moral past.

These were the positions involved in the doctrine already held and valued by the Church; and there was, strictly speaking, no pattern in existence to show the way in which they should be treated. The Jews, from whose theology they ultimately came, had never been philosophers; and the Greeks, who had, were not in presence of these particular issues. The phraseology of freedom and responsibility all presupposed the old view of human life. Any one could say when a man deserved punishment in the eye of the law for what he did; any one could describe the growth of habit and the gradual loss of free self-expression under its influence. But it was a new problem to decide how to meet the case of a man placed in the world without being consulted, confronted with a law which he did not make, with no power to act or to abstain except what he gained from his Maker, with this power maimed by an ancient sin which he had no part in committing, and with the issue of all foreknown. This was the problem which must inevitably have been brought up as soon as the Christian doctrine of sin and Redemption attracted attention; and it was to this problem that St. Augustine addressed himself.

The view of sin, of which we have spoken so far, is common

in St. Augustine. It is 'hominis inordinatio atque perversitas[1].'
It springs from the mind and not from the body[2]. It consists
in a preference of the world's pleasures to the knowledge of
God[3]. Man after the sin of Adam forms 'eadem massa
peccatorum[4]'; he struggles, but fails to carry out his will to
do good; he has not lost freedom, but has had serious injury
done to the will[5]. And this does not mean that there are
two separate natures at war in the man, as the Manichaeans
thought. 'Spiritus bonum est, et caro bonum: et homo qui
ex utroque constat, uno imperante, alio serviente, utique
bonum est, sed mutabile bonum. ... Verum in hac bona
hominis et bene a bono condita constitutaque natura nunc
bellum est, quoniam salus nondum est. Languor sanetur, pax
est. Languorem autem istum culpa meruit, natura non habuit[6].'
Thus the regular view of sin prevails; but St. Augustine
is alive to the problems it involves, and has a definite theory
to account for them.

It is probable that Augustine's own personal history had
much to do with the attention he gave to one part of the
problem. After many years of wandering, he was suddenly
converted, in a way which he looked upon as half miraculous.
The result of this experience, as frequently happens in the
minds of those to whom anything like a special providence
has come, was that he had the most vivid sense of the guiding
hand of God in life. The evil and rebellion that there is in
the world was to his mind as certainly overruled and moulded
by the Divine will as it had been to his knowledge in his own
case. The phrases he uses about the relation of God to evil,
the emphasis which he lays on the fact that God's will is never
thwarted, the certainty he feels that the obdurate are obdurate
of their own will, are an extension to the world's history of
his own experience. His Confessions contain also his theodicy;
that is the reason why they are worth writing. Looking back
over his life, he sees the manner of its working and his own

---

[1] *Ad Simpl.* I. ii. 18.
[2] *De Civ.* XIV. 2, 3.
[3] *De Agone Christ.* c. 13.
[4] *Ad Simpl.* I. ii. 17.
[5] *De Civ.* XIV. 11.
[6] *De Cont.* vii. 18.

responsibility in it; his response to the often-repeated calls of God is, he is sure, matter for gratitude to God; if he had failed, the result would have been due to his sin. The final reason of all is still obscure. Why God should have taken so much pains—why He made and ordered the world as He has—man can never know; he can only know the bearing of the revealed facts of God's discipline upon the conduct of life here.

It has been St. Augustine's misfortune that his doctrines on the subject of predestination and grace have been largely considered in separation from their context in his thought. It is true that in his later years, under the pressure of the Pelagian controversy, he himself lost the proportion between the various elements of the problem. In his fear of admitting any element of self-determination into the process of salvation, and of diminishing thus the supreme prerogatives of God, he seems to have fallen back more and more upon the secret counsels of God, and thus to have endangered the very existence of the human will.

That this was not so at all times is clear from the doctrines he put forward as to the nature and psychology of man. In the first place it is an error (in spite of the phrase quoted above, 'massa peccatorum') to suppose that Augustine regarded man in his fallen state as wholly evil. His nature is maimed and its balance disturbed, but still he exists. Augustine had inherited the doctrine from Plato that existence as such was a good— the gift of a good God who declared His goodness by giving it. So long, therefore, as a man has existence, he is not wholly evil. And further, he is placed in a world which is marked all over with signs of its Maker's hand. The invisible things of God are discerned by reflection in the created world. And again he is endowed with a conscience. Here also man is in a position to infer the goodness and love of God. The works of the philosophers and their partial attainments are a proof that this theory of man is true, and that he is not wholly forsaken, though by his own act his powers are modified and injured. Lastly comes the Incarnation, the supreme instance of the concern of God for man; in this the hand of God is most clearly discerned, and an opening is given by which the defect of his will may be restored, and man may regain the position he has lost. Thus man is at all points surrounded by the works of God; and not only so, but he is never wholly without a witness of the presence of God in the physical and moral world.

This view of man's position in the world is borne out by the Augustinian psychology. The will, says St. Augustine, does not start independently into action; it moves in response to some stimulus. 'Quoniam nec velle quisquam potest, nisi admonitus et vocatus, sive intrinsecus, ubi nullus hominum videt, sive extrinsecus per sermonem sonantem, aut per aliqua signa visibilia; efficitur ut etiam ipsum velle Deus operetur in nobis. Ad illam enim coenam, quam Dominus dicit in Evangelio praeparatam, nec omnes qui vocati sunt venire voluerunt, neque illi qui venerunt. venire possent, nisi vocarentur. Itaque nec illi debent sibi tribuere, qui venerunt; quia vocati venerunt: nec illi qui noluerunt venire, debent alteri tribuere, sed tantum sibi; quoniam ut venirent, vocati erant in libera voluntate[1].' Thus the call of God is not confined to such events as the conversion of St. Paul: it consists in the continual appeal of God through the continual assertion of His presence. In the *De Trinitate* there is a still more complicated account of the working of the mind and will. In this great work St. Augustine is searching throughout nature for some analogies by which to bring home the doctrine of the Holy Trinity more closely to the minds of men. The chief source of these analogies is to be found in the human mind. There are in the mind, according to Augustine, three powers or aspects: *memoria, intelligentia*. and *voluntas*[2]. The

[1] *De Div. Quaest.* LXVIII. § 5.
[2] In *De Civ.* XI. 27 and 28 the three aspects are called *essentia, et scientia, et utriusque amor*. The passage in the *De Civ.* is by no means so elaborate as that in the *De Trin.*; but the meaning of the two is, roughly speaking, the same. *Memoria* is equivalent to *essentia*. It means the single line of continuous self-consciousness which belongs to all personal life. St. Augustine has chosen the word because memory is

Note to Lecture V

soul as thus constituted acts in presence of the world of fact. Its simplest acts are really complex. Thus even simple apprehension is not merely the passive response to a stimulus from without, but involves a definite act of will. The mind, conscious of itself (*memoria*) and aware of various possible objects of contemplation (*intelligentia*), deliberately identifies itself with one of these (*voluntas*). Its threefold powers are at work, and it expresses itself freely in accordance with its constitution [1].

This more elaborate psychology is perfectly consistent with the passage cited above. And it shows that Augustine had grasped the idea that the will can never be isolated or treated apart from its environment; wherever it acts, it acts *in concreto*, and its freedom is only such as is consistent with the idea of an act as a concrete whole. The idea of such a concrete whole is peculiarly hard to articulate in thought, though it is simple enough in direct experience and patent enough to self-consciousness. For abstract thought separates for its own purposes the various aspects of the concrete with which it deals, gives these a quasi-independent value, and then finds it hard to reconcile them. It was this difficulty which proved fatal to St. Augustine when he became thoroughly involved in the Pelagian controversy. As this discussion developed, and as St. Augustine continually insisted on the operation of grace in all human activities, he was gradually forced to determine the respective contributions of the Divine and human will to the resultant human act. Under these circumstances he was logically compelled to insist on the power of God till the human element practically disappeared. So long as he analyzed human action and described the moral

the power which connects the past with the present in one continuous unity; it will therefore stand for the continuity of self-consciousness. It may be that the choice of this word is due to Augustine's Platonic education, and that it is an attenuated survival of the doctrine of ἀνάμνησις.

[1] Cf. *De Quant. An.* xxv. 48; xxvii. 52, 53; xxix. 56, with *Retract.* I. viii. 2. These passages deal with the psychology of thought; cf. also *De Trin.* IX. X. XIV.

environment of man, he was only called upon to refer the final disposition of all human life to the inscrutable counsels of God; but when he undertook to apportion the various elements in human action, the whole tended to disappear into the darkness of a seemingly arbitrary and unintelligent movement of the Divine will.

Strictly speaking, we have no concern here with the later developments of Augustinian doctrine. But it has been necessary to allude to them in order to emphasize the position adopted earlier in this note, that to St. Augustine we owe a new conception of the will. It must be plain from what has been said that responsibility and freedom have undergone a change of interpretation. The old view which belongs in spirit to Greek philosophy makes responsibility turn on individual agency, and leaves the question of the nature of the individual entirely out of sight. For ordinary legal purposes, for the purposes of ordinary conversation, this is all that is required. It is only when the final difference between right and wrong comes into view—when it is seen that a single alternative is placed before the will of man, to the decision of which all his actions contribute—that the further analysis of human action becomes necessary. This point of view was forced forward by the Church's doctrine of sin, and St. Augustine's philosophy of voluntary action is a serious effort to answer it. It is the old point of view which is still to be found in Origen. And it must be confessed that the old point of view is also a prevalent modern one. It is easier, because it is easier to conceive of the action and reaction of two independent forces—the will of God and the will of man—than to enter into the subtle way in which the will and its environment are intertwined. And the old theory satisfies all ordinary demands upon the mind; it is a good ordinary working hypothesis. But it fails in the end through its lack of fullness, leaving us to the alternative of bare deism or religious fatalism.

The peculiar difficulties raised by the question of sin have made it necessary to treat the will here rather than in the

Note to Lecture V

previous note. No man is inclined to contest an arrangement by which he gets credit for virtuous acts; but freedom is questioned at once if it is proposed to make him responsible for sins. And further, virtue is agreed on all hands to be in harmony with the Will of God: hence the independence of the human will comes forward most prominently in connexion with sin.

As in the former case, the theory of St. Augustine exercised a profound influence upon succeeding thinkers. The strong doctrine of Predestination excited Cassian into violent opposition, and has not been generally followed. Until the time of Calvin, who developed and stiffened the Augustinian doctrine, the predominant view of the will was that of Augustine's earlier works; and this view, extended and elaborately developed, is expressed by St. Thomas Aquinas.

It should be added that the final determination of the nature and position of the will came not from speculations upon its responsibility, but from the discussion upon the Nature and Person of our Lord. According to the old theory of human action it was unnecessary to distinguish between the man himself and his will. The actions he performed, he performed either voluntarily or involuntarily, and there was no more to be said. But the doctrine of the Incarnation affirmed, as it was gradually articulated, that the Word of God took human nature upon Him without change of Person. He was what He had always been, the eternal Son of God. He did not assume a human person. The question was then asked whether there were in the incarnate Christ two wills, the divine and human, or one only. All admitted that to the changeless Personality of the Son of God there belonged of necessity Divine will; but was a human will necessary to the completeness of human nature, or was it simply another name for a human person? The question was not, as might appear, a merely scholastic one. Upon the answer to it depended the sense in which it could be said that humanity was renewed. The decision of the Church was that will was necessary to the completeness of the human nature assumed by Christ, and therefore that the complete human nature including a human will was joined, never to be divided, with the Person of the Son of God. By this decision will was finally distinguished from personality in the Christian conception of man. A tract like that of St. John Damascene, *De Duabus Voluntatibus*, will prove how large a change was involved in the old language.

In view of this history it is not too much to say that the modern idea of human personality, with all its significance for ethical theory, is a gift to philosophy from the theology of the Incarnation and Redemption[1].

It has been said that the essential characteristics of Christian ethics lay in the doctrine of freedom, the sense of the social effect of sin, and the character of the practices now called sins. It will be necessary to add a few words on this last subject to what has been already said in this note and in Lecture V.

In the New Testament there are several lists of actions or habits which are condemned. One, which occurs in two forms (St. Matt. xv. 19; St. Mark vii. 21, 22), is ascribed to our Lord; it consists of the evil things which proceed from the heart of man. There is a list of twenty-one crimes in the Epistle to the Romans (i. 29-31); one of fifteen, the works of the flesh, in Galatians (v. 19); certain smaller lists in 1 Cor. v and 2 Cor. xiii, and a small one in Rev. (xxi. 8). Those in the Gospels are for the most part breaches of the Ten Commandments. Of those in St. Paul, that in Rom. i describes the state of the heathen world. It is difficult to find a principle of selection in the list here given. The first nine are names of vicious states, the rest describe vicious men. The characters mentioned seem to fall under the heads of selfishness, malicious speech and act, pride, and indifference to other men. In the other passages St. Paul is probably describing varieties of sin to which those to whom he wrote were given. Thus in 2 Cor. xiii. the list consists of varieties of quarrelsomeness. The works of the flesh are varieties of impurity, impiety, hatred,

[1] Cf. *Illingworth*, B. L. p. 8.

and excess. In the Revelation we have murder, falsehood, idolatry and unfaithfulness, impurity, and cowardice. On the whole, as may be seen by comparing the lists, they comprise sins and habits of a somewhat ordinary kind; the evils which are most likely to have been present, and to have been troublesome from the beginning. The New Testament doctrine of sin is, as Lecture V will have shown, dogmatic rather than disciplinary. Its peculiarity depends on the scheme of salvation which the Church had in hand to preach; it alleges new reasons and enforces new sanctions against old sins. Its additions to moral theory are rather in the way of new demands for virtue than new revelations of vice. In two cases, both of them in the Revelation, there are two new states condemned—lukewarmness and fear. Perhaps it may not be fanciful to see in these temptations dangers which arose as the Church grew and was coming under the unfavourable notice of the authorities [1].

But it is obvious that as the Church grew and came to include men of doubtful loyalty and various characters, it was necessary to define carefully the difference between various sins. In Clement of Rome we are still somewhat in the position of St. Paul; Clement rebukes the Christians at Corinth for their disposition to quarrel, and in various places names varieties of the sin of strife. But with Hermas we come into a very different atmosphere. The question has already arisen whether sin after Baptism can ever be forgiven[2], and it has become necessary to distinguish various kinds and types of sin. The tone of Hermas on these points is extremely severe. He seems to allow that in some cases the sin shall be removed and forgiven. According to *Vis.* II. ii. 5 there is a time fixed, after which there shall be no forgiveness. And in

---

[1] The former is constantly condemned in the early Christian Apocalyptic literature (*Visio Pauli*, c. 31). In *Test. Abr.* ch. xii the soul of a person whose good and evil deeds were equal is separated from those who go to the tormentors and from the saved (cf. Dante, *Inf.* Cant. iii). The soul is saved at the intercession of Abraham. The *Testament of Abraham* is published in the Cambridge *Texts and Studies*, vol. ii. No. 2.

[2] *Mand.* IV. iii.

the *Similitudes* VI, VIII, and IX it appears that some of those who have failed will have power and time to recover and repent. Those who are apostate, those who have followed this world's lusts and deceits, and have blasphemed the name of the Lord besides, have no hope of repentance. Those who have been hypocritical, who have brought in new doctrines, who have been double-souled, are in danger, but may yet repent. There is here a distinct division set up amongst the various classes of sins, and some are clearly regarded as infinitely more heinous than the others. But this is not all that Hermas conveys that is new. He shows a tendency to connect certain sins together as antecedent and consequent. Thus μνησικακία is connected with καταλαλιά [1]; and the latter with διψυχία [2]. Self-will or self-pleasing (αὐθάδεια) is connected with ἀφροσύνη and with innovation in teaching (ἐθελοδιδάσκαλοι). In *Sim.* VIII. ix. 1 the perils of wealth are described, and it is observed that wealth leads to ὑπερηφανία: ὑπερηφανίαν μεγάλην ἐνεδύσαντο καὶ ὑψηλόφρονες ἐγένοντο, καὶ κατέλιπον τὴν ἀλήθειαν, καὶ οὐκ ἐκολλήθησαν τοῖς δικαίοις, ἀλλὰ μετὰ τῶν ἐθνῶν συνέζησαν, καὶ αὕτη ἡ ὁδὸς ἡδυτέρα αὐτοῖς ἐφαίνετο. This suggests a picture that is indeed easy to realize—of the rich man gradually drawing away from his humbler fellow-Christians, finding the way of the fashionable world pleasanter—not forsaking God, yet not performing the works which faith demands. Further, there is in Hermas a strong sense of the importance of spiritual conditions. In the first Vision (ch. i. 8) Hermas describes himself as being severely rebuked by his heavenly visitor, because he did not know that sins of thought were as grave as sins in act. We have spoken in Lecture V of the importance given to λύπη and διψυχία—the state of the half-hearted man who looks both ways, and is not ready to commit himself wholly on the side of God to forsake all that hinders him in his approach to God. But Hermas is by no means scientific in his classification. In *Mand.* XII. iii. 1 ἀρετή occurs as one of a long list of virtues. In *Vis.* III. viii. there is a list of seven essential virtues.

---

[1] *Sim.* IX. xxiii. 3.   [2] *Ibid.* VIII. vii. 2.

Note to Lecture V

A parallel to this occurs in *Sim.* IX. xv., but the number has increased to twelve. In this context there is a list of twelve vices which are presumably the opposites of the virtues. In nine cases the opposition is obvious, but in the remaining three it is somewhat obscure. The three virtues in question are δύναμις, μακροθυμία and ἁπλότης; and the vices which hold parallel places in the opposite list are ἀπείθεια, ἀπάτη, and λύπη. ἁπλότης means simplicity; it is connected with ἐγκράτεια[1], and probably means the contented acceptance of what life brings. In this case λύπη (=accidie)[2] would be its natural opposite: but the other two contraries are by no means clear.

The general result of these notes on the moral ideas of Hermas throws considerable light on the growing ethical sense of the Christian Church. There are clear signs that a systematic view of ethical facts is being developed under the pressure of experience. Already there is a sign of a distinction between the sins which can and those which cannot be forgiven to the Christian man; and there is some disposition to class the various types of sin according to the element in human nature from which they proceed. Further, there is a good deal of corruption in the Church, against which Hermas feels bound to protest. What measures were taken to enforce discipline it is not easy to say, as the author does not enter into detail. He describes the spiritual nature of penitence[3], and the character of those who are capable of penitence, but no more. In *Sim.* V a rule is laid down for fasting, which is closely connected with the avoidance of sin; but a parable is immediately added which seems to imply that fasting is a work of supererogation: ἐὰν δέ τι ἀγαθὸν ποιήσῃς ἐκτὸς τῆς ἐντολῆς τοῦ θεοῦ σεαυτῷ περιποιήσῃ δόξαν περισσοτέραν, καὶ ἔσῃ ἐνδοξότερος παρὰ τῷ θεῷ οὗ ἔμελλες εἶναι[4].

The tone of these works, as we have said, seems to modern eyes extremely severe; but it was not severe enough for Tertullian. The author had unfortunately committed himself in the way of allowing second marriages, and speaking with

[1] *Vis.* III. viii. 7.
[2] See above, p. 231.
[3] *Mand.* IV. 2.
[4] *Sim.* V. iii. 3.

an uncertain sound in the matter of divorce. Hence Tertullian alludes to the 'pastoris scriptura quae sola moechos amat[1],' Tertullian's own views on discipline are the least attractive and authoritative part of his work. It was on this subject that he broke off from the communion of the Catholic Church. But they are important, for it is to Tertullian that we owe some of the distinctions which have become prevalent in later theory. In *De Poen.* c. 3 we find sins divided into two classes: *corporalia*, which means overt acts, and *spiritalia*, which means movements of will only. Penitence is required for both. In the Montanist treatise *De Pudicitia*, Tertullian applies the Johannine distinction of sins unto death and not unto death, and denies the possibility of absolution to all the former. Thus he quotes a list of things which are of constant occurrence which are capable of forgiveness[2]: 'Cui enim non accidet aut irasci inique et ultra solis occasum, aut et manum immittere, aut facile maledicere, aut temere iurare. aut fidem pacti destruere, aut verecundia aut necessitate mentiri? In negotiis, in officiis, in quaestu, in victu, in visu, in auditu quanta tentantur? ut si nulla sit venia istorum, nemini salus competat. Horum ergo erit venia per exoratorem patris Christum. Sunt autem et contraria istis, ut graviora et exitiosa, quae veniam non capiant, homicidium, idololatria, fraus, negatio, blasphemia utique et moechia et fornicatio, et si qua alia violatio templi dei.' In the same way Tertullian quotes the letter of the Council of Jerusalem in Acts xv as defining sins which are 'non remissibilia[3].' Tertullian's exaggerations, however, affect his whole conception of sin. Now and again he makes remarks of serious moral value. He shows, for instance, with great clearness the range of sins of impatience[4]. He connects *luxuria* and *gula*[5]. In the commentary on the Lord's Prayer he remarks that overt acts begin in the spirit, and that it is there that the real purification is required. But his extreme view of sin and of

---

[1] *De Pudic.* c. 10. [2] *De Pudic.* c. 19.
[3] *Ibid.* c. 12. [4] *De Pat.* c. 5 and following.
[5] *De Jej.* c. 1.

Note to Lecture V

the discipline of the Church makes his moral code an elastic one. It is impossible to carry it out without condemning all men alike. Hence the list of venial sins above quoted, which are in most cases the germs of those called deadly, conveys not a moral but an external distinction. Admitting that these occur constantly, he cannot sustain his theory of discipline without diminishing their moral significance. Thus, though the distinction of mortal and venial sin is largely due to Tertullian, his use of it is unsatisfactory and without principle.

The attitude of St. Cyprian is less severe than that of Tertullian, but it is beyond the level which eventually prevailed in the Church. Cyprian is primarily a practical bishop. He deals with the situation of the Church as he found it, and does not trouble himself as to the remoter principles of things. He scouts the idea that all sin is of the same moral guilt, a theory which he ascribes to the Stoics[1]. He recognizes that sin against God, by which he means sin against the Holy Ghost, is unpardonable[2]. In dealing with the lapsed, he refuses all hope of ecclesiastical reconciliation to those who have fallen except under the most violent pressure, and even these he holds to severe penance. These are they who have fallen through the weakness of the flesh: 'Quos videmus non animi infirmitate cecidisse, sed in proelio congressos et vulneratos per imbecillitatem carnis confessionis suae coronam non potuisse perferre, maxime cum cupientibus mori non permitteretur occidi, sed tamdiu fessos tormenta laniarent quamdiu non fidem quae invicta est vincerent, sed carnem quae infirma est fatigarent[3].' Cyprian further distinguishes between sins of ignorance and self-will[4], and has much to say of the spiritual value of patience as a protection against mortal sins, and, on the other hand, of the perilous effects of envy. There is not, however, in Cyprian any extensive advance towards a systematic treatment of sin, its causes and varieties. Cyprian accepts the language of his day, and regards the Faith as providing an answer to all difficulties[5].

---

[1] *Ep.* LV. 16.   [2] *Test. ad Quir.* III. 28.   [3] *Ep.* LVI. 2.
[4] *Ep.* LV. 26.   [5] *Test.* III., *Praef.*

With St. Augustine, as in previous cases, we reach a completely new stage in the history. He is prepared with a precise distinction between the various kinds of sin [1]. There are three kinds of sin, he says: that which comes from infirmity and is opposed to virtue, that which comes from ignorance and is opposed to wisdom, that which depends upon viciousness of will and is opposed to goodness. Moreover, Augustine entirely takes leave of the legal or judicial aspect of sin. The moral guilt of sin, he says, depends entirely on the will with which it is done [2]. The decision of Christ has made a difference in the estimate of things. Who would suppose that one who says to his brother, 'Thou fool,' was liable to Gehenna unless He who is the truth had said so [3]? The ordinary daily sins are forgiven by means of prayer, especially the Lord's Prayer; others, if the life is also changed, through confession and giving of alms [4]. The unpardonable sin is to deny to the Church the power of absolution [5] or to persevere in impenitence.

It must not however be supposed that St. Augustine had devised a fixed and unalterable classification, from which he never allowed himself to diverge. He is guided in most cases by the needs of the moment, by the opportunities offered by the passage he is interpreting, by the requirements of the argument he is expounding, as the case may be. Thus in one passage [6] he finds the entire range of temptations covered by the three vices, voluptas carnis, superbia, et curiositas. In this case, he uses these three as a means of interpreting the words in Ps. viii, 'pecora campi, volucres caeli, et pisces maris qui perambulant semitas maris.' Elsewhere he traces all sin to the two motives, cupiditas and timor [7]; and this again is ruled by the needs of interpretation. In another place he gives a more careful account of sins, dividing them into three classes, sins of thought, of word, and deed; and all alike he ascribes

[1] *De Div. Quaest.* XXVI. [2] *Cont. Mend.* § 18. [3] *Ench.* 79.
[4] *Ibid.* 71. 19; cf. 2 Clem. xvi. 4; *Ep. Polyc.* x. 2; Cyprian, *De Opere et Eleem.*
[5] *Ench.* 83. 22. [6] *Enarr. in Ps. VIII.* c. 13.
[7] *Enarr. in Ps. LXXIX.* § 13.

to concupiscentia[1]. Considered as efforts at a formal classification of sins, it must be admitted that these cannot all of them be worked into a consistent system. The arrangement he adopts depends upon the occasion, as we have said.

But though he is thus irregular in formal divisions, there is no essential variation in his view of the nature and significance of sin. In an endless variety of ways he continually asserts that it depends solely on the rebellious will. The suggestion of the evil act, even the desire for the object as such, do not reach the point of sin. That is attained when the will finally consents[2]. And so it is that a number of small things which are not in themselves sufficient to constitute a grave sin against God, may become so by repetition, if the soul comes to take pleasure in them[3]. This gives a moral interest to the difference between venial and mortal sins, which might well have been kept more steadily in view than it has. This would have avoided a danger which afterwards became serious.

The novelty of the Augustinian view of the question, therefore, lies not so much in the actual order of the various moral ideas, as in the vast range covered by the works of St. Augustine, the profundity with which he has dealt with the problems belonging to moral action, and the spiritual insight by means of which he has detected the drift and bearing of various moral acts and tendencies. He has the preacher's desire for clearness, and this leads him to break up his ideas into something like a scientific order; but he is not primarily a scientific writer, and therefore he is willing to adopt different points of sight, according to the nature of the readers for whom he writes.

In the note to the last Lecture it was pointed out how very powerful the influence of the mystical method of interpretation was upon the systematization of moral ideas. A similar account may be given of the origin of the classification of deadly sins. It seems to have been developed by the monks

---

[1] *Cont. duas Epist. Pelag.* I. xiii. 27.   [2] *De Gen. c. Man.* II. xiv. 21.
[3] *Enarr. in Ps. CXXIX.* 5; *Cont. Mend. ad Cons.* viii. 19, 20; *Serm.* 58, § 8; 71, § 7, &c.

of the Egyptian desert on the basis of this method of exegesis. Origen regards the nations whom the children of Israel were to overcome in Palestine as types of the sins which occupy the soul of man. 'Intra nos etenim sunt omnes gentes istae vitiorum, quae animam iugiter et indesinenter oppugnant. Intra nos sunt Chananaei, intra nos sunt Pherezaei, hic sunt Iebusaei[1].' Later on in the same chapter, a list of such sins occur, most of which appear afterwards in the familiar catalogue of seven. These are ira, superbia, invidia, libido, avaritia, iniquitas, ceteraque similia[2]. In like manner the last six plagues of Egypt are interpreted as means of eradicating various sins: 'per errorum suorum figuras mundo supplicia temperantur[3]': the earlier ones typifying the various temptations to which the old world gave way[4]. There is thus a disposition to interpret the history in terms of the various kinds of sin, but the scheme of sins is not precisely defined.

The earliest mention of the classification in the form which it finally assumed is in the East, and it comes from the Egyptian desert. Evagrius Ponticus, who retired thither about the year 390 and died there in 398, has left a work on the subject called *Antirrheticus*. The list consists of eight states which are called ὀκτὼ λογισμοί. They are not called sins, but represent the hidden motions of the soul out of which all kinds of sin arise. A little later we have a similar short treatise on these eight λογισμοί by Nilus of Constantinople, a friend and supporter of Chrysostom, who retired to the Egyptian desert with his son in 390, and spent forty years in the practice of asceticism[5]. Both these works are short, and are clearly representative of a tradition of teaching rather than an original speculation on the part of the authors. They are parallel in many minute details, such, for instance, as the

[1] *In Lib. Jes. Nave. Hom.* I. 7, ed. Lomm.
[2] Cf. *Lib. Jes. Nave. Hom.* VIII. 6, where a slightly different list occurs.
[3] *In Exod. Hom.* IV. 6.
[4] The water turned into blood represents the philosophers; the frogs are the poets; the lice stand for dialectic; and the flies, for those who identified man's true good with pleasure.
[5] Published in Migne's *Patrol. Graeca.* vol. lxxxvi.

Note to Lecture V

effect of various sins upon the outward demeanour; and they contemplate the same conditions of life.

The period covered by the two (Evagrius 345-398, Nilus died 430) is, roughly speaking, that of the great Fathers in East and West, Basil (329-379), Chrysostom (347-407), Augustine (354-430). And there is no trace in any of these three of the list of deadly sins. All three of them have much to say on the subject of sin. Of St. Augustine's theory we have already spoken, in general terms. Of the other two, we say with truth that Chrysostom deals with sin from the point of view of the preacher, and that Basil, where he is not the preacher, is rather the canonist than the moralist. Chrysostom scourges the vices of his own day; he denounces the wickedness and wilfulness of sin. But he is not interested in setting out theoretically the various primary forms which it may take. Some which belong to the regular list occur and are condemned in his works, but he is guided by the circumstances of his hearers and the meaning of the passage he is expounding, and not by any formal account of sin.

Basil, in like manner, preaches, and in the course of his sermons assails various types of vice; but there is more in his writings of definite moral theory than in those of Chrysostom. He attempted the organization of the monastic life, and to that end put forward two bodies of Rules, dealing with the various questions to which life under vows gives rise. Besides these, there are his canonical letters to Amphilochius and the work called the *Moralia*. The last named consists of a string of texts quoted in answer to a variety of moral questions; it has no obvious principle of arrangement, and makes no attempt at precision of system. The other works are chiefly of an administrative character, dealing, like the *Moralia*, with isolated questions. The consideration of them must be postponed for a few moments.

We must now return to Western writers. In the *Collations* of Cassian, Bk. V, we find described the views of sin entertained by Sarapion, a hermit or abbot of the desert of Scetis, in Egypt. Sarapion affirms that there are *octo* principalia vitia, but explains that the seven nations of Canaan overcome by the Jews typify the deadly sins. Germanus, a friend of Cassian's, who travels with him, calls upon Sarapion at once to explain why, if there are only seven nations, there are eight sins. He answers as follows: 'Octo esse principalia vitia quae impugnant monachum cunctorum absoluta sententia est. Quae figuraliter sub gentium vocabulo nominata idcirco nunc omnia non ponuntur, eo quod egressis iam de Aegypto et liberatis ab una gente validissima, id est Aegyptiorum, Moyses vel per ipsum Dominus in Deuteronomio loquebatur[1].' The sojourn in Egypt, therefore, stands for the elementary condition of the soul under the influence of sin. It is the soul as yet wholly unredeemed from the trammels of the body—the soul under the influence of gastrimargia, or ventris ingluvies. This, which is the first evil to be overcome, is, according to Sarapion, the temptation of all who have not found their way into the monastic life. The other seven are fought and vanquished when this first contest is over.

The list in Cassian, as in the case of the Greek writers named above, is a list of vices besetting the monastic life. The fate of this list was widely different in the East and in the West. In the East its originally monastic character clung to it throughout. In the West, largely through the influence of Gregory, it was applied as a moral test alike to the secular and religious life. Thus St. John Climacus (flor. A.D. 596), who makes use of it in his *Scala Paradisi*, restricts (apparently) the possibility of attaining the ideal life to those who renounce the world in the monastic sense. So too St. John Damascene in his two letters concerning these vices addresses a monk, and mentions among the virtues some specially monastic characteristics[2]. On the other hand, Johannes Jejunator (died 596), who wrote a manual for confessors, makes no mention in it of this list, but bids the confessor

[1] *Coll.* V. xvii. 1 (ed. Vindob).

[2] E.g. ἀλουσία. It is difficult to believe that these short works are really to be attributed to John of Damascus. They look much more like excerpts from some monastic work. The longer one, *De Virtutibus et Vitiis*, contains three inconsistent classifications of sins.

Note to Lecture V 263

inquire concerning the ancient triad of heinous sins, adultery, idolatry, murder. This restriction of the classification to the monastic life was rendered more difficult in the West by the use Gregory made of it in his Moralia on Job. Alcuin, who follows Gregory somewhat closely, definitely calls attention to the fact that laymen as well as the religious can attain the life of virtue, and then mentions these in his account of vice. Their use in the *Penitentials* of Egbert and Halitgar, and still more in such works as Myrc's *Instruction to Clergy* (published by the Early English Text Society), show how widely the list spread in mediaeval times. The use of the list disappeared in England with the Reformation.

There are some slight differences in the number and names of them. Cassian and the Greeks speak of eight: superbia, ὑπερηφανία; inanis gloria, κενοδοξία; acedia, ἀκηδία; tristitia, λύπη; ira, ὀργή; philargyria (avaritia), φιλαργυρία; gastrimargia or ventris ingluvies, γαστριμαργία; fornicatio, πορνεία. In St. Gregory[1] superbia is separated from the other seven, which are represented as its followers or consequences.

Gregory is explaining the allegorical meaning of the description of the horse in Job, and pictures him in conflict with the powers of darkness. These are under the leadership of superbia, and there follow, in high office amongst the soldiery of Satan, the seven principalia vitia. Each is at the head of a rout of sins, which apply in various directions the principles inculcated by their superior. But Gregory is not contented with describing these seven as rulers, so to speak, of independent provinces; he also sets forth the close connexion between them: so that they seem to stand as a kind of Rake's Progress in abstract terms. Pride causes vainglory; vainglory causes envy; envy leads to anger, anger to spiritual melancholy (tristitia), melancholy to avarice. And then the two carnal vices, gluttony and luxury, appear on the scene. This list is closely parallel to that in Cassian, differing from it chiefly in nomenclature. Luxuria in Gregory answers to fornicatio in Cassian; acedia and tristitia in

[1] *Mor. in Job.* XXXI. xlv. 87 sqq.

Cassian take the place of tristitia in Gregory; and Cassian does not mention invidia.

The list of sins as thus defined prevailed for the most part in the West after the time of Gregory. It does not occur always in exactly the same form. At times the nomenclature of Cassian is followed, at times that of Gregory. In one respect, indeed, Cassian prevailed over Gregory. The word acedia or accidia was most generally chosen in place of tristitia. But this was not quite invariable. For instance, Isidorus Hispalensis and Alcuin, both of whom certainly read Gregory, speak of acedia; while Halitgar, who is later than Alcuin, returns to the Latin name[1]. A difference of treatment also appeared in connexion with superbia. In Gregory this vice stands alone, and the other seven are represented as its offshoots. The first of these—inanis gloria or cenodoxia—is but slightly different from pride itself; and it would probably have been hard to sustain for any length of time a real distinction between them, quite apart from the desire of the number seven. Accordingly we find that cenodoxia tends to drop out, and the list is reduced to the familiar form of a series of seven co-ordinate states.

It is plain that there are two different ways in which the question of sin can be approached. Emphasis may be laid on the outward facts or upon the mental conditions out of which the outward acts proceed. Roughly speaking, this difference serves to distinguish the provinces of law and casuistry. Law assigns fixed penalties to various transgressions; casuistry, though it too may deal with fixed rules, allows a larger range to the differences between men, and recognizes the fact that no two persons are precisely the same, however closely they may resemble one another in their acts. The three sins condemned in the Council of Apostles and treated as the most heinous are all of them of the nature of outward acts, and are therefore naturally suited for treatment in canons. The classification of seven

---

[1] Isid. Hisp. *Quaestt. in Deut.* XVI, XVII; Alcuin, *De Virt. et Vit.* c. xxxi.; Halitgar, *Poenit.* Bk. I.

Note to Lecture V

deadly sins, especially in the form given to it by Gregory, belongs more closely to the province of casuistry, or applied ethics. The Easterns, if we are right in maintaining the predominantly monastic connexions of the ὀκτὼ λογισμοί, seem to have dealt with the moral problems of the Church largely by means of canons, and to have concerned themselves in large measure with the external acts named above, and cognate acts. The canons of Councils, the canonical letters of Gregory Thaumaturgus and Basil, are chiefly occupied with questions arising out of some one of the three crimes. They lay down penalties and, in a certain degree, distinguish cases. There is, moreover, a considerable element of casuistry in the Poenitentiale of Johannes Jejunator. In the canonical letter of Gregory of Nyssa there is a division of sin (which reappears in John of Damascus) based on the Platonic division of the soul. Yet he too is largely concerned with varieties of penance.

Much would, of course, depend on the way in which a system like this was administered. There is nothing to suggest that the process was external or lacking in depth. The questions put in the mouth of the priest by Johannes Jejunator, though they comprise a catalogue of extraordinary and horrible sins, and seem to relate to a life of extremely low tone, do not fail in sincerity or directness of moral intuition. They are not restricted to overt acts, but deal with the actual moral condition of the soul. At the same time, it is difficult to avoid the feeling that, considering the inward character of the list of seven, and the real practical use made of it in the mediaeval Western Church, it is a pity that the Easterns tended to restrict it to the monastic life. It would seem difficult to avoid creating the impression that the monastic life was a thing wholly and entirely distinct from that of the layman. It is certain that this impression was created in the West, owing to various causes, which it is not necessary to specify here. But at least it was plain that the life of the monk and that of the ordinary layman were to be tried by the same moral standard, and that meant the same thing spiritually for both.

This short account of the list of the seven deadly sins is, of course, very far from being complete. To make it so would require considerable space, and is not necessary for our present purpose. It has been observed above that the list is not exhaustive, or, at least, that a number of the moral conditions which are treated as secondary and derivative seem to have some claim to an independent position. Lying, for instance, though it may be true that it is usually the outcome of avarice, does not easily fall into the derivative position; and its absence from the list is, perhaps, morally unfortunate. But though this and possibly many other criticisms may be made upon the list, it still affords a most valuable illustration of the theory of sin prevailing in the Church. It includes obvious and notorious sins, but it also traces them to the point at which the human will breaks off from God. This is the moral significance of fixing superbia as the source of all. For superbia includes all those acts of self-assertion in which the soul refuses due honour to God. And out of this all other forms of sinfulness really flow. The others do not all lie so far back in the inward nature of man as this, but in the classification they are described in their most elementary forms. And a survey of their history and use will show how readily the list was adapted to the practical needs of Church life. It is impossible to read some of the treatises upon the deadly sins—Chaucer's *Persones Tale*, for instance—without feeling that the use made of this scheme was really of spiritual value in the ordinary work of the Church. The old simple list of peccata irremissibilia could easily be brought under these heads, and it was not hard to combine the list of seven with expositions of the Decalogue. In the Middle Ages the Church undertook the guidance of men's consciences, after a manner which we may think tyrannous, but which was really well meant. And it is difficult to understand how the work could have been done without some simple classification of wrong-doings, which, while it should bring to light the real spiritual importance of sin, should at the same time keep before men's eyes the ordinary dangers of life.

LECTURE VI.

'We preach Christ crucified, unto Jews a stumblingblock, and unto Gentiles foolishness; but unto them that are called, both Jews and Greeks, Christ the power of God, and the wisdom of God.'—1 COR. i. 23, 24 (R.V.).

THE Christian revelation is not primarily an abrupt assertion of facts not known before; still less is it merely the authoritative confirmation of hopes which men had entertained in earlier days: such aspects of it belong purely to its relation with the contents of the human mind. It moves on a higher level. It is a stage in the whole purpose of God—so far, indeed, as we have been permitted to see, it is the final stage under the existing conditions of spiritual life. The facts upon which it rests, the historic juncture at which it appears, are a manifestation of certain universal principles. It is not merely imposed upon man's mind, like any other fact or body of facts which may come into his possession; it is not merely placed before the mind like an item of new information about the world; but its principles are revealed as being there, and having always been there, in operation on the field of history, men being now admitted into an intelligent appreciation of them. The movement of history is declared to be not accidental nor purposeless; the events of history are shown not only in reference to the condition of things out of which they arose, but also in reference to a consummation to be still realized; and the correspondence of the Incarnation to the desires of all peoples in the past, and its growing adaptation to the needs of each successive present, are offered as an earnest or proof of its adequacy to the spiritual needs of this dispensation. The preaching of Christianity, as it has been said, rests upon a philosophy of history.

It is clear that this point of view arises necessarily out of the relations in which Christianity stood to Judaism. Christ had come to fulfil and not to destroy, and the faith of Christ had therefore to be brought into some sort of intelligible continuity with the earlier creed of Israel, seeing that at first sight it seemed to be destroying so much more than it fulfilled. So long as the apostolic preaching was concerned with Jews alone, it would seem sufficient to show the real affinities of the new faith with the true spirit of Judaism. But the Gentile influx made it necessary to take a wider sweep over the history of the world, and present Christ not merely as the Jewish Messiah, but also as the desire of all nations. The Church was to claim its rightful place in the whole system of the world's order. Though the scene of its foundation was the chosen place where the chosen people had enjoyed, and sadly misunderstood, their privileges, the reception of the Gentiles meant that their history also had a rational explanation, and fell into its place in the Providence of God.

It involved no unfaithfulness to the widest of Jewish traditions to maintain that there was a future in store for the Gentiles. The prophets had asserted it, and it is with definite reference to their words that the apostles first announce the possibility of an equality of privilege for the Gentiles. But it was required not only to show that the admission of the Gentiles was anticipated by, or at least not inconsistent with, the older dispensation, but also that the days of ignorance formed part of the consciously chosen plan of God, Who waited until the due time came, before He made Himself fully known to the nations outside the covenant.

The ordinary conceptions of God which appear in the Law, and which ruled the Jewish mind for the most part, are closely bound up with His self-manifestation to the chosen people. But there was one ancient idea which lent itself with exceptional readiness to the purpose: I mean, of course, that of the Wisdom of God.

It is not necessary to trace the development of this notion among the ancient Hebrews, nor to prove its connexion with the general ordering of the world. It has been discussed and described frequently. It was the Wisdom of God which brought man out of his first Fall, and guided the wanderings of the children of Israel; and it was also Wisdom which was present at the creation, and 'ordereth all things sweetly.' It is the force, mysterious and irresistible, which controls all the history of the world. It is, therefore, without surprise that we find St. Paul speaking of the Wisdom of God in close association with all such references (as that in the text of this Lecture) to the scheme of the divine Providence. The occurrence of events at a particular point in time, the spiritual destiny of Jew and Gentile, the call even of the individuals who compose the Churches, spring from the divine Wisdom. As of old, it is unfathomable; it confounds the anticipations of those who are wise merely with this world's wisdom. Concealed in large measure before, and obscurely described in prophetic writings, it is partly made known now, in the person of Christ, upon whom the whole purpose of God hinges and is concentrated. This idea of a wise Ruler, Who, with wisdom which man cannot fully grasp, carries out His purpose, underlies the references in the New Testament to the counsels of God, to the divine necessity which determined the course of Christ's life; it explains such a constant habit of language as the use of ἵνα with telic force in connexion with the fulfilment of prophecy. Relatively to the lives of men and the order of the world God is conceived as working firmly with a definite unswerving purpose, which St. Paul describes continually as a manifestation of wisdom. Such an idea is the justification of that philosophy of history which, as already observed, is essential to the Christian view of things.

It is important for our purpose to dwell somewhat carefully upon this aspect of the divine nature. What exactly is meant by regarding God as a wise Ruler? To speak in human terms, the Wisdom of God is practical wisdom; it is essentially reason regulating, and embodied in, act. It is the rule, as it were, according to which the will of God acts, that which prevents the good pleasure of God, if I may reverently say so, from being an arbitrary exercise of absolute power. It is not occupied in the contemplation of the abstract reality of things; it does not deal with a world of bare ideas, but it guides a world of spiritual beings. In short, it is only distinguished from the unmotived exercise of free-will by being radically rational; however effectual in act, it is always wisdom.

There is good reason for bringing forward the thought of the divine Wisdom in connexion with the subject of Christian moral ideas, for in the ancient writers it supplied a sort of philosophical sanction for the moral life. It was Wisdom who was with God when He prepared the heavens; who was by Him, as one brought up with Him, when He gave to the sea His decree, and appointed the foundations of the earth. Wisdom again it is who crieth at the gates at the entry of the city unto all men; who hath furnished her table and sent forth her maidens, and calls to all men to feast with her—to forsake the foolish and live. For the fear of the Lord is the beginning of wisdom for men; by it their days are multiplied and the years of the life increased. They that sin against Wisdom wrong their own soul, they that hate her love death. The wise man was he who lived in accordance with the demands of God and of conscience; the fool was the man who followed his own inclinations like an ox to the slaughter, and was at all points deceived by them. If the full knowledge of the drift and bearing of the Wisdom of God was known to God alone, yet man through the habit of innocency and holiness could come nearest to such wisdom. As the Wisdom of God was expressed in the due order of the world considered as a whole, so the wisdom of man lay in correspondence with this order. Such correspondence, if things happened rightly, would end in earthly happiness and prosperity; but even apart from these, though the righteous seemed to die, and to have wasted in self-denial time that might have been spent in self-indulgence, such a verdict upon his life was only the superficial judgement of the ungodly and the fool [1].

It is true that this connexion of morality with the divine attribute of Wisdom is not insisted upon in the New Testament. For the most part, as I have already said, the Wisdom of God is associated with the historic process of the world. It is not, as in the Old Testament and especially the Apocrypha, placed closely in relation with the earthly life of man. It is important, however, to bring this particular attribute into connexion with the life of man, as it points the way to a legitimate explanation of a difficulty that would otherwise become rather serious.

Throughout this whole discussion I have been insisting that Christianity takes the ultimate sanction of moral life out of this world, and represents mankind, so far as they are in union with Christ, as united in a spiritual society under the immediate rule of God: and it asserts that the ultimate rule for the moral life is the nature and character of God. This

[1] Prov. viii; Wisdom i, ii.

assertion is contained in the phrase from the Sermon on the Mount—whether it be a promise or a command—'Be ye, or, Ye shall be perfect, even as the Father which is in heaven is perfect.' The ideal of man, the goal towards which he is to move, is nothing less than the perfection of God. And the same thought appears in the more profound promises in the last discourses in St. John, where the love that is the nature of the Holy Trinity is taken as the type of the love that is to prevail among the members of the Church.

And as soon as this is said a difficulty begins. Is it not, we may ask, a mockery to attempt to clear up the problems of our life here by referring to the Life of God as supplying the rule for it? How can we, who are men, profit by merely knowing that the unity of God is our type of unity? What meaning can the unity of God—the love of God—have for us? How can we understand the promise that we shall be perfect, even as our Father which is in heaven is perfect? The explanation, we are inclined to say, is too lofty to be of any use; it is raised above us like the Idea of Good in Plato, and lies out of our reach in some super-celestial sphere. The life of God, the unity of God, the love of God, must necessarily be different to anything that we can know under those names. Must we not, as Aristotle did, deny to God all virtue, simply because His mode of being transcends all our powers of conception? And then, is not the command to follow after Divine Perfection little better than an unintelligible arbitrary order, of which we can give no rational

T

account? Such a command is laid upon us; an ideal like this is held out to us; but can we say more of it? It can never help us to fight our battle with sin, to curb our selfishness, and love our brethren. It has been urged that the essence of Christian morality lies not merely in the extension of the moral law, but in the communication of the new life. But neither this nor even the doctrine of grace will help us at this point. It may be and is an unspeakable comfort to know that as a matter of fact we are not left alone, but are strengthened and led by the Divine Power. But a new life might be in us—grace might be given to us to fulfil a command of which we know only that it is commanded: that is, our moral nature on its practical side might have felt the consequences of the Incarnation; but these consequences might have stopped short with the will. Moral life might still be a problem solved only by obedience, and that obedience irrational.

The idea of love is, in a sense, a mediating term. It brings, at any rate, the nature of God close down to the area of human life. For it is obvious that St. John thinks of the love of men as an exercise in preparation for the love of God. 'He that hateth his brother whom he hath seen, how can he love God whom he hath not seen?' The love which men owe to God is in some sense the same with that which they owe to one another. And the issues of the two kinds of love are the same. Both involve sacrifice, to which love itself places no limit. And the love of God further involves obedience, if indeed that is not merely another name for self-sacrifice; it is quite impossible for those who love to be self-willed, defiant, sinful. This idea defines, as previous lectures have shown, the character of the life to be pursued; the new life given quickens the will to the point of obedience. It must be observed, however, that though the demand for love on the part of God is practically intelligible—though, further, God has Himself set a pattern of sacrifice before us which we can but faintly copy, love usually appears in the New Testament in the form of a command or law. It is the new commandment; it is the royal law: the fulfilment and sum of all the precepts of the earlier dispensation; it is enjoined upon us as friends and not as servants, in the hope that we may obey not blindly and unintelligently, but as reasonable men. It is a command, rising mysteriously out of the depths of the Being of God, enforced by the example of the action of God; but it is a command still. It is a law which transcends the old dispensation and appeals with a wholly new directness to the heart, and is met by a gift which makes obedience to it in some degree possible; but so far as it is a command, it does not contain within itself its final sanction. It does not by itself throw on life all the light that is to come upon it from the dispensation of the fullness of the times. It addresses all men, it is true, so far as it is universal; but it addresses them as individuals, and commands their personal life.

It is not, we may be sure, due to any accident that the new commandment is haunted still by some of the associations of the old Law. For, indeed, it is true that the aspect of man's life, which this commandment accentuates, is not in itself complete. However true, however final it may be in its own region and within its due limits, it could not claim to exhaust all that can be said of the moral condition of mankind. It requires to be filled out and rounded by reference to that other attribute of the divine Nature of which I have spoken, the Wisdom of God.

For the life of man has not merely an individual outlook. Its interest is not merely to test the individual will—to build up individual character for better or for worse. No man's life is without a significance that falls beyond himself; no man can fail to contribute in his measure to the consummation of the wise purpose of God. A man lives here and acts; he chooses to serve God or to reject Him. Day by day his character declares itself, till the end comes inexorably, and he dies. And it has all meant something more than just an experiment on the individual character; more than just a trial of the effect of this particular combination of will and circumstance. By the time the end arrives, every man has entered into some relation with the whole course of history as God has planned it. The march of events required his contribution; the purpose of God would have been incomplete or other than it is, if he had not lived. Even if he has failed under the test, if he has given himself over to the evil, his life and its issue still fall under the supreme control of the divine Wisdom. God is not thwarted by sin, nor forced to adopt some hasty expedient to remedy its mischief. He works unswervingly through it all, though the changeless march of His purpose carries with it the discomfiture of those who rebel. The Wisdom of God saves the world through the Crucifixion, though it convicts at the same time the human agents concerned in it of heinous sin. The whole of life becomes rational and purposeful in relation to the divine Wisdom. There is no caprice about it, not even such caprice as might not be wholly unworthy of love. The whole course of things is rationally ordered, and moves on infallibly to an end which Wisdom has foreordained.

This point of view, if it be true at all, cannot fail to affect the moral obligations of man. The principles which guide his life, no less than the particular details and events of it, must find their final explanation in the wise purpose of God. As the events and decisions which go to make up a man's active life have not merely a reference to the development of his personal character, but also serve a wider end, so the moral laws which guide these acts and decisions cannot be merely arbitrary commands addressed to the individual will: they cannot but embody some principle or uniformity in the working of the divine Wisdom itself. They do not stand merely as commands, to break which is an outrage upon love, and of which the sanction is the threat of some ultimate loss or punishment; their sanction lies in their relation to the divine Reason. They are enjoined because it is in this way that the will of man can be brought into harmony with the purpose of God, not merely because God arbitrarily wills it so. An arbitrary enactment, however great the authority upon which it comes, is never final; it must always throw us back upon the investigation of the will which issued the command, and the examination of its motives. Hence the command—even to love—so long as it remains in that form is not the final resting-place of the mind; life is only brought under the control of the mind when this ultimate form of the moral law is itself seen as the necessary expression of the Wisdom of God.

This result is in no way affected by the fact that the moral law has found expression in very various forms. An objection based on this variety, indeed, could press hard only upon a conception of morality which is destitute of all character of finality. Any view of the moral law, for instance, which rests for its ultimate justification upon expediency or pleasure or any of the essentially changeful elements in life cannot escape from the changefulness which they bring with them. Expediency or even pleasure can give but a rough rule of thumb which will satisfy the conditions of life so long as they remain much the same. It will serve to distinguish between actions, and to guide the choice, so long as fashion does not change. Even if it should prove that much the same objects continue to be thought desirable, much the same pursuits thought honest and the reverse, yet still this fact is not an explanation of the life of man, it simply calls attention to the fact that an explanation is wanted. Why is it, we may ask, that, in spite of all the endless variety of circumstances in which men are placed, there is still some degree of rough agreement as to the expedient or the pleasurable? It is no answer to say that man's nature rules it so; that answer falls entirely within the bounds of human nature, and is simply a summary reassertion of the fact of which the cause was required. But it is an answer to refer the whole of life, its principles and its order, to the decision of the divine Wisdom, even though such an explanation raises at first sight as many difficulties as it solves. For such an explanation draws the various strands of this life together and binds them into a fabric displaying a rational design. Life as a whole is gathered up in it, and placed in contact with the providence of God. The bounds of inquiry are not set up within this earthly order; the whole earthly order is shown as a stage in the fulfilment of a purpose of which the consummation is not yet.

And that means that the earlier and less developed conceptions of morality are rationally explicable. Something is known of the end to which they converge, and they can therefore be brought within the category of evolution: in that light they have a meaning and a discernible drift; they lose their apparent arbitrariness and eccentricity and fall into order: their contradictions and antinomies are solved.

There can be no question that those who first were attracted to the new religion found in it this finality. After the first disorganization was over, which was caused by the expectation of an immediate Second Coming, and the Church was settling down to its place in the world, this belief produced in the Christians that temper of quiet and undisturbed tranquillity which meets us in ancient writings and has been so admirably described by Mr. Pater in Marius the Epicurean. They had the sense of problems solved, and anxiety allayed, which cannot arise so long as the world is held to be in any degree the scene of accident. And they are free from the dull lack of interest which comes of fatalism, because the Purpose which shapes their lives is one of divine Wisdom and Love.

But it will be said—and it is a serious objection—that such a view as this tends to separate the divine Wisdom and the divine Love, and thus runs the risk of throwing them into antagonism. To attempt to allot, as it were, a separate province to these attributes, and to reserve for the divine Wisdom the task of ordering and planning the universal course of things, introduces, it may be argued, a principle which may prove dangerous later on. The danger is not by any means an unreal one. It has seriously affected, in one period at least, the progress of theological thought: and it requires some notice.

In theology, of course, whether it be speculative or practical, everything depends upon the theory adopted of the divine Nature. The contact with Greek philosophy, which occurred early in the history of the Church, had seriously affected the doctrine of God. Christian thinkers found themselves in face of a system of thought and a vocabulary in many respects similar to that of the New Testament. And this doctrine in particular of which I have spoken to-day, the doctrine of the divine Wisdom, had much in it that would seem to suggest reconciliation between the new faith and the old ways of thinking. For Plato had found wisdom in the Most High; his conception of Deity was of a Being of whom wisdom could be predicated without any reserve. This Deity, like Jehovah, stood at the head of things: from Him all the whole course of the world's history took its start. His thoughts gave the rule for all that happened, and were the sum of the truth which the world in part expressed as an ectype or copy. As it stands in the *Timaeus* there is much language used in connexion with this theory which implies definitely creative, originative acts of will; and though it may be true that Plato's own intellectual bias lay in the direction opposed to ascribing such activity to God, the work as it stands admits of the other interpretation. But those who followed in his steps and looked to the *Timaeus* for their inspiration laid more and more exclusive emphasis on the speculative and intellectual element in the mind of God. More and more the activity for which God could be held responsible was exclusively regarded as a thinking into existence of the abstract ideal world, while He tended more and more to be excluded from the management of details, from contact with that which was material or individual.

It will be obvious at once that a development such as this might reveal an incompatibility with the Hebrew view of God. But for a long time the close allegiance of those Fathers who made use of Plato's thought to illustrate the text of Scripture prevented the elements of disunion from becoming apparent. St. Augustine, for instance, explains the first verse of

Genesis in accordance with the opinion that had prevailed since Philo[1], but he never suggests by his language that he has the slightest difficulty in thinking of the immediate influence of God upon the course of human life. A large part of the interest of such a work, for instance, as the *Confessions* consists in its exhibiting the wondrous way in which the hand of God had been upon him, guiding him through tortuous windings into the light of the Gospel. And this activity is conceived not as belonging to a remote Deity whose archetypal ideas are the hidden and inexorable principles of the earth's movement, but it is the personal activity of a God who loves infinitely and is infinitely wise.

Thus far the two ideas of wisdom and love, though distinguished, are not separated. But in later days the influence of the works of 'Dionysius the Areopagite' among other things tended to produce separation. The theory of a remote God beyond the reach of all possible experience or knowledge, higher than existence, higher almost than goodness, approached by speculative reason, was put forward under the authority of a companion of St. Paul, and acquired impressiveness from its supposed author rather than from anything peculiarly convincing in itself. From this time forward the prevalent conception of God in His own Nature felt the influence of 'Dionysius.' It seemed to provide a simple and rational solution of a serious problem, and was popular accordingly. In

---

[1] Philo held that Gen. i. 1 contained the assertion of two acts of creation: that of the ideal and the actual world.

the West it became involved in the discussions rising out of the controversy between nominalists and realists, and then its inherent one-sidedness became apparent. The divine Mind, according to the prevalent theory, was engaged in the perpetual contemplation of the ideas of things: i. e. their truth as opposed to their semblance. The question then arose of necessity whether God had any power over these ideas, whether He could have ruled them to be other than they are. Those who found their highest conception in the category of wisdom practically denied that He had any such freedom. Even God Himself, they felt, was not free to depart from the truth of things; and the truth of things depended not upon will, but upon the absolute wisdom which was embodied and took shape in the creation and controlling activity of God. Things are as they are, not so much because God willed them so as because, being absolute reason, He could not think them otherwise. This was, on the whole, the verdict of St. Thomas Aquinas. On the other hand, his great rival Scotus, though he did not seriously depart from the realistic position, recoiled from the fatalistic tendencies of the doctrines just described. He asserted the absolute freedom of God in all His actions, and made freedom of will in the widest sense the essential feature of the nature of God. The full consequences of this change did not appear till the days of Ockam, who not only followed Scotus in his conception of the nature of God, but also denied reality to all universals. Thus existence, truth, and morality depended entirely upon the free and arbitrary fiat of God. Ockam did not shrink from the logical result of this position, that it was in no way in contradiction with the true nature of God for Him to attach His approval to adultery or murder, or even blasphemy. The moral condemnation of such acts depends, according to Ockam, entirely upon the mere unexplained immediate fact of their prohibition by God[1].

I have made this short digression in order to make plain the peculiar danger which haunts all such speculations as these. It is my intention to amplify it in the notes to these lectures, but I hope I have said enough here to indicate the danger and its cause. The first perilous step is taken when the speculative conception of wisdom, which is always contemplative and not active in the practical sense, is allowed to overpower the idea of practical wisdom. From that moment a real separation has begun between two attributes of God, which reflection can only widen by degrees till it reaches the point of open and glaring contradiction. There is, indeed, no final halting-place between the first step and the last. Unless the love of God, the free-will of God, the wisdom of God, are held together in the grip of a personal conception of God, distinguished, as we must distinguish, as aspects or attributes, but never pressed to the point of separation, we must relapse in the end into a distribution of provinces amongst the various separate attributes of God: and this always involves us in some of the difficulties of Polytheism; it becomes as hard to define the relations of the attributes

[1] See note to this Lecture.

as it was of old to keep the peace among the deities of Olympus.

I am far from admitting that the dangers just mentioned are equally great on both sides of the controversy. To identify the wisdom of God with the contemplation of ideas undoubtedly carries with it the tendency to fatalism, for it subordinates the divine Mind to an intractable object of thought which conditions all His activity. This is, of course, an impossible position for Christian theology to adopt without serious modifications. But its evil is nothing to the chaos which follows upon the assumption of the other alternative, which derives all the activity of God from arbitrary will, even though that will be aglow with love. For this can only mean in the end that the action of God is not merely non-rational in relation to us, but irrational. It does not mean merely that these things *seem* irrational to us, not merely that we are incapable of finding the formula which affords the solution to all our speculation: but that the most elementary of our moral ideas are wholly without rational justification. If the thought of God's mere command, backed up by habit and the pressure of society, helps us to continue in the path of right, even if some never care to press for a further solution, it still is not true that this is a final position for the mind of man. The time must come when he will demand, and be right in demanding, some hint or suggestion, at the very least, of a more satisfying and rational explanation. Mere authority exists and is justified only as preparing for reason. If the sense of being under the rule of an omnipotent power satisfies us for a time and silences all question, it can only secure our allegiance so long as our reason happens to be in agreement with the commands imposed.

The tendency of thought displayed by Ockam did not die with scholasticism; it is alive and active at the present day. The unthoughtful and one-sided insistence upon the Christian doctrine that God is love, the dislike of an inexorable law and of the inseparable connexion of action and consequences, the conviction that a God who is love can be lightly overcome by prayer, are all forces tending to draw us away from the belief that the principles of moral life are as irrevocably written upon the system of things—as true a product of reason, as the laws of space or matter. Quite recently we have been bidden to take comfort in the fact that though there is no rational sanction for progress, though reason can never explain the surrender of individual interests to those of society, the religious beliefs of man are the natural and inevitable complement of his reason, providing an ultra-rational sanction for his conduct[1]. Or again it has been skilfully argued that authority is the source of most of our beliefs, and that it is idle and misleading to look to reason to justify them; that most of them rest on reasoning applied to convictions which we have accepted unquestioningly from our 'psychological climate,' the validity of which we have never seriously attempted to test[2]. It is true that at

[1] Kidd, *Social Evolution*, p. 116.
[2] Balfour, *The Foundations of Religion*, pp. 205-212.

present we are not invited to say more of them than that they are supra-rational, or that the failure of reason is not more than was to be expected. But we may be sure that a much larger demand lies hidden in that invitation. We may satisfy ourselves at present with the reflection that we are not asked to surrender much, and that the effect of our admissions is for the moment encouraging, in the way of solving difficulties and easing the strain of opposing impulses. But to accept this solution involves ultimately a surrender of an intellectual ideal. It may be true that the complete articulation of a rational system of thought is an ideal which is unattained, and, as the history of philosophy suggests, still unattainable. But it is this unattainable ideal which is present, consciously or unconsciously, in all intellectual processes and gives them their value. Each step is made in the conviction that the whole universe will justify the first venture, and that this belief is more than a blind, half-instinctive belief, which may be defended on the ground of its convenience; it expresses the truth that the divine Wisdom rules all things both in nature and in life, and that the reason of man reaches out to it as deep calls unto deep. Though we may believe and rest in the love of God, our view of His Nature will be inadequate unless we find in Him also our ideal of reason. The order of the world, the laws of life, the march of history—all of them flow out from the divine Wisdom—from wisdom interpenetrated with divine Love.

And here must arise a difficulty at which I glanced

a little way back. 'Granted,' it will be said, 'that the divine Wisdom ultimately rules all things, yet there are many occurrences in the world which do not suggest wisdom at all. The purpose of God is strangely obscure on the whole; we cannot characterize it in any complete and articulate form: how then can it be a guide or help in life? How can we gain from the mere belief that there is a purpose, from a blind confidence that the world is rational in spite of appearances?' This difficulty would be fatal if it were not for one fact. We should be in the position of those who manage well enough with generalizations from experience, but fail when experience shows signs of leading out of itself—out of this world into some region beyond. The saving fact is the fact of the Incarnation. And it saves us here because it presents us with a typical instance of the divine Wisdom and the divine Love. It was because God so loved the world that He sent His only begotten Son; and, at the same time, it was in Him that all the wise purpose of God was concentrated. In Him the Wisdom and Love of God combine and are manifested.

In whatsoever sense therefore Christ is an example for us, in that sense the loving Wisdom of God is our guide. If the appeal of His purity, His patience, His utter sacrifice of self moves us and wins our hearts, the explanation of its power lies in the fact that these are the laws of the world's ideal order, and they speak to the true manhood in all of us, which the Fall has blurred and distorted, but not destroyed. It is perhaps hardly possible to miss these lessons, but they are not all. Through all the manifestations of self-sacrificing love and endless patience there runs the thread of a stern and inexorable purpose. There is nothing casual, arbitrary, or unforeseen. He is set for the rise and fall of many in Israel. The burden of His Father's business lies upon Him even as a child. There is a divine necessity in all that He does and suffers: His life has moments, epochs, hours that are fixed and that culminate at the Passion. Moved by the Holy Ghost, holy men of old have seen what must be in regard of Him: to the very last jot and tittle, to the very detail of the vinegar and the sponge, all their prevision must be verified. And why is all this? Is it because He alone of all men displays a divine order in His life? Are our lives the sport of chance, and His only the scene of a fixed and steady purpose? Scarcely that. It is just because in His life the comely order of divine Wisdom is fulfilled without the disturbing force of personal sin—because in Him God has made known the mystery of His purpose—to sum up in Him all things whatsoever, the things in the heavens and the things upon earth. That is then the reason why the life of Christ has a real meaning for our lives, because in it the whole Wisdom and Love of God were manifested in full in their inseparable union. It is not merely that self-sacrifice and all that it involves have a natural attraction for man, and that he therefore finds something divine in their perfect manifestation: but rather the other way. The law of the divine Wisdom expresses itself in this form necessarily and naturally, and men acknowledge its supremacy in proportion as they are spiritually able to read the signs of the spiritual world. There are some still to whom the Cross is foolishness.

Thus Christian ethical philosophy, as it begins with, so it must return to, the Life of Christ. The new epoch of moral history dates from there. The life of man beforehand had been guided by ideals, by generalizations from experience, by the efforts of thoughtful men to lay hold upon the central principle of human action. They had defined virtue, they had estimated the value of various motives, and they had devised rules for good living. Men had laid down their lives rather than depart from the leading of the best that was in them; they had striven to rouse their fellows to a higher sense of right and wrong. And they had had a measure of success. Yet for all that the world remained an enigma: they waited the coming of a divine Word. On the other hand, the Jews had sought in patient waiting and careful technical obedience for the solution of their problem: until Christ came, revealing by the searching test of His presence the thoughts of many hearts. With Him there came a wealth of new knowledge which transformed the life of man. Men knew himself as a son of God, no longer a slave. He knew himself as a spiritual being, whose life was not bounded by the limits of the world, but stretched out beyond it into the very presence of God. He knew himself as a member of a spiritual society, united to all other members in virtue of his relation to Christ the Head. In the strength of these thoughts he sets himself again to solving the riddle of his life with new hope and new possibilities of success. New principles have to be added, which the old world has overlooked, which the spiritual order demands. The old rules which served for guidance under the old conditions have to be reinforced and interpreted. The grave and terrible fact of sin has to be deliberately faced, and the full seriousness of it deliberately stated. And when all this is done, rising as it does out of the Life and Death and Rising again of the Son of God, the reconstruction of life is still not quite complete. One other thought is still required that the 'whole round world may be every way bound by gold chains about the feet of God.' This is the thought of wisdom. It is in this that the process is completed. Whatever happens, even though it be a death upon a cross, man is unperplexed. God Whom he loves has known it all before, has provided for it, and understands it. And His ruling wisdom is not a blind, inexorable fate—careful of type, careless of the single life—for man has found at last that neither height, nor depth, nor things present, nor things to come, nor any other creature, can separate us from the wise Love of God in Jesus Christ our Lord.

NOTE TO LECTURE VI.

THE functions of religion in human life, from the philosophical point of view, are twofold. It is the medium through which man expresses his ideas both of the origin of things, and of the sanctions of moral life. The cause of the natural world and all that is in it, is to be found in God; and, at the same time, God is the source and the champion of the moral law. These two interests are not kept always fully distinct. It is probable that, though different always, the distinction between them is merged in the earliest forms of religion. But the state of fusion is not final. The metaphysical interest develops first into mythology and then into pure metaphysic, and the end of it is the idea of God as Substance. From first to last the moral idea of God is superior in freedom and directness of reality, and in the light of it God is always conceived, not as Substance, but rather as Subject.

It is not asserted that these two ideas are necessarily incompatible. God conceived as a Person may be the Cause of the universe still, though it is more difficult to see how God the First Cause can play the part of God the Friend. It is, however, affirmed that the two are different; and it may be added that in the course of history the difference becomes accentuated. On the whole, those systems of religion of which mythology is to us a leading feature, of which the explanation of nature is the most prominent motive, end naturally in metaphysic. The most obvious instance is that of Greek religion. On the other hand, Hebrew religion, of which the prominent characteristic is its close connexion with morality, keeps steadily in view the Personality of God. The Hebrew mind, as has frequently been observed, seemed entirely indifferent to the claims of speculation, even in regard to the bases of moral life, and trusted to the observances of religion for the satisfaction of all the higher impulses of the soul. The character ascribed to God varied as the consciousness of the people changed: but the idea of a Ruler and Lawgiver was never lost.

The progress of Christianity carried with it the necessity of a combination of these two points of view. The new faith arose directly out of the old Hebrew monotheism, and inherited the associations which lay round the name of Jehovah. The life and work of Christ, moreover, riveted the bonds which connected morality and religion. But again, the philosophy which prevailed in the world when the Church had to settle its attitude towards such speculation, was the attenuated result of a development which had begun with religion. The various forms of Greek philosophy had arisen out of the criticism passed upon Greek religions: and thus, though the philosophies had, as it were, religious relations, and could easily be persuaded again to take on a religious appearance, they were associated with the presuppositions of a particular type of religion—and that not the same type as the new faith with which they were asked to combine. It was obvious that the combination would not be achieved without difficulty.

The difficulty appeared quite early in connexion with the attributes of God. Jew and Greek agree in the assertion of the changelessness of God: but there is a wide difference in the application of the term. To the Jew the changelessness of God is moral: it is a changelessness of Will and Love [1]. It involved no curious questionings as to the possibility of creation; it rendered even the problem of evil practically intelligible, and it ignored almost entirely the theoretical aspects of the difficulty [2]. But it was otherwise with the

[1] Cf. Mal. iii. 6: 'I am the Lord. I change not: therefore ye sons of Jacob are not consumed.'

[2] Thus there seems to be no sense of danger or contradiction in such phrases as Amos iii. 6 or Isa. xlv. 7. Though the same writers affirm the entire responsibility of man for his own sin, yet they do not hesitate to use such language as that in the passages cited. 'Shall evil befall a city,

Greeks. The idea of creation seemed to carry with it the notion of a change in the Unchangeable—a longing fulfilled—a state of incompleteness succeeded by perfection. So the presence of evil seemed more adequately explained as an inevitable effect of finite existence; and this again seemed to make it impossible to believe that God desired and created a world involving this result. The Gnostic controversy, therefore, whatever other interests it had, brought this question forward also, viz. the determination of the attributes of God.

The answer of the Church from this point of view may be regarded as the first attempt to deal with a very serious and difficult problem. It will not be possible here to detail the whole process by which the result was attained; it is desirable however to call attention to two points in regard to it, (1) the actual result itself, (2) the general character of the method which led to it.

1. The outcome of all the discussion which Gnosticism set in motion was the strong assertion of a particular view of the Nature of God. It was clear beyond all dispute that God is capable of action comparable in some sense with that of a human will. He creates and He keeps His hand on the whole progress of things throughout history. And this was not peculiar to any one writer or school; it is characteristic of almost all who can be called Fathers of the Church[1]. Origen and Athanasius are no less clear than Tertullian or Augustine that the Nature of God is founded in love, and that it is out of this fact that we explain (so far as we can explain them at all) the Creation and the Incarnation[2]. God acts, because He wills to act, and can. To say this, of course, opens up various problems of considerable subtlety. If God

and the Lord hath not done it?' 'I create evil.' The strong conviction that God controls all things saves them apparently from feeling the paradox which their language suggests.

[1] The widest divergence from this point of view is to be found in Clement's speculations as to the Nature of God, *Strom.* V. xi. 72.

[2] Cf. Iren. IV. xiv–xvi., ll. xxx. 9; Orig. *c. Cels.* iii. 70; *De Princ.* II. ix. 6; Athan. *c. Gent.* c. 35; *De Inc.* III. 3, X.; Tert. *Adv. Marc.* I. xxvi.; Aug. *Enarr. in Ps.* CXXXIV. 10; *Tract. in Joh.* ii, iii.

Note to Lecture VI

can do all things, can He do wrong? Certainly not, reply Origen, Tertullian, and Augustine alike. It would contradict His essential Nature, says Origen[1]. God is supreme Reason, says Tertullian, and the supremely rational is also the supremely good[2]. He suffers evil and controls it, says Augustine. Out of His love He created the world; and no finite will has power to thwart His purpose[3].

2. The result of the consideration bestowed on the subject was thus comparatively simple. But it was dogmatic rather than demonstrative. It affirmed that God was of a certain nature: it did not deal with all the problems that such an assertion could suggest: it was not always clear how far the Will of God acted on the analogy of arbitrary or reasoned action. This limitation was due in large measure to the way in which the result had been attained; in other words, to the influence of the dogmatic tradition. The opposing systems were speculative first, and historical or scriptural afterwards. The Church began by being the exponent of Scripture and tradition; it was speculative only so far as was necessary to make the truth intelligible to speculative minds. It was confronted with a metaphysic of nature, and it answered with a philosophy of history. It laid emphasis on the work of God in the history of the human race. It dwelt on the selection of the Jews, the long succession of prophets, the fulfilment of their hopes in the coming Christ, and the work of Christ when He came. All this was asserted in Scripture, formed part of the Church tradition, and was certified in the religious experiences of all who were true Christian men. The philosophies had to conform to it; they were enlarged or modified, as the case might be, in order to take in the operations of God in history.

With all this, there was still a problem unsolved. It was agreed that the Nature of God was such that the Incarnation was possible, and the Doctrine of Christ as the Word was

---

[1] *C. Cels.* iii. 70; cf. Greg. Nyss. *Or. Catech.* c. 20.
[2] *Adv. Marc.* II. vi; cf. *Adv. Prax.* c. 10.
[3] *Ench.* cc. 100 and 101; *De Civ.* XI. 21, XIV. 27, XXII. 2.

connected with the philosophical theories of the Word and Wisdom. The climax of philosophy as well as of prophecy had been found in Christianity; but yet there was a problem still unsolved. The two interests of religion had come together in the theology of Christendom, but the formula which was to adjust the two had not yet made its appearance. If it were true that in the faith of Christ the philosophical impulse found its completion, and at the same time that the God of the Christian religion performed functions not contemplated by philosophy, it was necessary to decide in some way how these two aspects of God were to be reconciled. If it were granted that He was the supreme Essence, the underlying Reason of the world, yet it might still be asked in what sense He was the universal Will. It was necessary to decide where and how the metaphysical conception of God would have to be modified to allow room for the other; and this was a matter of speculation, requiring some other method of exposition than the mere interpretation of tradition. Questions were raised early as to the exact meaning of Omnipotence, and these would not be left unsolved.

It is this interest which underlies the inquiry into the attributes of God in the Scholastic Age. While it apparently means nothing and is nothing but an arbitrary discussion of things beyond the range of men's thought, it is really a most important stage in the history of a question that is involved in the very existence of Christianity.

In order to make this clear it will be necessary to speak shortly, by way of digression, of the theological ideas introduced through the works of 'Dionysius the Areopagite,' and of the influence of the Realistic controversy on theology proper. In the earlier centuries, as we have already said, the philosophical opinions professed by Christian thinkers were eclectic. They did not profess to follow any school wholly and without reserve. Philosophy was to them a partial and undeveloped embodiment of truth. It had its place in the order of the divine counsels, and was useful, in its degree and kind, within the range of theology. Augustine, for instance, though he was strongly under the influence of Plato, and of the Platonism current in his day, was not, strictly speaking, a Platonist. Plato had, to his mind, come nearest to the truth of Christ of all those who had speculated in ancient times.

But this is all changed in the works which appeared in the fifth century under the name of 'Dionysius the Areopagite.' In these the Platonism of Proclus and the later Athenian school appear with little modification; and the doctrines of the Church, so far as they are discussed, are expressed in terms of philosophy. The position assigned to Christ is required by the philosophical system; the meaning given to redemption is merely philosophical, and the whole is Christian rather in language than in idea. It is, perhaps, a mistake to press hardly on the author of these works for such theological shortcomings as he displays. His interest is clearly a philosophical one. He aims at solving by his theories the opposition between the unknown transcendent God and the ordinary course of human experience. In the view of 'Dionysius' God is entirely inaccessible to all the human methods of knowledge. He is beyond existence and thought: terms which are used to describe God may quite as truly be denied of Him. But through the various processes of human experience men acquire such knowledge of Him as is possible to them: for God, while He is none of existing things, is also all. This, which seems to be a fundamental position in the theology of 'Dionysius,' determines his attitude towards the two questions or problems above mentioned, the changelessness of God, and His relation to evil.

Together with his Platonism 'Dionysius' inherited all the inferences as to the Nature of God which that philosophical position carries with it. One of the reasons why none of the names which we assign to God is adequate to His Being, is that they are derived from experience of changeful things, and God never changes. He must therefore be isolated from the world, lest the purely transcendental and immaterial Nature should be affected. Between God and the individual beings of ordinary experience we are to conceive a series of grades of being, which depart in successive stages from the divine mode of existence, until in the Person of the God-man they are brought into the unity of God again. This view almost necessarily carries with it a fatalistic doctrine of the order of the world, and it makes it impossible to deal with evil, except by peremptorily denying its existence. That which is called evil is always some limitation of good : pure evil is inconceivable, it could not exist. So we find it laid down that τὸ ἀγαθὸν ἐκ τῆς μιᾶς καὶ τῆς ὅλης αἰτίας· τὸ δὲ κακὸν ἐκ πολλῶν καὶ μερικῶν ἐλλειψέων [1].

It would not require much elaboration to show how closely this doctrine is allied with Pantheism in its crudest form. It is probable, however, that such a pressure of its meaning would be an injustice to its author, and would certainly lie apart from our purpose. All that need be done here is simply to call attention to this very important fact; namely, that under an almost apostolic name, there had come into vogue a purely speculative theology, based on the philosophical conceptions of what the Nature of God should be, and not so exclusively or primarily upon the items of the Christian Creed ; and that this speculative theology tended, at the very least, to merge all finite existence and activity into the being of God. The circumstance which interfered to suspend this result was probably its mystical character. The processes of pure reason were not the truest ways of reaching God, nor was reason the highest term that could be found to describe Him. He was beyond reason and beyond being : and therefore intercourse with God lay beyond the range of definite consciousness.

The controversy between Realists and Nominalists is primarily a logical one : relating simply to the meaning that may be ascribed to general terms. But though its origin is sufficiently humble, it acquires a profounder importance in the end, when the answer given to this logical question is treated as a principle of truth. It is obvious that if universals are

[1] *De Div. Nom.* IV. 30.

Note to Lecture VI

mere *flatus vocis*, and there is no reality to correspond to them, our whole knowledge is of individual things, and universals are banished for ever from the range of the human mind. This seems to open the dreary prospect of pure materialism before us. God Himself becomes a doubtful object of knowledge, and the universal principles of morality must necessarily disappear.

On the other hand, the idea that universals are real, and, in fact, are the reality to which we get access by our individual acts of thought, has a tendency in the direction of Pantheism. The highest reality would belong to the most abstract thought. There would be remaining but a single substance expressing itself in various forms in the world.

There are thus three lines of speculation at work in the Scholastic Age. There is the negative and mystical Transcendentalism of Dionysius, the crude Materialism flowing from the premisses of the Nominalists, and the scientific Pantheism from those of the Realists. It is in the light (if that is a suitable expression) of these presuppositions that the further question of the relation of God to morality is discussed. It will be well to consider typical cases of the arguments alleged, and then endeavour to reach a conclusion as to the significance of the discussion.

The first author who will claim attention is, of course, Thomas Aquinas. In Thomas Aquinas we find the combination of a realistic philosophy with the mystic agnosticism of 'Dionysius.' Aquinas accepted these writings as the work of St. Paul's convert, and therefore ascribed to them an authority which they would not, perhaps, have acquired by their own intrinsic merits. Hence he admits in general terms the doctrine that God is beyond the reach of any created intellect. But 'Dionysius' had allowed, besides this, some possibility of attaining a partial knowledge of God, though he does not wholly succeed in harmonizing the two sides of his theology. It was here that Aquinas enlarged and developed the principles of 'Dionysius' in a strictly scholastic fashion. He distinguishes between various methods and kinds of knowledge, and he converts the negative exclusions of 'Dionysius' into the assertion, on reasoned grounds, of positive attributes. Thus he asserts the simplicity of the divine Nature, and from this proceeds to develop a list of other attributes which, he maintains, are involved in this or flow out from this. Hence we find ourselves led almost imperceptibly to a position exactly the opposite to that of 'Dionysius': a series of attributes, precisely defined and sustained by argument, is asserted of God.

But the mere assertion of attributes is not all. Aquinas also defines in some degree the relation between them. He affirms that God is identical 'with His *essentia* or *natura*,' and that the *essentia* and the *esse* are the same[1]. From this it is argued further that all such perfections as we rightly attribute to God—the Reason and the Will without which we cannot conceive Him—are part (if such a phrase may be allowed) of the divine Nature. The Reason, says Aquinas, from the point of view of a Realist, is concerned with ideas which are 'principia cognitionis rerum et generationis ipsarum,' and these are adequate to the whole process of the world[2]. These, therefore, are the rules or principles which guide the divine Will, or through which it acts.

In answer to the further question whether God wills of necessity Aquinas makes a distinction. As Will has been shown to be of the *esse* of God, He wills its due object, 'bonitas divina, necessarie et absolute.' Other things, which He wills to exist for their sake, and not because they are necessary to the fullness of His own being, He wills 'non necessario, nisi ex suppositione tantum: supposito enim quod velit, non potest non velle[3].' This doctrine is still further

[1] *Summa*, Pars. i, qu. iii, arts. 3 and 4. The former point depends on the fact that God is not, like man, a form embodied in various individual material shapes, but is pure form: the latter, on the fact that there are no accidents or unrealized potentialities in God. This is probably only a scholastic way of saying that God is pure Spirit, and that His existence is not limited by external conditions.

[2] *Ib.* P. i^a, qu. xiv, art. 4; xix, art. 1; xvi, arts. 1–3.

[3] *Ib.* qu. xix, arts. 2 and 3.

Note to Lecture VI

explained later on [1], where it is ruled that God, though omnipotent, and not bound by any law to have produced the world exactly as it is, cannot do anything which involves contradiction or derogates from His own Nature. This is an important decision, because it proceeds from the original position adopted by Aquinas in regard of God; namely, the unmixed and uninfringed unity of His Nature. 'In nobis,' he says, 'potentia et essentia aliud est a voluntate et intellectu, et iterum intellectus aliud a sapientia, et voluntas aliud a iustitia,' and therefore 'potest esse aliquid in potentia, quod non potest in voluntate iusta, vel in intellectu sapiente.' But in God the whole works in harmony. 'Potentia intelligitur, ut exequens: voluntas autem, ut imperans: intellectus et sapientia, ut dirigens:' hence the acts and the limits of the power are alike the product of the one Nature of God. There is no possibility of variance, and that which is willed expresses the final and changeless Nature of God. From this point of view it is clear how the question as to the final validity of the moral law will be treated. It will be impossible that a law which expresses the actual Nature of God as we find it in the moral law should take any other form than that in which we know it. And this will be so, not because the moral law is necessary *ex suppositione* and absolutely contingent, but because the true Nature of God is expressed in it, both in regard to Reason and Will. As the Will is not separable from the Reason, there will be nothing arbitrary and nothing contingent in its utterances: the moral law will have the force of a rule of which the contradictory is absurd.

The great rival of Aquinas, John Duns Scotus, rejects this notion of God. He accepts in some measure principles similar to Aquinas, but he derives conclusions from them which are completely different. Thus he assumes and proves in scholastic fashion that God is one and simple in nature; but when the further question arises as to immutability, Scotus, though he affirms the presence of this attribute in the divine Nature, gives it a very different meaning. He deduces it from the simplicity of the divine Nature, but he applies it only to the

---
[1] *Summa*, P. i, qu. xxv.

divine Nature itself and not to the order of the world. When Scotus comes to apply the conception he has of God to the creation, he uses a very curious piece of argument. There is certainly, he says, contingent action in the world. But if the world's creation proceeds from the natural or necessary action of the divine Will, the whole process from beginning to end must be necessary. This conclusion being out of correspondence with known facts, Scotus accepts and emphasizes the alternative view that there is contingent action even in God ; in other words, that the essential Nature of God is Free Activity. Hence all that we know as necessary and fixed owes its character not to any inherent qualities or grounds, but simply to the free choice of God [1]. It is obvious that this theory leaves a good deal unexplained. There is no true reason offered why God should choose one side rather than the other of a pair of contradictions. But if pressed with this difficulty Scotus has a simple answer ready: 'Indisciplinati est, quaerere omnium causas et demonstrationem secundum Philosophum [2].' There is no reason except the mere fact of the Will of God. On these grounds it becomes necessary to affirm that will is the primary element or power in the Nature of God, because will is a power to which contingency naturally belongs. Thus the moral law falls under the control of the final characteristics of the divine Nature and depends upon His arbitrary fiat. This theory does not imply in Scotus any uncertainty as to the validity or certainty of the moral code. Nor again does it point to a nominalist theory of universals. Scotus expressly excepts from the category of contingent activity the operation of intellect, and asserts the reality and certainty of the primary laws of thought. It would seem as if these had for the intellect, even the Intellect of God, a necessary character [3].

---

[1] The arguments on this subject may be gathered from the *Commentary on the Sentences*, Lib. I, dist. ii, qu. 2, and dist. viii, qu. 1 and 5.

[2] *Op. cit.*, p. 763, ed. Paris, 1893.

[3] The most fundamental difference between Aquinas and Scotus turns on the Nature of God. The point ordinarily mentioned as in

Note to Lecture VI

Both Aquinas and Scotus have assumed the reality, in some sense, of universals: and both alike allow a certain knowledge of God to be possible to man. The difference between them turns on the different development given to principles in which they are closely similar. But with William Ockam we pass over into a completely different set of principles. Ockam is a nominalist pure and simple: he absolutely denies the possibility of any knowledge except the direct knowledge of particular things, and this he applies equally to God and man. A principle like this carries with it, of course, the conclusion that God cannot be directly known; for it is obvious that God does not express Himself immediately to the senses of man. And it further tends towards the conclusion, which Ockam adopts, that there is nothing but arbitrary will to account for the presence of the moral law. The system is not easy to manage consistently with itself; for the whole process of deductive argumentation on which Ockam relies assumes universals, and uses them to prove the conclusion. But he is alive to the absurdity of giving universal significance to the moral law when positive commands will be sufficient for its support[1].

debate between Thomists and Scotists is of secondary importance, and arises out of their differences in the idea of God. The question was whether the Incarnation was to be regarded as necessary in itself, or as dependent upon the course of created things. Aquinas, who, from the principles already described, might have been expected to treat it as necessary, here deserts his usual point of view. He maintains that if the Incarnation is to be founded in the absolute Nature of God, it must necessarily have been eternal: this is obviously impossible, and therefore he accepts the alternative which bases it on the free decision of the Will of God. The fact that in Scripture it is usually placed in connexion with the Redemption leads Aquinas with some hesitation to assign human sin as the cause of it. On the other hand, Scotus, though he has affirmed, as we have seen, that the essence of the divine Nature is free-will, explains the Incarnation in connexion with the predestination of God. The Incarnation is a necessary means to the blessedness of the human race— the end which God has freely chosen to achieve: hence it is an inherent necessity in things prior to the existence or even the prevision of sin. Cf. *Comm. in Sent.* Lib. III. dist. xix.

[1] Cf. *Comm. in Sent.* Lib. I, dist. xxxv and xli-xlvii; Lib. II, dist. xix.

The language and associations of this controversy make it appear sufficiently remote from all human interest. This impression would only have been deepened, if the quotations had been multiplied and the philosophical positions involved in them more fully set forth. It has been necessary, however, to enter into scholasticism only so far as would make the nature of the problem apparent. It will be clear from what has been said that the question is a real one, and is concerned, as was said above, with the inter-relation of the two interests of religion. In an age like that of the Schoolmen the merely dogmatic solution of questions was clearly inadequate: the temper of the time required the systematic exposition of all the contents of belief. It is sometimes said that the Schoolmen did wrong in attempting a philosophical construction, on the basis of pure thought, of the whole world of nature and religion. They doubtless made many errors of judgement and of fact. But their real danger was much more that they criticized their creed too little, than that they felt too much confidence in reason. There were two very strong dispositions prevalent at the time. One was the desire for a completely systematized account of things, and the other the desire for orthodox belief. It was not that there were no sceptics ; there were sceptical thinkers enough, and the influence of Arabic speculation was sceptical. But the Faith had an antecedent right to acceptance, which would not generally be accorded to it now ; and this, more than anything else, seems to have been the difference in atmosphere between the present and the Scholastic ages. The philosophical points at issue then are at issue still under other names, and it is rather a superficial criticism which deals chiefly with the bulk of the works and the cumbrousness of the style of the great Scholastic authors, and ignores their significance in the history of thought.

A time such as this was exactly the right one for the discussion of the problem before us. The strong desire for philosophical completeness ensured the discussion of the philosophical conception of God, and His relation to nature ;

Note to Lecture VI

while the universal prevalence of the Christian Faith brought decisively forward the rule of God in life. It would have been impossible under the conditions to avoid approaching the question of combining the two points of view.

But we may still ask whether it was worth while, and whether any result that was more or less permanent for theology emerged from the discussion, and this is a question that is far from easy to answer.

There is always a strong inclination, in any reasonable theology, towards the mystic agnosticism which we have seen to be characteristic of 'Dionysius.' It seems much safer and much more consistent with the limits of human capacity to refrain from discussing too anxiously or defining too precisely the attributes of the divine Nature. It looks like presumptuous and crude anthropomorphism to profess any knowledge whatever of the meaning of personality, or attributes, or essence, or existence in regard to the Nature of God. For indeed, it might be asked, do we know any of these things clearly in regard to ourselves? Can we define beyond all possibility of doubt what we mean by personality as applied to our own life? Can we distinguish the essential from the accidental characters of human existence, by infallible criteria? Can we describe our own existence, at all faithfully and exhaustively? And if not, how can we pretend to decide peremptorily and dogmatically any final question as to the method of operation of a Being wholly outside the range of our experience? How can we profess to solve about God problems of which we can barely understand the terms in regard to ourselves?

It would be a matter of serious difficulty to meet these questions, if the problems thus criticized really meant all that they say and had no other aspect. If it were really true that we set out to discuss and decide the laws and constituent elements (so to say) of the divine Nature, there would be but one prospect for the inquirer: he could look forward only to failure. But, as a matter of fact, these problems represent merely the theological method of raising questions which are inevitable, and have a profound effect on our whole conception of life. As in the case of the problems about our own way of being, it may seem futile to ask the questions, yet it is inevitable, and makes a good deal of difference how we answer them : so it is in the case of the Nature of God. It may seem presumptuous to inquire whether the divine Reason or the divine Will is supreme; but this is the theological method of asking whether we can trust our moral sense as an unerring guide, or whether its utterances, apart from all question of degradation and perversion through vice, are liable to an inherent lack of rational necessity? And not only is it true that this is the theological method of asking the question, but also that in this case, as in all others, the theological method is the real and ultimate form in which the question may be expressed. The existence of God may be denied, as it is by some. But if it be admitted, it can only appear as the final ground of all experience, the source of all knowledge and all being. And in the same way morality, like scientific thought, finds its ultimate explanation in the Nature of God. The end of life, as has been urged in the lecture, is that we should be perfect as our Father in heaven is perfect; in other words, that our moral life, like our intellectual life, must lead us back to God, and must be, like our scientific knowledge, a source of information about God.

There is, in reality, no alternative between admitting these theological relations of morality, and denying that God has any influence over it, or any place of self-revelation through it. Obviously, intellectual and moral life must be expected to stand on the same basis. If the denial that our ordinary intellectual knowledge leads us to God means atheism on intellectual grounds, it is difficult to see why moral life should not be subject to the same reasoning. If anything, there is more need of some ultimate and decisive principle in morality than in science. Science works with axioms, of which the contradictory is inconceivable. It may easily claim to take its start from these, and close its eyes to all questions of their origin and ultimate validity. But there are no axioms of this

Note to Lecture VI

sort in morality. To ask for them in morality is a μετάβασις εἰς ἄλλο γένος; it is to assume that scientific order rules in practical life. Where the object is scientific truth a start must be made with intellectual principles which are assumed to be unquestionable : otherwise scientific procedure would be like playing a game without rules. Morality does not aim primarily at scientific truth, and therefore does not in itself require procedure which only scientific truth demands. Moreover the rules of morality are notoriously not axiomatic. Under these circumstances we may adopt one of two positions. We may find the sanction of the moral law in the general good of society, or we may take moral life, like intellectual life, into connexion with God.

If we do this, the question cannot but be pressing, in what sense are we to bring morality into connexion with God? And here we are back in our Scholastic disputes. Is morality a mere system of unexplained and arbitrary commands, or is it an embodiment of the divine Reason? To this question, as we have seen, three answers were given. It remains to translate these into some more modern phraseology. Of Ockam we need say little. His language on the subject can only be fully explained in terms of pure materialism; and it entirely deprives the moral law of any rational sanction. His theory, moreover, if the materialistic interpretation be avoided, demands a strong Calvinistic theology[1]. And reason is throughout an unexplained mercy. It is there and it somehow rules the thoughts of men : but it is not easy or natural to account for it on the basis of pure caprice; yet this is really the only solution open to Ockam. In his reckless theory of things the attempt of scholasticism to combine the dogmatic tradition and reason into one system broke down, and the need for a new method came prominently to light.

---

[1] The section on the subject of Predestination (*Comm. in Sent.* P. I. dist. xii) contains language which is strongly suggestive of Calvin. It would be interesting to inquire how far Calvin was affected by later scholasticism in the development of his theories.

There is the widest possible difference between Scotus and Ockam, though superficially they seem to be in agreement. Scotus maintains the priority of will on principles diametrically opposed to those of Ockam. Ockam finds will the natural force to account for the presence of a complex of individual rules and facts, from which the whole conception of universality is excluded. Scotus conceives that will is the necessary presupposition of contingent action in the world of experience. In other words, he assumes the principle that experience gives some clue to the being and attributes of God, and believes that experience requires this order. The predominance of reason seems to him to be indistinguishable from fatalism. He does not reject, but assumes the prevalence of universal principles; but he hopes by his emphasis on the presence of deliberately chosen contingent action to save his theory from a serious danger, which seemed to him (not altogether, perhaps, without reason) to lie near the doctrine of Aquinas.

It would seem, however, that, of the two, Aquinas is on the truest lines. The principle of Scotus assumes too sharp a division between contingent and necessary action. In our own experience there is no difficulty in distinguishing between the product of reason, the purely contingent, and the necessary. And, though it might be fairly argued that this experience cannot be applied without reserve to the discussion on the Nature of God, it would still be true that the argument of Scotus assumes too much. It loses its force, unless the contingent and necessary belong to wholly different regions of activity. But this reasoning lies entirely within the limits of Scholastic thought. A more modern aspect of the question emerges when we reflect upon the results of the two theories upon morality itself.

A theory which puts reason in the subordinate place can never secure the operation of reason over the whole field of experience. The region which lies outside it is *ex hypothesi* non-rational: and it is impossible to define its limits by reason. There is a region over which reason works and

Note to Lecture VI

there is a region beyond : and this is all we know. It may, of course, be the scene of a rational operation of another and unfamiliar type ; but the presumption is that it is not this, but simply a non-rational province. This is diametrically opposed to our experience of life. However clearly we may distinguish reason and will in ourselves, it is obvious that reason covers in a sense the whole of life. The objects upon which reason, in the narrowest sense of the word, exercises itself are different from the objects of will : and their procedure is different also. There is therefore no room for mistake as to their separate functions. But still reason is our only means of obtaining a conscious realization of anything at all. The difference between reason and will is itself a rational difference, and reason colours and permeates every action in which the will expresses itself. As regards human nature, therefore, while we can in a sense conceive abstract operations of reason which should lead to no action, we cannot conceive of moral action which is not at all points interpenetrated with the processes of reason. And this is simply another way of saying that reason is the ultimate ground of our whole experience, scientific and practical—the fundamental presupposition to the unification of all life. But it is just these fundamental principles which give us our notion of God : if, therefore, the order of our own experience demands this relative position of reason and will, if the consequences of depriving moral principle of rational basis are as serious as we have seen, we shall do well to use this guidance in our conception of God. For, though we cannot deduce *a priori* that which must be true of God, we shall never attain to any knowledge of Him by depreciating or passing by our own experience. The belief in God is the cumulative result of experience, philosophically speaking, and, for us, that which is finally necessary to the full validity of our experience is necessary to our doctrine of God.

LECTURE VII.

'Love not the world, neither the things that are in the world. If any man love the world, the love of the Father is not in him. For all that is in the world, the lust of the flesh, and the lust of the eyes, and the vainglory of life, is not of the Father, but is of the world. And the world passeth away, and the lust thereof: but he that doeth the will of God abideth for ever.'—1 ST. JOHN ii. 15-17. (R.V.)

THE moral forms and theories described in the last four lectures prevailed in the Church throughout the Middle Age. The types of virtue which grew out of them, especially in the West, the conceptions of sin, and the general principles of life were accepted as the rule by which moral conduct was to be guided. An elaborate system of interpretation was necessary, as must be the case with any formal rule, in order to secure its application to new circumstances as they arose. But there was no serious variation of practice in regard to the outlines and ruling ideas employed.

This fact gives considerable importance to a set of ethical conceptions which has now passed out of fashion. For, in view of the position they held, and the use that was made of them, they were little less than the moulding forces which shaped the modern world. The political factors in this process are well known. The removal of the seat of empire from Rome to Byzantium, the failure to maintain a dual

Ethics and the Reformation

system of imperial rule, the gradually intensifying divergence between the Easterns and the Westerns, and, lastly, the appearance of northern invaders, are familiar features in the history of Europe, and I need only call attention to them. To the vacant throne of the Roman emperor, the Roman bishop succeeded of necessity, and it is this fact which colours all the subsequent Western history. It was the action of the Popes of Rome in allying themselves with the northern peoples against the Eastern Emperor that gave the decisive turn to events. Without involving ourselves in the necessity of deciding to which power —the ecclesiastical or the civil—the initiation in the matter really belonged, it may be said without hesitation that, as a mere political fact, Pope Leo III in crowning Charles the Great threw over old things, consciously or unconsciously, and cast in his lot with the new. It was not important merely because Charles was a Frank. For a long time the citizenship of Rome had been attainable by barbarians : more than one foreigner had already occupied the imperial throne. The coronation of Charles by Leo stands apart from all these in significance : for it determined, more perhaps than any other single fact, the order of modern European history.

But if the alliance between the Emperor and the Pope was politically important, its moral significance was no less striking. It reinforced and established the hold of Christian moral ideas upon the people under the imperial sway. The Church, already recognized as the one supreme spiritual organization, gained the right and the power to carry out in practice the code which had grown up within it.

It would not, of course, be true to suppose that the Church had waited till the formal support of the civil power was obtained before it asserted itself in matters of moral right and wrong. Far from this, there are various signs of the actual success of the new moral ideas in moulding the conceptions of the northern peoples before this date. Christianity, in other words, using the theological and moral principles of which we have said so much, had been actually successful on a great scale in dealing with the moral problems presented to it, and its success, so far as it went, underlies all that has happened since. There are various signs in the history of the time which go to prove this, and I must here dwell on two.

I. There is the rapid spread and prevalence of monasticism. In modern times this is usually regarded as a fact which is somewhat doubtfully creditable to the Church. Society, it is felt, would be at an end if the monastic ideal were represented as the only true ideal of human life. Such a pursuit of Christian perfection would mean not that the Church was leavening the world, but that it was improving society off the face of the earth. There can be no doubt that errors were made in this direction. Though there was certainly more discouragement given than is popularly supposed to the choice of the monastic life, yet it was not limited severely to persons who had a real vocation for it. Kings were allowed to forsake their kingdoms, husbands to leave their wives, and wives their husbands, in order to seek for the peculiar blessing which was believed to follow upon the literal fulfilment of Christ's command, to forsake all. And in all this there was a serious danger of self-pleasing under the guise of self-sacrifice. But when every allowance has been made, it remains that the monastic life cannot have been much more pleasant to men of strong passions or high position or great wealth than it would be to men similarly situated in modern times. Life was less luxurious in those days, but the luxury that there was must have appealed to human nature then very much as it does now. And it requires no very strongly developed sense of historic perspective to see that the immense prevalence of this custom, the numbers of persons of various ranks who were attracted by it, and the level of high saintliness and simplicity which many of them attained, point to the fact that the Church had placed before uncivilized and passionate people a very high ideal of self-denial, and that it had great success in so doing.

II. The spread of monasticism, however, is not the whole of the evidence for its success in this regard; nor is it perhaps the strongest portion of it. Those who entered the monastic orders formed after all a special class. Though they were drawn from the ranks of the laity, their proceedings do not throw much light on the influence of the Church upon laymen in general. Such evidence is afforded indirectly by the Penitential literature which remains to us from this period. Much of this contains regulations which apply only to the ordained and to those under monastic vows: but there is also a large portion of it which is definitely applied to the laity, and in this may be clearly seen the uncompromising and stern attitude adopted by the Church towards prevalent sins. From the nature of the case we gain more information from these works as to the sins condemned than as to the virtues encouraged, and it is impossible to say from merely reading them how far the penances enforced or the rules laid down were actually carried out. The analogy of civil codes, however, in regard to which the same difficulty might be raised, the fact that the Penitentials are in many cases a register of decisions rather than a code of laws, together with occasional references to the working of this or that enactment, enables us to use their evidence with a considerable amount of confidence. And there can be no doubt as to the code of moral action which guides the decisions. In some cases outward acts are more prominent than inward moral conditions, and then the scheme follows the rule which dates back to the Apostolic Council at Jerusalem; acts of idolatry, fornication, murder, are condemned and penance is assigned to them. To these there are often added regulations concerning food, prohibitions to use the bodies of animals which have died of themselves, or of which the blood has not been removed, such as things strangled. Besides this, other sins prevalent at the time are condemned, such as drunkenness, against which sin the authority of St. Paul is sometimes cited; and rules are laid down for crimes which have a partly civil aspect, such as perjury and theft. In some cases distinctions are made between the desire to commit a sin and the actual accomplishment of the act; and again in others the list of the seven (or eight) deadly sins, which, as I showed above, turn rather upon the state of a man's mind than the character of his act, forms the principle of division of the various classes of sins. But whatever be the form or principle of classification and the attitude maintained towards social life, there is no question as to the view adopted of sin; it is a taint which excludes from the fellowship of the Church until, by endurance of hardship and pain, the restored purity of the man's will has been tested and approved. The penalties were meant to appeal to and strengthen the spiritual nature, and restore it to a healthy tone.

The existence of this copious literature, with its many indications of its practical usefulness, proves that the Church had really taken in hand, and really in part succeeded in, the task of coercing and civilizing the rough wills of those rude peoples. The copiousness and elaboration of the books is in itself an evidence of the difficulty of the problem. The more orderly people of Greece and Italy are more easily guided by the isolated decisions of Councils or of Popes: but the case of the northern peoples required a systematic use of stern discipline, and it was this which the Penitentials aimed at supplying. The Church was a social as well as a spiritual force, and amidst all the confusion that reigned in those days it may well have seemed to be the only body which gave hope of real stability. It was natural enough, therefore, that a king like Charles the Great, who was bent on bringing order out of chaos, should welcome the alliance of the Church and use the sanction of his political power to enforce its decisions and spread its ideas.

For the Church such an alliance involved considerable risk. There is a certain irrelevance in the application of legal penalties to spiritual misdemeanours; and even the use by the State of the already existing sanctions of the Church in the interests of social order brings with it the danger that the Church may learn to rest on social forces, or tend to allow merely political and popular moral standards to govern it. And surely to yield to either of these temptations is a vast mistake. The Church, we have insisted, looks at the spiritual side of things, and at this only. Sin is a spiritual breach of spiritual unity, and its treatment must be wholly spiritual. The fact that sin also affects the comfort or well-being of men in their social life is not, for the Church, the primary count against it. Impurity, murder, drunkenness, are all of them things which make against social order, and any ruler who has the welfare of his people at heart must wish to crush them. But whatever the view which the legal ruler takes of them, the attitude of the Church is unchanged. It is not necessarily satisfied if a culprit has paid the penalty which the law demands; that does not in itself fit a man to receive absolution and be admitted to communion. Still less can the Church engage to punish only crimes which the law recognizes as such, or to allow social rank to excuse or mitigate, as it so often does in civil life, the commission of acts which are condemned in men of low estate. But the closer the alliance between the Church and the State-power, the nearer lies the danger of confusion on this point, and the more necessary is jealous watchfulness against it.

This danger was far from being imaginary in the times of which I have been speaking. Cases would necessarily arise in which a legal penalty would be imposed as well as spiritual censure or penance. And it might seem impossible to avoid taking this fact into consideration. So, for instance, in Theodore's *Penitential* it is enacted that a person who has committed a murder, but has voluntarily paid blood-money to the relations, may have his ecclesiastical penalty mitigated. As it stands, this does not involve a departure from the true spiritual attitude of the Church. The readiness to pay, when it goes with a voluntary confession of the fault, may be taken, and reasonably taken, as a sign of reality of penitence, which was precisely the point which the spiritual penance was intended to test. But the practice of thus commuting penance was fruitful of perilous consequences. Though this was almost the only case allowed by Theodore, and though the practice was altogether uncommon in England, it became, especially in the Frankish Church, a means of evading the discipline of the Church altogether. Men who were wealthy paid other persons to perform their penances, or satisfied the demands of the law by some perfectly external and valueless act. This was a real departure from the true functions of the Church, flowing from the adoption of a principle which may work perfectly well in secular courts. The State may find it sufficient to give the wrong-doer an option in regard to his penalty. But the Church has to do with the spiritual aspect of things: it aims at producing a spiritual tone of mind and character, not merely at producing due balance among the contending claims of men. Commutation, therefore, is likely to counteract the purposes of Church discipline. It should be noticed, however, that the system of commutation was not invented by the Church, but was adopted when political influences had begun to affect its proceedings. The old and more strictly ecclesiastical point of view was never wholly lost. From the position of the Church, the theological and cardinal virtues, the seven deadly sins, interpreted in the sense which St. Augustine had done so much to determine, were the dominant factors in the moral theory of the Church. Even so late as Archbishop Peckham they are all set down in one of his ordinances as the proper subjects for the instruction of parishioners by parish priests; and I need only mention the use of them by Chaucer, William Langland, and the Schoolmen right on to the time of the Reformation.

With the Reformation there comes a change, and a change which, for our purpose, is one of very serious importance. It raises a grave question as to the validity of the whole position here adopted. It has been argued that the one basis of Christian morality has been the new life bestowed in Christ: that the presence of this, and of this alone, saves men from the failures which beset moral efforts of ancient times, and makes real moral achievement possible. Further, it has been mentioned that the forms of expression which were seized upon by the moral consciousness of the Church, drew their peculiar character from their relation to Christian theology. The scheme of moral ideas, in fact, was in principle and essence the practical expression of theological ideas underlying it. Hence, though it is not necessary to insist upon reducing all moral life under the scheme of seven virtues and seven sins, yet the theological principle which dictated the selection of these virtues and sins, and decided the particular character ascribed to them, is essential to all Christian moral teaching as such. Moreover, it has been argued on the basis of the actual history of the early Middle Age that the principle in question was effectual in practice, so that it is to its presence that we owe it in an especial degree that order emerged out of chaos in Northern Europe. But, as I have said, a serious problem is raised by the Reformation. For, from that date, there has tended to grow up a gulf of separation between the doctrine of the Church and morality. It is customary to regard it as almost a paradox that the creed should be in any way necessary or advantageous to high moral life. Not only have the particular forms of Mediaeval and Patristic ethical theory disappeared, but the principle which, as I have maintained, underlay them has also gone out of fashion. The Pauline habit of enforcing a moral precept by reference to a strictly theological consideration, which I do not think would have seemed strange in former days, has come to look strange now. Christianity is very widely regarded as being merely a name for a particular type of moral practice, to which doctrine is simply an irrelevant appendage. While I cannot but think that such a theory as this is only tenable on the assumption that Christianity began abruptly with the Reformation, I am no less certain that the fact of this divergence does require explanation, the more especially as the theological Reformation was accompanied by a strong movement in the direction of a strenuous and wholehearted yearning for good. It will be necessary therefore to inquire into the cause of a divergence which the beginnings of the Reformation seem so very slightly to suggest, but which most certainly has resulted; and which, if notorious in England, is still more so in Germany, the other country in which the principles of the Reformation have had their fullest freedom.

The Reformation is the name for a variety of changes, both religious and secular, of which it is peculiarly difficult to describe the causes and the effects. The remoter causes lie far back in a period which few people study—the Dark Age, it is called: the nearer causes are still capable of exciting violent party passions, and, though it is possible to indicate some of the effects, the full results are still to come. In spite of the difficulty, however, an effort must be made.

It is probable that the causes which lie furthest back and were productive of the most permanent effects were political. Not that the Reformation itself when it came was primarily or wholly a political movement: but still it was the political shaping of things in the past which gave occasion to much of the religious controversy. Much of the corruption which led to the great revolt came from the political power claimed and enjoyed by the Church. And this, as I have already implied, arose out of a particular response made by the Church to a very definite call. Europe was in confusion. A struggling crowd of various interests was in violent conflict. And the Church was the one power that transcended them all. The Church was neither Frankish nor Celtic, Saxon nor Spanish. It was everywhere, and was everywhere the same. It had been engaged in its own way for centuries in pressing the claims of the moral law and sustaining a high ideal. The work it was already engaged in was civilizing, orderly, and social; the successes it had won had all told in these directions, in humanizing war, in rousing a sense of responsibility for all human action, in curbing passion. And hence its value, to any one who attempted work of this kind from the civil side, was that it removed him, or tended to remove him, from the narrow issues of tribal emulation. Alliance with the Church gave such a ruler a kind of universal authority, a significance outside his own immediate area, a power of unifying contending elements, amidst the strife of which he would otherwise be lost. The old prescriptive prerogative of universal sovereignty belonging to the Roman Empire could never have been revived if it had not been for the actual universality of the Church. In the Church there stood before men's eyes a concrete embodiment of a universal power, a society which was not afraid of stern discipline, and wielded spiritual powers which were valid beyond the horizon of this world. It had every quality which marked it out as the body to which a ruler with great ideas would appeal. It is difficult to conceive how the civilization of Europe could have been achieved if the Church had declined to listen to the appeal [1].

Out of these conditions the theory of the Holy Roman Empire was developed, the universal earthly sovereign and the universal spiritual ruler. But the great call was too great for the men through whom the Church's response was made. The experience of power, the practice in ruling, the inspiring sense of great chances and great capacities in the better men, the lust of worldly success and influence in the worse, brought about corruption of the grossest kind in the Church itself. The growing concentration of the authorities of the Church upon politics, their jealousy of all attempts on the part of the State to perform its proper functions, their readiness and even anxiety to take secular employments and privileges to themselves, materialized and demoralized them, as such things must always do. Forgetting the high and spiritual mission of the Church, which alone had justified its summons to help in the organization of society, Churchmen entered eagerly into the struggle for merely material interests. And it was this that produced the spectacle of a corrupt, unspiritual, inactive Church—the result, far from inevitable, of the misuse of an inevitable call.

The corruption took various forms in various con-

---

[1] Cf. Bryce, *Holy Roman Empire*, chs. vii, xv, xviii; Stubbs, *Lectures on Mediaeval and Modern History*, pp. 214 seqq.

nexions. For the neglect of spiritual things avenges itself in many forms and in many ways. In the first place, it opened the door to positive immorality. The spiritual world occupied less space in the horizon; for the restraining force of holy things dwindles as they are less exclusively pursued, with less single-hearted devotion. Doctrines and expedients were developed to mitigate the severity of the conflict between the Church and the world—a conflict the sharpness of which the close alliance of the world made it desirable to limit. It is not that the methods still professed by the Church in public had grown old or obsolescent, but simply that they were no longer set in motion, no longer treated seriously, but used only professionally, and evaded wherever an opportunity offered. And secondly, as worldly advancement became the object of the lives of many Churchmen, there was hardly time to look after the unremunerative poor. To treat them as of equal importance with the rich and powerful would be clear waste of time, seeing that no good result could possibly come of it: and it might be positively harmful, since it would produce, not unnaturally, irritation among those in whom the power really lay.

Further, the drift of speculation had moved in the direction of a very sharp division between reason and faith. Quite apart from definitely sceptical influences, of which there were plenty abroad, the inner movement of ecclesiastical speculation had been such as to fit in with the moral severance between profession and practice.

It must not be supposed that all this development

moved on without protest from the more spiritual members of the Church. To mention only one or two instances, St. Bernard condemned in the strongest way the absorption of the Pope in worldly cares, declaring that if he allowed himself to be so preoccupied he was fulfilling the office of Constantine and not St. Peter. Dante follows him in the same line, and bewails the fatal gift of Constantine, upon which, as was then believed, the temporal functions of the Church depended[1]. Nor were the poor forgotten. The rise of the great mediaeval orders was an attempt to reclaim for them their birthright, and it is because this is so that Grosseteste takes pains to allow the Franciscans a free entry into England. Everywhere the conscience of men was stirred by the contradiction between the immorality and self-seeking of many Churchmen and their high profession. And in many cases, notably in that of Wyclif, the assault was made not merely upon the doctrines of the Church, but upon the political order—the unchristian misuse of riches, the struggle after worldly advancement, the eclipse of all spiritual interests, and the consequent moral degradation. Thus the corruptions, even when they were moral and religious in form, ran back upon political causes. The Church, in some of its most conspicuous representatives, had shifted its centre of gravity: from this the mischief had arisen.

Once more, these various conditions of will and

[1] Bern. *De Consid.* I. ix-xi; Dante, *Inf.* xix. 115-118. Reference may also be made to the books and passages cited in Note iii to this lecture (pp. 344, 345).

mind explain the ravages made among the higher orders of Churchmen by Humanism. It was not merely because Cicero wrote better Latin than St. Thomas Aquinas, or because the Greek sense of beauty came as a revelation to the age which re-discovered it. Something there was, no doubt, in the charm of novelty and change, but not enough to account for all. The faith that had overcome the pagan spirit in the early centuries of the Christian era was not really overcome by it in the fifteenth. The truth was that the spirit against which the Church had originally contended had found its way within the circle of the Church, so that when the old literature which contained it was brought back from the grave, it was greeted and welcomed as a friend. It attracted and secured those who had sunk under the temptations of the world and sold their souls to it already. It relaxed the strain of moral obligation and made the worldly life easier; gave a cultured and polished justification to the neglect of the strict code of Christian life, which the exigencies of political self-seeking had already made desirable.

It was natural that the moral results of the false policy of the leaders of the Church should arouse the conscience of men to a revolt, and this moral repulsion from organized and flourishing hypocrisy was one of the most prominent causes of the Reformation. But there was also a distinctly political cause which we must consider shortly here. When the Church undertook the task of promoting social order it had to deal with a number of tribes, who, if not savage purely and simply, had no sense of national life. They fought and struggled rather as tribes than as nations. And the value of the work of the Church and Empire lay in the fact that, within this inclusive unity, there was room for development and for the growth of the sentiment of nationality. This sentiment had grown up in the intervening years, and the claim of the Roman Church to political supremacy was therefore an anachronism. The Empire had already been reduced to the limits of Germany, and it was thus openly declared that the old political idea was out of date, but the peculiar spiritual character of the ecclesiastical claim made its failure to correspond with the new order less glaring. The Roman bishop went on demanding that which was obviously convenient for him, but which the beneficent action of his predecessors had helped to make impossible. The rule of Rome had educated men to the point of dispensing with itself. It may be doubted whether the Church of Rome has ever really learnt the lesson of recognizing national feelings and peculiarities. With steady and relentless pertinacity, as it seems from the outside, it deliberately and as a matter of policy enforces Roman practices and ideas, so that everywhere, except in Italy, and to a certain extent even there, it runs the risk of looking like a foreign Church. It tends to impose itself upon national sentiments rather than encourage these into a free and yet Christian development, and in so doing it departs from that policy of the ancient Church, which prevailed before political influences had led it astray.

In all this there was ground enough for anticipating a change, the more especially when to these various sources of dissension were added dogmatic difficulties. It may be doubted, however, whether these last would have been sufficient by themselves to produce so tremendous a convulsion. If it had not been that they were imposed upon men by persons who claimed also the right to interfere politically, it is hard to see why they should not have been settled, like so many theological disputes in the past, by discussion and by reference to the ordinary common sense of the whole Church. It was the political element in them that rendered them so acute, and has helped to make the resulting differences so inexorable and permanent.

It is time now to return to the problem put before us by the Reformation, and inquire whether we can see any hope of solving it. Unless the account I have here given of the predisposing causes is wholly at fault, the Reformation is more than a reaction against immorality or theological error or authority. It is all these; but, inasmuch as the head and source of these corruptions lay in the false assumption of political supremacy, the true opposite to the position rejected lies in the profession of Christianity apart from the worldly distortions, which had done so much to discredit the whole faith of Christ in the eyes of the Christian world. The creed had to be reasserted, shorn of its erroneous interpretations; but no new creed was wanted. The truly spiritual work of the Church had to be resumed; but this was another way of saying that much of its political and temporal work had better be laid aside. The faith of Christ had to be again a reality to the individual soul, not a mere external profession, or the motive principle of a semi-political machine; but this, though it involved the assertion of individual responsibility, of the need of individual experience, and of the rights of individual reason, was not necessarily a rejection of all authority. In fact the Reformation was an effort to restore primitive belief and practice, to bring morality again within the range of Christian teaching, and to get rid of the shameful spectacle of a Christendom which was morally debased.

There was, then, no reason inherent in the Reformation movements which could suggest *a priori* a separation between morality and religion. It was in its essential features an attempt to restore the connexion which had once existed between them, which political and other causes had tended to sever, but which was necessary to the effectual existence of Christianity in the world. But since that date a divergence has occurred, and it is necessary to inquire into its character and meaning in the light of what has been already said upon the Reformation movement.

Those countries, let us notice first, which followed the old paths to a large extent escaped being more than stirred by the Reformation. It is true that the Council of Trent was a reforming Council, and ordained the alteration of many abuses by which much scandal had been caused. But it did not penetrate to the heart of the false position in which the Church was placed. It condemned, for instance, the sale of indulgences, and limited their use; it passed canons concerning the residence of dignitaries and the more careful regulation of the morals of the clergy; but it did not succeed in bringing the Christian faith more closely into relation with the ordinary life of the layman, and it left the claims of the Church in regard to secular authority as they had been before. It improved certain details, but it left the causes of corruption as they were.

On the other hand, in those countries which gave in their adhesion to the changes, a renewed power of moral achievement seemed to have arisen. Christ was very near to men's souls. They had a personal conviction of salvation: they felt that the power of sin in them was broken. But the Reformation was more than a process of change; it was also a revolution. And its revolutionary elements limited and have partly counteracted its better effects. A revolution tends to produce exaggerations; and it was the exaggerations of the revolt against Rome that have seriously affected the work of the Reformers.

I. It was right and necessary to revolt against wrongful authority. The Church in its later mediaeval form had usurped functions to which it had no right, but in raising the cry of freedom the whole conception of authority came into danger. It is clear from many indications that the greater Reformers—even on the Continent, where a much more drastic view prevailed than in England—had no intention of abolishing the principle of authority altogether. They appealed not only to the Bible, but also to the authority of the Church. Thus the Augsburg Confession cites the Council of Nicea in support of the doctrine of the Holy Trinity. There was no question but that the wilder forms of fanatical revolution were to be suppressed. Anabaptists and such disorderly sectarians were dealt with, after the manner of the times, by the formulation of articles and by legal pains and penalties. Yet the fact remained that the most imposing system of Church authority had been assailed and its claims rejected, and it was excusable, even if it were wrong, to infer from this that the principle of authority was at an end. It seemed to follow, though as a matter of fact it does not follow, that because the Church has no right to determine directly any questions of ordinary policy, it has therefore no right to determine, and determine decisively, what is and what is not of faith, what does and what does not constitute a breach of unity.

II. It was right to reassert the position of the individual in the Church. Through the changes which had come in course of time, the organization had more and more completely excluded the individual. From being the natural and necessary visible expression of the unity of all Christian men in Christ, the Church had tended to become a barrier between Christ and the soul. Just as language, which is the necessary means of interchange between a man and his fellow, may act first as a summary of thought, then as a substitute for it, and finally as a positive hindrance to it. Thus it was necessary to call attention again to the essential rights of the individual within the outward order. But it was an exaggeration of this truth to infer from it that a man's religion is his own affair, and that there is no need for him to stand in relation with any outward body at all. From the fact that religion is more than a process carried on by some ordained minister independently of the individual, it does not follow that the whole prerogatives of the Church of Christ are in every man's hands by natural right, for him to use them or not, just as he likes. Pure individualism is not essential to a true Christianity; it was not necessary as an answer to the exaggerated Roman claims; it is a principle of revolution and anarchy, not of reformation.

III. Throughout the Middle Age the state-life of the European nations was somewhat in abeyance. The clergy held the highest offices in the State and in large measure controlled public policy. It was right and necessary that this should come to an end, and that the exclusive claims of ecclesiastics should disappear. It was right that, from the point of view of the State and its life, they should take their place as ordinary citizens, with the same right as any one else to an opinion, but no more. But this truth is distorted into an error if it ends in the substitution of the State for the Church as the true home and the natural sphere of action of the human spirit. For that is to return to paganism: to concentrate the attention of men upon the transitory and material, and leave the unseen world to the taste and speculative powers of particular individuals. Socially a man lives in a state and interests himself in its fortunes and its policy.

Without such an area to move in his powers are only partly in operation. But unless his spiritual nature is a mere accident, it requires, with no less insistence than any other part or power, its proper atmosphere and food. Without these the man's life is not complete: it is not converging upon a single end. And religion can only be supreme. It cannot be subordinated to the political society. For this deals only with man's life here on earth; his connexion with it is hopelessly and irretrievably broken the moment that he dies. His works live on for good or evil, but he does not; even though some few out of the whole population of one generation may attain what in this life we loosely call immortality.

All these three exaggerations were unnecessary to the truth of the Reformation, and were unfortunate; but they occurred. And it is easy to see how closely they are connected with one another. If there is no authority anywhere in matters of religion the individual conscience or the individual taste must necessarily be the only determining power in this region. If that is so, the functions of the Church as a society disappear; it is an accidental aggregation of loose atoms, joined and separated at will. And if the functions of the religious society disappear, the political environment is all that is left for man's social life. The mischief is done as soon as ever the religious life of the individual is withdrawn from all social associations and centred within himself. For then an antagonism arises in his life. His ordinary political life, with the morality which the existence of a community demands, occupies, so to speak, one-half of him; and the other—a secret, withdrawn, externally ineffective part—is reserved for the operation of religion. The external ordinary moral life of the man tends to be separated from his religion. This result, though (as it seems to me) it is logically inevitable, is, like many other logical results, frequently delayed, and in some individual cases suspended.

Individuals, to speak of them first, are not all required to take a complete survey of the position in which they find themselves. In times of crisis like that of the Reformation their course of action is governed by some one definite and strong conviction. As Luther was led by his strong condemnation of the scandal of indulgences to make an assault upon the system which sheltered the practice, so others are moved in a similar way to take decisive action. It may cause serious disturbance in the world, as Luther's action did, or it may be merely the choice of one whose mission is to follow where others lead. But however this may be, the action taken never stands alone. For the individual at any rate it means a new departure. He acts in the light of his previous history, with the character that his history has produced in him, of which some part is, and some is not, profoundly affected by the decision taken. In some regions of his being life will move altogether on new lines; in others, even if in strict logic these also ought to be influenced, life will go on very much as before. The Reformation was ostensibly an attempt to restore the connexion between morality and religion, and was at first successful in so doing: it might have continued to succeed, provided that the tendency of certain principles which came to light with it were not yet manifested. Even when the perilous principles have been asserted and have already begun to produce their effect, men still in individual cases connect their religion and their morality. But the connexion is an accidental one, springing rather from habit than from the reason of the case. A man connects morality with religion upon the ground of some positive precepts of Christ: and this, compared with what Christianity will do for life at the best, is a relapse upon the position of the Law. Or he is moved by the example of Christ's life and strives to follow it: here too we have the presence of an external ideal working from without upon the will. Or, and this is the highest case under this category, a man may believe that his sins are washed away in the blood of Jesus; he may see in the Resurrection an analogue to a moral change in himself: but this belief in past facts, as past and standing alone, though it inspires, falls short of the power and width of appeal that lies in the presentation of the risen Life of Christ in the visible society, and the display of all moral activities under this consecration. Religion, on the basis of pure individualism, is not naturally and cannot be the supreme motive and the synthetic force which binds together and makes rational all the various elements of life.

The effects of individualism have thus been delayed in the case of individuals; they are delayed also, especially in England, on a larger scale and by a more permanent cause. In England the Church has occupied a very peculiar relation to the State. It has never yet been reduced to the position of one sect among many; it has always had a stronger claim than individual taste and preference. It has been the official spokesman of the State on all religious questions; its creed and order have been the rule in all parishes; its services have been at the disposal of all men, so far as this is consistent with definite principles of creed and order. There has been loss as well as gain in this arrangement. Issues that are really distinct have been confused, and it is sometimes difficult to see how they can ever be cleared up. For various reasons, into which I need not enter, the ideal has not been adequately maintained. But it has been there; and it is the old ideal which has dwelt in the Catholic Church through the ages which preceded Charles the Great—the ideal of a life over which at all times and in all relations the faith of Christ has its legitimate influence. The reformed English Church has never dealt so systematically as the Church of the Middle Ages with moral questions; but its moral decisions, where they have been expressed, are essentially the same. We are accustomed to the modern state of things in which the separation of religion from morality has taken place, and we forget, therefore, that moral theology did not cease in England at the time of the Reformation, but was studied and formed the subject of books till after the Restoration. It was in the dead period intervening that the separation was effected, when men forgot to care for the creed they professed, and reduced Christianity to the dull mechanical performance of uninspiring and ordinary routine. The separation of morality and religion has occurred to a very serious extent, but the means of restoring unity to life are, as I hope to show in the next Lecture, still in the hands of the Church: and so long as it retains its present position, the worst result of separation can always be forestalled by vigorous and faithful efforts of Churchmen to practise what they preach, by simply using the powers and giving open expression to the ideas already in their possession. But, as things are, it is often difficult to see how we shall avoid the existence of two moral ideals in one State, the higher and more exacting one professed by the members of Christ's Church, a lower one ruled by the fluctuating utterances of the popular voice. The whole State is, in name, governed by the Christian conception of virtue; but there are signs in more than one quarter that some portions of the Christian code, e. g. the marriage-law, are found irksome, and are denounced as wrong because they are irksome. Were this due merely to the presence of unbelievers there would be less cause to fear it; there is danger if some who profess the faith dissociate it from the ordinary social and moral life. It is the State that would suffer most from the existence of two standards. It rests with Churchmen to make the nation's nominal adoption of the Christian code a reality.

Thus, as things are, it seems as if the worst effect of the separation of the faith from the external moral life of man—the presence of two conflicting codes—is still suspended, and may, we trust, be altogether averted.

But there are many signs that not all the other evils of it have been counteracted. I will mention, in conclusion, two of them which fall in most naturally with the course of my subject.

(1) Moral philosophy has largely ceased to be definitely Christian. It has gone back upon Greek models. The old questions which the Greeks found incapable of definitive solution are with us again: Is virtue knowledge? Is virtue pleasure? The existence of Christianity so long in the world has not, of course, gone quite for nothing; there is a disposition to maintain that virtue may be neither of these things, but rather self-sacrifice that looks for no reward. But for all that we have relapsed upon the pagan mood; the State, and not the kingdom of God visible and invisible, is for modern thinkers the area of moral life; religion, though it is recognized by all as a persistent fact which has to be reckoned with, is no longer an essential element in the whole life of man, and that element which enables us to present him in relation to his environment in its truest and widest sense; it is, for the most part, left to the individual to profess or not, as he pleases, a thing of which one can only speak generally and by the use of highly abstract terms.

(2) The separation seriously limits the good that we actually do: morality itself becomes affected by individual preferences. The various sects, as they are based upon some preferential selection out of the whole body of Catholic truth, are apt to develop some peculiar corresponding character, representing the intense prevalence in the mind of some over-

mastering idea. The general relation of religion to life has been lost; but the surviving impression that such a relation ought to exist gives force to the doctrine intensely held, and leaves the others ineffectual, though they are often formally retained. Or again, men forget that religion should correspond with all life and govern all its relations, and find in it instead simply a confirmation of their own moral hobby. It is a convenient controversial instrument in such cases, and, no doubt, also a positive practical help. In the last century, for instance, the moral danger which seems to have been most feared was enthusiasm. And Christianity was accordingly commended because it was not based on enthusiasm, the Apostles because they were not enthusiastic men, the Church because it preached a comfortable doctrine that never disturbed or startled men. And is it not true that in our own day the virtue of tolerance, construed almost in the sense of indifference, and that of temperance, narrowly confined to one particular region, are often treated as if they were synonymous with Christianity and everything else were irrelevant to it? It is right to preach temperance, for no drunkard has a part in the kingdom of God: right to denounce intolerance, for it is an insult to the gentle example of Christ our Lord. It is right to be on guard against ill-regulated fervour of emotion, for God is not the cause of disorder. There is moral beauty in the stern severity of a Covenanter or a Calvinist. But it is a sad falling short from the ideal of Christian manhood if these, and such things as these, virtuous though they are, are put in its place.

They can never be substituted for it unless the supreme claim of Christianity over all man's life has been forgotten, and with it has departed that unity and system which only the Incarnate Word of God has power to convey.

NOTES TO LECTURE VII.

I.

THE social effect of monasticism is frequently estimated from the point of view of its decadence and failure. Its ruinous consequences, its inherent liability to give countenance to hypocrisy, the positive scandals which arose in connexion with it, have received such ample attention as to exonerate me from the necessity of doing more than allude to them. The purpose of the present note is simply to call attention to the presence at different periods of limits to the general impulse towards monasticism. It is a further question, too wide for the present work, whether human nature is strong enough to endure the practice of monasticism on a large scale, and, at the same time, secure freedom from the dangers which surround it.

The ascetic ideal of life found place in Christianity from the earliest days. As we have already seen, there were writers in the Church who laid down the strictest rules against all possible dealings with worldly life. The existence of this state of mind is largely accounted for by the presence of heathendom and the necessity of keeping Church-life secure from its influences. It is however easy to show, by reference to Canons and other evidence of various kinds, that this severity was not acceptable on all terms. If it proceeds from a general disdain of all material being, it is severely condemned[1]. It was then clearly understood that asceticism, if it was to be tolerated, must proceed from one set of motives, and these only. In the same way, writers whose whole interest

[1] See *Apost. Can.* 51; *Syn. Gangr. Can.* 21. εἴ τις ἐπίσκοπος ... γαμῶν καὶ κρεῶς καὶ οἴνου οὐ δι' ἄσκησιν ἀλλὰ διὰ βδελυρίαν ἀπέχεται ... ἢ διορθούσθω ἢ καθαιρείσθω, καὶ τῆς ἐκκλησίας ἀποβαλλέσθω, ὡσαύτως καὶ λαϊκός.

Notes to Lecture VII

lay on the side of ascetic profession emphasize the necessity of true vocation, and the need of care in acting upon it[1]. Even Jerome allows that all men are not equally called to the ascetic life. And so Gregory the Great[2]. We have already spoken of the attitude of Chrysostom in the *De Sacerdotio*[3]. From the Penitential literature it becomes plain that it was thought necessary in some places to enforce by ecclesiastical censures the prohibitions upon vows unwisely made. So husbands and wives were forbidden to make vows without one another's consent. This regulation appears in Theodore's *Penitential*[4], and in the two other collections bearing his name[5]. It is repeated in two Frankish Penitentials, which are obviously (according to Wasserschleben) later than, and influenced by, Theodore[6]. The principle is laid down also by St. Thomas Aquinas[7]. It reappears in the *Instructions for Parish Priests*, by John Myrc, Canon of Lilleshall. This work, which belongs to the beginning of the fifteenth century, is said to be based on earlier works covering the same ground. The priest is enjoined to preach diligently the law concerning husband and wife in relation to vows[8]. A similar restriction upon the whole life of devotion is noted in the beginning of Rolle of Hampole's work, *The Abbey of the Holy Ghost*[9].

[1] Cf. Ambr. *De Virginitate*, cc. 7 and 39; *De Virginibus*, i. 35. Augustine elaborately defends the married state: though he considers that of celibacy higher, and likely to achieve a higher point of glory. Cf. *De Bono Conj.* xi. 12, 13; *De Virg.* xxi. 21, 22.

[2] *Hom. in Evang.* II. xxxvi. [3] Cf. pp. 203, 204, above.

[4] Lib. I. xiv. 7. This is the collection of Canons which seems to have the closest connexion with Theodore. See Wasserschleben, *Die Bussordnungen der Abendländischen Kirche*, pp. 19 foll.; Haddan and Stubbs, *Councils and Ecclesiastical Documents*, vol. iii. pp. 173-175.

[5] *Can. Greg.* No. 69; Dach. 38, 39.

[6] *Poen. Martin.* §§ 65, 5; *Poen. Cummeani*, §§ 37, 38.

[7] *Summa Theol. Secunda Secundae*, 88, art. 8, 9.

[8] Cf. the introduction to the edition in the Early English Text Society series, and lines 384-400 of the poem; cf. Robert Manning of Brunne, *Handlyng Synne*, ll. 1876-1880.

[9] Edited by Horstmann, p. 321.

II. THE COMMUTATION OF PENANCE.

It is plain that this practice arose out of the exceptional value assigned by the Church to the act of almsgiving. In the time of the Didache this had proved itself a noticeable character of the Church, and its misuse had led to legislation. Cyprian wrote a work extolling the value of giving alms, and Augustine treats it as a means of putting away sin[1]. It was not therefore a difficult step from this doctrine to the practice of pecuniary commutation of penance.

A further reason for the development of the practice may be found in the extreme severity of the ancient laws of the Church. The penances imposed, especially on the graver sins, were found practically impossible[2]. The method of commutation provided a way of escape from this difficulty. The priest or the bishop who administered the penitential system would have the right of modifying the penalty within certain limits, and, in later days, would be expected to adjust it to the character of the individual penitent; but the other plan, by which a person could pay his liabilities in full, though in another kind, was naturally an attractive one.

Clearly a system like this would be precarious from the first, and would depend upon the most relentless sincerity of application to keep it free from the dangers which beset it. Theodore, as has been said in the lecture, restricted its use to one single set of cases. But the Irish and Frankish Penitentials allowed the practice to a considerable extent. In all cases it would seem that the regular tariff of exchange, so to speak, was based on practice already existing in the secular law. Efforts were made from time to time to provide against abuses of the system. A strong protest was made against the misuse of commutation in the Synod of Cloveshoo, A.D. 747[3].

---

[1] Cyprian, *De Opere et Eleemosynis*; Aug. *Ench.* lxx and elsewhere.

[2] Cf. Balsamo's *Comm. on Basil*, Ep. Can. ad Amph. Can. xiii.

[3] Haddan and Stubbs, *Councils*, &c., vol. iii. pp. 371-3; cf. Wasserschleben, *Bussordnungen*, p. 50.

Notes to Lecture VII 343

In the *Penitential* of Bede[1] the ninth chapter deals with the question. The penalties are named for various crimes, and they are to be imposed in all cases, 'si pauper aut dives, si liber aut servus, si iuvenis aut adulescens, si minus sapiens aut gnarus, si clericus aut monachus, si in gradu vel sine gradu.' The *Penitential* itself notices differences in age and responsibility, and in the chapter here cited the priest is recommended to use discretion in the administration of his office, for the good of his own soul and that of those to whom he ministers[2].

The tendency to make penitence easier for the rich, which the principle of commutation permits, and which is faintly recognized in the chapter from Bede's *Penitential*, was too strong to be met by protests. It took the form at length of hiring persons to do the penance: thus the idea of almsgiving disappeared, and that of the exchange of one external performance for another alone remained. This is expressly justified in the following passage[3] from the *Penitential* of Edgar: 'Haec est potentis viri et amicorum divitis paenitentiae allevatio. Sed non datur pauperibus sic procedere, sed debet in se ipso illud requirere diligentius. Et hoc est etiam aequissimum, ut quilibet propria sua delicta diligenti correctione ulciscatur in se ipso. Scriptum est enim. Quia unusquisque onus suum portabit.'

It is easy to understand how the extension of the plan of money commutation to purgatorial penalties might produce startling moral results.

---

[1] 'The only work of the kind appearing under the name of *Bede* of which the authenticity can be maintained with any probability.'—Haddan and Stubbs, p. 326. But cf: *Baed. Opp. Hist*: ed. Plummer, vol. I. p. clvi.

[2] This chapter is followed by a list of alternatives allowable for certain penalties. Wasserschleben regards it as spurious: and Haddan and Stubbs remark that 'the nature of the contents of the added portion suggests a like conclusion' (p. 333).

[3] Quoted by Wasserschleben, p. 51.

III.

The view taken in the Lectures of the mediaeval Church is not intended to suggest that it in any way attained to the true ideal of a Church. Nor is it based on the principle that there must be a soul of goodness in things evil. It is maintained that, together with the corruptions which impressed the mind of Langland so grimly, there was a real Church-life going on, and that there were real efforts made to save the souls of men. If it had not been so, it is inconceivable that any serious persons would have defended the Church when it came to be attacked. The truth of this position is supported by the large number of works on the subject of moral life which belong to the later Middle Age. The Schoolmen, of course, treat the question from the point of view of theory. But besides their work there is also a great number of books of a purely practical kind dealing with the problems of life. Examples of these would be found in the following: Bonaventura's *Diaeta Salutis*; Robert Manning of Brunne's *Handlyng Synne*; Dan Michel's *Ayenbite of Inwyt*; *The Book of Penance*, published with the *Cursor Mundi* by the Early English Text Society; or, again, the *Homilies* of Richard Rolle of Hampole, and other such works. Besides these, there is a variety of works entitled *Summa de Vitiis*, or *De Virtutibus et Vitiis*, such as those by Peraldus or Guillermus of Paris, Vincentius of Beauvais, the *Speculum Spiritualium*, *Destructorium Vitiorum*, &c. It would be a matter of interest, though of very considerable labour, to produce a complete bibliography of this moral theology. It would seem that there was a large demand for such works, and that the doctrine contained in them was more or less traditional. The same scheme of virtues and vices, for the most part, appears in all: the ancient authorities are used in much the

Notes to Lecture VII

same way, and, as a rule, the order of treatment is the same.

But the most striking fact about this literature, so far as I have been able to study it, is the tone of simple and direct piety which pervades a large portion of it. There are, of course, in some of the Homilies and Prayers, expressions which imply doctrines now rejected in England. The saints, and especially the Blessed Virgin, are invoked, and their activity is assumed as an aid to religious life. But, for the most part, it would be hard for the most captious of critics to find fault with the theological position adopted in these writings. There is an air of deep seriousness about them: the eternal issues involved in human life are continually set forth; and there is the most evangelical assertion of the unique value of the Sacrifice of Christ, to redeem men from sin, and to strengthen them for virtue. We do not find here the morbid dwelling upon outrageous sins in endless variety, which characterizes some of the later Penitentials and some modern books of moral theology; the frailties of men are touched firmly and gently, often with considerable humour and subtlety of observation. In short, the general impression produced by such a book as the *Ayenbite of Inwyt*, or Myrc's *Instructions for Parish Priests*, is that of a clergyman doing unpretentiously the work that he finds to his hand. It may have been that the priest who neglected his parish and went to London to seek his fortune, whom Langland condemns so severely, was the rule rather than the exception; but it is difficult to believe that the exceptions were not more numerous than is often supposed.

LECTURE VIII.

'Whatsoever is not of faith, is sin.'—ROM. xiv. 23.

CHRISTIANITY makes a complete and supreme claim over the whole life of man throughout all ages. It claims to rule and test every movement of his will. There is no act which is so elementary and seemingly indifferent to religion, that it cannot be brought within the purview of the Christian moral ideal. This fact, which is continually asserted in the New Testament, is explicable if the essential character of Christianity is the introduction of a new life, and not otherwise. Had Christ come promulgating a law or offering a philosophy, the immediate bearing of His teaching must have been limited by the circumstances of His own actual life. It would have been idle and unending to attempt to forecast all the conditions to which His teaching would come to be applied. He would have dealt with the problems of His own age, and given commands which the occasions arising in His life required of Him: and then He must have trusted to others to perceive the principle of His ruling and apply it to events not originally contemplated by it. As in the case of the old Law, a system of casuistry would have been required to make the words of Christ applicable to new cases as they arose. The world would have changed, though the Law did not, and would have made constantly changing demands upon the Law for guidance. If we can imagine ourselves in the position of being bound to live by the old Law, we shall understand the difficulty that would have arisen. Granted that the whole ceremonial section were thrown over, yet even in the more strictly moral or political parts we should have much ado to adjust the rules to life. How, for instance, could the rules relating to usury be tolerated under the conditions of modern trade? And if the Law rested upon a divine sanction, how would it be possible to venture upon its revision in any particular? There is no power of sufficient authority to revise it. Coming from God it can only be regarded by man from beneath. He would never know the secret principle which determined the relation of its parts: there would be a perpetual fear that by altering some detail which seemed to have grown old, a more serious loosening of bonds would be effected than was in contemplation. Casuistry, as the example of the Pharisees shows, has its dangers. If we assume, and I think we fairly may, that the origin of the Pharisaical casuistry lay in the binding necessity of making the Law applicable to the course of human life, still this method of interpretation is a double-edged weapon: it lends itself easily to the eminently human desire to evade rather than to apply the Law. But the risk of casuistical evasions must be run by any one who seriously proposes to lay down a written code.

Something of this sort must have occurred inevitably if Christ had come merely promulgating a law or system of philosophy: and I may remark in passing that the casuistical problems to which Christianity gives rise always appear in connexion with the most legal parts of Christ's work—conspicuously, therefore, in connexion with the Sermon on the Mount. In some quarters this Sermon has been taken, rather oddly as I think, to be the sum of the Christian religion. Efforts have been made in very different quarters to use it as the guide of all practical life, but with strangely disappointing results. It always has to be explained. Its sharp decisive utterances, if taken literally, would destroy the existing order; and this is felt to be impossible. Moreover, the efforts which have been made to carry out principles like those embodied in it have not lasted long or succeeded. The Apostolic community of goods has ceased by the time of St. Paul's First Epistle to the Thessalonians. The universal readiness to lend and give hospitality has produced a crop of evils by the time of the Didache. In later ages the vow of poverty actually proved remunerative, and has come into suspicion; the impulse to it and the passion for such renunciation have usually depended on an inspiration from some spiritual genius, and have died out after his death.

And yet Christianity still makes its universal claim, to govern and control the whole life of man under all circumstances and at all times. In the region of conduct it professes to be never at a loss: never to anticipate a condition of things for which it has no answer, or the appearance of a nation or an age for which it has no message. And it makes this claim boldly because it is, as I have argued, a force of life working from within, and not simply commanding, however well and wisely, from without. It does not, therefore, provide by a legislative code for circumstances yet to arise; but it places at the disposal of the Christian society and, through this, of Christian individuals, a power which will enable them to detect and desire the true course to be pursued. In this regard it appears not merely as an internal instinct, relative merely to individual action, but as an instinct which takes definite shape in the world, and is definitely embodied in a Christian society. It governs, or should govern, the whole body of Christian people dispersed throughout the whole world. As the impulse to change their home comes upon a flock of migratory birds, sways them as a body, and yet seems to live in each, so the power of the life of Christ lives, or should live, in the society as a whole, and in each and every individual Christian. The Christian idea should take shape in individual lives; and, at the same time or in the same breath, as it were, it should be embodied as a society of persons holding of necessity the same faith, and guided in action by the same principles. It should be a strong and vigorous organization, living in the midst of the world, and drawing its material life from thence, but inevitably determined in its attitude to all secular questions by the principle of life which calls it into existence and holds it together. It is not enough that here and there an individual should take a particular view of moral or social questions: that method leaves the whole practical aspect of Christianity to accident and idiosyncrasy, and is the evil under which, as I argued in the preceding lecture, we are at present labouring. What is required, what was attempted with some success in ancient days, is that the Christian body should express itself in some definite shape in regard to moral and social questions—naturally and necessarily, as an organism reveals its governing force or principle in its acts.

It will not be relevant to my purpose to discuss the question how far such a condition of things involves a particular external organization. The immediate question for us to-day is, in what way the Church of Christ is to make itself felt in the moral sphere. We saw in the last lecture how actual moral corruption, the intrusion into the Church of the forces of the world, and again the separation of the Church's activity from all immediate connexion with life, had hindered the development of the Christian type of life in the world. If we ask then, how the Christian view is again to be made effective, the answer will be in brief, that the Church idea must be quickened and the function of discipline resumed. That is, (1) the sense of unity and sympathy which follows from a conviction of membership in the Body of Christ must be renewed and strengthened. It must be confessed that there is some lack of this sense among us. The *esprit de corps* which holds classes together, and determines their likes and dislikes, has made its way into all denominations of Christians. The conception of the parish church in which rich and poor alike bow down in worship of the Father of all is rhetorically set forth at times; but it may be questioned whether the unity implied by it goes further, in many cases, than the bare accident of being under one roof occasionally. It certainly does not always carry with it more friendly intercourse, or a sense of a common cause, still less a sense of spiritual oneness. And on the other hand, it may be questioned whether the stronger social sense which prevails in some of the sects may not be partially due to the identity of feeling naturally to be found among men approximately of one class, with similar social and political aims. There is nothing in modern England which precisely corresponds to the strong sense of fellowship with all Christians as such—with 'the brethren'—which we find in ancient writings. And yet it would seem that unless this sense of Christian fellowship can be restored, quite independently of mere politics or class feeling, there will be a considerable obstacle in the way of the Church's progress. The Church of Christ will not make itself felt as a force moulding society and leading it in its moral perceptions, unless its members are filled with the zeal of persons who have one object at heart, and therefore work together without any hindrance from merely secular considerations. To a certain extent the exigencies of party warfare in politics show how this may be possible. For electioneering purposes the barriers of social distinction are to a certain extent broken down; and surely that which is possible temporarily for such a purpose as this, might be more conspicuous, at least as an ideal, within the Christian Church. Such a change would certainly give force to the work of the Church to-day. The evils of disunion among various Christian bodies are being constantly placed before our minds just now; the desire for reunion seems to be stronger and more real than ever before. But we are likely to provide obstacles to our own progress, so long as our sense of Christian fellowship is merely a vague sentiment, and not a definite and real feeling of unity in the Body of Christ.

(2) If this seems a hard saying, and I am afraid it may, it will probably be easier than the assertion that the Church must resume its function of discipline. For while the demand for an intenser feeling of Christian unity merely cuts across certain feelings, in which in our best moments we are not very confident, and which we know we cannot justify on grounds of reason, the other assails our feelings of independence, of which we believe ourselves to be justly proud. For the right of the Church to exercise discipline seems to break into the charmed circle of individual independence. The picture rises before our minds of a priest-ridden people: of men doubtful and hesitating in action, until the verdict of the Church has indicated the course they may pursue. And all our deep-seated resentment against such pretensions is raised to its highest point. Or, perhaps, we think of the failure of such sacerdotalism as displayed in the immoral system of casuistry that has given the Society of Jesus its bad name. And we seem to be between two alternatives of which neither is satisfactory: a good system which crushes

Church Discipline

out all individual effort and initiative, and an immoral system of ethical doctrines which is no less destructive to the individual self.

Both these terrors, casuistry and sacerdotalism, are terms which cover a wide range of ideas, not all of which are of equal importance. It will be well therefore to determine, first of all, what exactly are the dangers of these two tendencies, and then to inquire how far an increased activity of discipline on the part of the Church would be likely to involve us in them.

There are two conspicuous instances of casuistry on a large scale which have generally shocked the conscience of the world and brought the whole practice into disrepute: I mean, of course, the casuistry of the Pharisees and that of the Jesuits. But the error of these lay, not in their endeavour to determine precisely the difference between right and wrong, but in the fact that they used their intellectual ingenuity to delude the conscience into sin. A plausible argument may often, perhaps I may say may usually, be made out for acts, of which the outward appearance is entirely immoral. Sometimes the excuse turns on the legitimate influence of circumstances, the agent's state of knowledge, the intensity of his temptation: accidents which are used to conceal the moral issue raised by the action. Again, there are, as the phrase is, exceptions to every rule; occasions when an universal command or prohibition seems to break down. And it is right to take all these into account. Within these limits casuistry has a legitimate range. But the moment that the power of the intellect to develop the consequences of some aspect or accident of an action is used, without due regard to the fixed issue of right and wrong, casuistry becomes immoral. In other words, the danger of casuistry, as of everything else, lies in a certain moral temper or condition which it is apt to encourage, and not in the mere casuistical discussions themselves. And the mischief, which casuistry, when wrongly used, conspicuously embodies, is present in full force whenever the intellect exercises a paralyzing or distorting influence over the will.

That the intellect has this power is beyond all doubt. The effect of its vicious action is perfectly well known and condemned under various names. It is a common charge, for instance, against the academic mind that it tends to be indecisive in action. An excess of education, it is said, devoted purely to the sharpening of the mental powers, produces an abnormal clearness of vision, and discourages that sense of proportion which is brought about by experience of the way in which things actually happen. Hence, when a decision is required, a host of contingencies start up before the active and acute mind, which lead to hesitation and compromise, and spoil the effectiveness of the action when it comes. Whereas, on the contrary, the mind that has been trained chiefly in affairs, though it is acting with far less information and with far less wide prevision of possible contingencies, is yet more likely to be effective as a general rule, though its lack of information may lead occasionally to ruinous blundering. This charge, wherever it is truly alleged, convicts the person accused of the casuistical temper—the temper in which the capacity of the intellect for abstract reflection is perverted to the paralysis of the will.

The same explanation holds good of the paradoxical effects of over-conscientiousness. There are men whose conscience seems so abnormally sensitive that it is a positive hindrance to them in dealing with their circumstances. They are alive to the most subtle indications of good and evil, and, in their anxiety to tread securely, they shrink from the venture which action often involves; and either hold back from action altogether, or delay till the chance is gone by. That the conscience should be a positive hindrance to effective action is a more complete paradox than that this should be the result of education. And indeed it is not as a rule the conscience that is in fault. It is again a case of the casuistical temper, through which the power of developing the possibilities of a situation *in abstracto* paralyzes the power of decision and action.

In these two cases the intellectual capacity of anticipation and analysis has been used, not for positively immoral ends, but simply towards the suppression of action. In the case of the Pharisees and of the Jesuits the same power was used in the interests of moral perversity, either to concentrate moral effort upon merely ceremonial acts, or with the definite object of establishing a plausible defence for the human desire to sin. It is possible that the inefficiency which is the result in one class of cases, and the immorality which is the result in the other, may ultimately be accepted by the conscience, at most with occasional protests and surprise, as its guiding rule. When this is so, a grievous moral ruin has been achieved, which may well make men shy of all casuistry whatever. But such a universal exclusion of moral analysis would, nevertheless, be an error. It would condemn indiscriminately a whole district of moral thought, and would fail after all to indicate precisely the real source of the wrong. This lies, as I have argued, in the presence of a particular temper, in a particular distortion of the relations which should subsist between the various capacities or elements which produce the moral action of man.

As this is true of casuistry, so it is also true of sacerdotalism. What we have to fear in this regard is not a series of overt acts of a particular kind, but the presence of a particular temper in a certain class of Churchmen. The evils of sacerdotalism arise whenever the laity and the priesthood are separated in idea and in the conception of the Christian life. For then the priesthood becomes the representative of a point of view which lay brethren disclaim. At the best, their moral demands seem excessive; at the worst, domineering and offensive. It is easy for either party to misunderstand the other: for the one to suspect, and the other to make exaggerated pretensions. And to this may be added, of course, the effect of personal disposition, and the survival of the ancient conception of a mysterious intermediary between a distant unapproachable God and mankind; these will appear from time to time within the Christian Church. But apart from the personal characteristics of individuals, the originating cause of this development is the separation of two elements in the Church in ideal and in practice. So long as the unity of the whole Christian body is retained as a guiding principle, the differentiation of functions, however elaborately carried out, will not produce the dangerous separation of the necessary elements in the Church. It will not matter that certain functions of the whole body are performed only and always by commission, provided the implication is not allowed that this commission separates those who hold it by a distinction in kind from those whose vocation lies in other lines. It will not matter if it be maintained that Ordination conveys an indelible character, provided this is not construed in a quasi-magical sense, as excluding all unordained men from the union with God in Christ, which is the essence of the Christian character.

It is obvious that this bad result may be produced equally from either side. It may be, and it has been, brought about by the superstitious misconstruction on the part of the priesthood of the significance of their Ordination. They have dealt with the laity as being hardly Christian in the same sense as themselves. They have used the powers which they undoubtedly possess in their own material interest or to promote their advancement in secular power. They have failed to keep alive the responsibility which is on all Christians alike to forward the work of Christ, and have acquiesced in the surrender by the laity of many of the functions which they are specially qualified to perform.

But there is another side to the picture. From various causes the laity have allowed themselves to become largely secularized. The obligations of the Creed and of the Christian moral ideal are often practically supposed to affect the clergy only. The continuous presence of the spiritual order is treated as being a matter which concerns only the clergy : the need of constant communion with God is ignored ; and persons who as laymen fix for themselves a more distinctly Christian ideal are labelled ecclesiastical laymen, given to works of supererogation. From whichever side the separation comes, it is the separation which is the danger and the mischief of sacerdotalism ; for it is this which begets the spirit of exclusiveness in that class of Churchmen to whom certain functions are by the act of the whole Church extended.

So far from encouraging these unfortunate developments, the restoration of discipline in the Church is the most hopeful way of avoiding them. For the recovery of discipline should mean not the restoration of inquisitorial intrusion into affairs legitimately held private, but the reawakening of the feeling of the Church as one Body united to one Head, following one law in the strength of one Spirit. The loss of this unity of feeling has meant the loss of any definitely Christian conception of right and wrong. We most of us accept the standard of the class in which we live, and apply to life the casuistry which that standard involves. Doubtless the world has been considerably affected by the presence of Christianity ;

but it is idle to pretend that it or any part of it has been fully christianized. It accepts too many conflicting standards, concedes too much to pleasure, shrinks too naturally from pain, and, in a word, believes far too confidently in its own order to be a true guide for Christian men. But the recovery of discipline would mean that it would be a recognized fact that Christians would take a Christian view of all things which came under their cognizance. There would be a recognizable type of character displayed by Christians as such, which would be the outward manifestation of the working of the one Spirit. In the presence of moral problems they would act inevitably by Christian rules, not under compulsion, but in virtue of the Christian spirit all of them possess. If then this plan of action came to prevail in the world so that men could safely fall in with the standards all around them, so much the better for the world, it would have already become christianized. If not, still this conception of life would stand out in contrast to all others, as necessary and natural to the Church in its dealing with life, and as distinguishing the followers of Christ from all who follow other teachers.

In proportion as this Christian view of life is a direct and immediate outcome of the indwelling of the Spirit, in that proportion the casuistical temper will be discouraged. The Christian attitude towards things will not be the logical exposition of a fixed code; nor will it be guided by an elaborate analysis of moral and immoral possibilities. But it will be the inevitable practical comment of the spirit of the Church upon things as they pass. The more men trust wholly to this inward force, the more closely they will be bound together in Christian unity, the more unerringly they will be guided, the less they will be liable to deception, arising either from their own casuistical speculations or the plausible suggestions of other men. The general sense of Christendom, which is their spiritual home, will be their guide. And again, in proportion as this temper pervades the whole Church, in that proportion the danger of the separation of priesthood and laity will be reduced. There will be the less danger that the two elements in the Church will be moving on different lines: that to one will be assigned the function of following an exalted ideal, while the other needs only to avoid conspicuous failure. For each and all will be moving towards the same end in their several ways, all alike in the strength of the life which holds the Church together.

But it will be said, Is this restoration of an internal spirit in the Church rightly described as a recovery of discipline? I think it is: though the associations of the word 'discipline' are rather with its negative and severer aspects. For these primitive associations with the word belong to it not by nature, but in consequence of the evils which have arisen in the course of history. Punishment, exclusion, curtailment of freedom, are not of the essence of the idea. What is essential to it is this—that the Christian moral character should be recognized as something perfectly definite and positive, in which the lives of Christian men are to be trained. It is the mission of the Church to produce this character, and the object of all its efforts. If it were to come about that membership of the Church of Christ necessarily carried with it an obligation to pursue this course, and to strain every nerve after this ideal, that would mean that the Church had resumed its functions of discipline—that it had again undertaken the extremely complicated and difficult task of bringing men's lives into some conformity with the pattern of Christ.

This would doubtless have a negative as well as a positive bearing. If the Christian character is a positive thing, following necessarily out of the presence of the Spirit in the one Body, it will by the same necessity exclude inconsistent moral ideas and practices. Certain dispositions, acts, and beliefs will be necessarily held to be destructive of the Christian life, and must necessarily be incompatible with the continuance of Christian privileges. However large may be the liberty of free choice within the circle of the Christian society, every act of adhesion to the forces that make against Christ will be a matter for repentance and reconciliation to God. It is not necessary that this reconciliation should be formal and open, especially when the sin has not been public and notorious; but it must be real and carry with it the promise of amendment, or else the sinner is acting in regard of his fellow-Churchmen under false pretences. It may well be that a Church may trust its members with the task of dealing personally with their own failings, and straining in secret after the level of the Christian demand; but if, accepting this grave responsibility, they use in their self-judgement a standard which is lower than the best they know, if they test themselves from some purely secular standpoint, then the confidence of the Church in them will have been misplaced; they will be a drag upon the progress of the cause of Christ: by their misuse of the privilege of communion they will act as poisonous spots in the society, endangering, perhaps ruining, others as well as themselves. Such things will happen the more rarely, the more fully the spirit of the Church is alive among its members, the more successfully the discipline of the Church is carried out.

This description, short and incomplete as it is, of the meaning of the discipline of the Church is sufficient to bring clearly into view its very numerous difficulties. It may seem that to put trust in the common feeling of the Christian community is to confide in a very intangible power. But this has not always been found so in the past. It is due to this intangible common sense of Christians that the Creeds have grown into their present shape, and that the presence of the Christian Church has had its effect upon the world around it. But it is a thing of which the evidence lies in its activity. The more prevalent and effective it is, the more obvious its presence will be. But there are other far more serious difficulties than this, and I must speak of one or two of these.

It will be said, for instance, that the idea of a Church exercising discipline is entirely alien to the modern spirit. Of course, the old universal claim of the priesthood to direct the moral lives of men is, in

England at least, an obsolete custom, dead beyond all hope of rising again. But, more than this, even the indirect exercise of discipline, it is argued, is justly extinct. That the Church should claim the right to exclude from its communion persons who in the exercise of private judgement have pursued certain courses of action, or persons who entertain, for reasons satisfactory to them, particular opinions, still more that it should expect such persons voluntarily to stay away, is beyond all reason, and will never be tolerated again. If it obtains here and there, among a few enthusiastic individuals, it will never be again the normal rule of any extensive Church. This point of view, I think, depends ultimately on an assumption that each individual is absolutely and solely responsible for the conduct of his life—that his proceedings have no bearing upon other men; and that, again, other men have no right to interfere or interest themselves in what he does. It may be said, no doubt, that this assumption is rarely put in such unqualified terms, and would not be accepted by many of those who revolt against the exercise by the Church of all discipline whatsoever. And there is no doubt truth in this. But it does not affect the fact that it is this assumption and this only which will explain the denial of all right on the part of the Church to control its members. The Church exists as a body of men joined together upon certain conditions with a view to certain ends, and the whole theory of it depends upon combination in this sense. It is therefore bound, as in another degree and region the State is also bound, to insist upon compliance with its fundamental principles of association. A person, therefore, who claims to belong to it, and yet resents the bearing of the general Church feeling upon his way of life, is really asserting the unmodified separateness of each individual soul; a position which is hard to sustain even in political theory, and is not consistent with a complete adhesion to the New Testament, or with the principles which emerge throughout Church history. It is only by this isolation of each individual that the right and the obligation of the Church to enforce discipline upon its members can be validly set aside.

But a yet more serious difficulty has still to be considered. It may be urged, and not without considerable show of reason, that the exercise of discipline will mean in the end a pernicious interference by Churchmen with all kinds of matters—social, political, commercial, aesthetic, and the like—with which as such they have no concern, and in regard to which they have no special capacity of judgement. If this objection could be sustained it would be fatal to the exercise by the Church of any disciplinary powers whatever. Discipline would be simply a modern instance of the interference by the Church in alien matters, which, as I showed in the last lecture, has been productive of so much disaster in the past. But as a matter of fact the objection does not lie against the process of discipline which I have been describing. Discipline should bear purely on the moral aspect of things, and deal with a situation not from the point of view of its political expediency, for instance, but as it offers an opportunity for the development of the moral character of the agent. This, which at first sight seems to restrict the Church to the individual life, is really the ground of its universal claim. It encourages to moral effort: it condemns nothing but moral error. And all the various junctures of life may offer an opportunity for moral rise or fall.

The Church, as we have noticed all along, directs life to a spiritual end, and estimates motives according to their bearing on this. It is concerned to insist that its members direct their lives to this end, and to this end only. It dwells on the temptation to prefer the readier attractions of this world to the claims of the spiritual order, and recognizes that this sinful yielding may take many forms besides those of coarse and violent sin. Hence it has nothing to say to a system of social order as such; but it insists with relentless severity upon the law of love between man and man, and the perils of selfishness. It has no concern with the possession or acquisition of wealth as such; it has no mission to denounce riches as such, or extol poverty as such. But it is bound to insist upon the truth that all property is to the Christian a trust from God, given to him as the material furniture of his passage through this world to that which is beyond. It does not aim even at separating men, except in the spiritual sense, from the movement and the society of the world, but it assures them that they enter upon all the interests of life bound by the conditions of the faith they profess. If they join in the pursuits of other men, they do so with deliberate reserves. For the world has no authority over them: its voice has no command for them. Things which it may justify, or at least allow, are not on that account sanctioned without question for any Christian man. His conscience as a Christian is the only authority to which he can bow.

The same is true of politics. The Church has no call to discuss or to promote any political programme as such. Still less are the clergy charged with the duty of pressing or denouncing any political scheme. But it is an infringement of the moral order of the Church —it is a surrender to the temptations of the world— if a man who professes Christianity places the interest of his party above that of his country, or gives his vote on whatever side for motives that are not pure. With that Christianity is concerned, and that it cannot choose but condemn. And it condemns it not merely because it affects the political atmosphere and degrades the whole tone of public affairs, but also because it is a breach of Christian order and is an act unworthy of a true follower of Christ.

So again the temptation to reject Christ may come through art and literature. Far from condemning these, the Church has continually employed them for the furtherance of its own purposes. Both literature and art have owed a vast debt to the fostering care of the Church in times past. It has been far more directly concerned with these, and from the nature of the case must continue to be so, than with the details of State policy. But both literature and art can stand alone: they may preserve the appearance of indifference to all spiritual questions, or they may claim to provide a complete and satisfying atmosphere for the human spirit. In the last case they convey the temptation to prefer this world's readier attractiveness to the exacting claims of the spiritual order. And here again the Church can speak in only one way. It must recall men continually to the one end of all their efforts; and to those who find in particular forms of art or literature a real temptation, it can only say that to yield to such a temptation is to imperil the soul, that it is a comparatively small thing to forgo some part of the attractive pleasures of literature or art, for that the whole of them are but a poor exchange to man for his soul. It passes no judgement upon literary or artistic form; but it has no choice but to condemn the use of these to obscure the purpose of the soul, and bind it to the material world.

In none of these cases has the Church any call to interfere with men's free action or enjoyment: it never aims at forcing forward a particular programme. But it is a fact most patent, one would think, to any observation but the most recklessly superficial, that there is no pursuit in this world, however dignified or intellectual, that may not serve as the barrier to separate a soul from God. It is in this way that the claim of the Church of Christ covers all the provinces of life.

If it should seem that the Christian ethical ideal is calculated to have only a slight effect upon the world, the impression will, I think, soon disappear on further reflection. Certainly, it operates indirectly; it deals with the soul of man and concerns itself only with his moral relations. But it has an immense advantage in the fact that it is guided by one idea and brings all things to one test. This leads to concentration of purpose, and avoids the dissipation of moral force, which inevitably occurs when life is only partly unified in principle. This is, of course, a gain to those whose aim is to lead the highest and best life they can; it is a loss only to those who wish to shelter their desire of self-indulgence under the variety and separation of the different interests in life. To these it comes easily to argue—and it is by no means a rare form for modern casuistry to take—that in each district of life we must be content to follow the principles that we find ruling there. So that, for instance, religion or the religious view of things, which is justified to those who approve of it in its own sphere, must give way to the principles which in politics or commerce or art are found necessary by those who professionally pursue these ends. The obvious result of such specialism is a constant condition of moral conflict, a waste of effort in the ceaseless endeavour to keep the peace among the various interests that are at war, and, at the worst, a surrender of the conscience in numberless cases, where it ought not to give way. Men whose moral sense is disturbed by some custom which largely obtains in trade, or by some tendency that they find loudly proclaimed as the teaching of some popular phase of art or literature, are not comforted by the assurance that their morality and religion are well enough in their place, but that trade is independent of such considerations and has its own laws, upon which no external criticism can be tolerated; or by the assurance that art must be pursued for art's sake. For all such formulae leave the conflict still undecided, and are therefore useful to those who would make the best of both worlds. These depend for their whole position upon an unresolved conflict: it is only this that can make respectable their pursuit of worldly satisfaction apart from morality and religion. But those who are minded to give full freedom to the principles which rise out of the Christian faith, are helped and strengthened only by the severe Christian rule, 'Whatsoever is not of faith, is sin.' That is, that the faith governs the whole life without exception, so that there is no room in it at all for any region of indifference, for any comfortable place of retirement, where the spirit may indulge itself at will. It is the knowledge that there is but one principle which rules over all the affairs of life that is one peculiar source of the strength and effectiveness of the Christian conception of moral life.

The Christian view of life, then, is effective, though it works indirectly, because it rests upon one principle which is applied to all things: and it is effective also because it is, in the best sense of that word, an ascetic view of life. We know how this aspect of it has been misrepresented. I need not remind you how pain and squalor and feebleness and purposeless self-torture have been supposed to be characteristic of the more excellent way. We have all been long persuaded for various reasons—reasons which are not all, perhaps, of equal value—that this was a hopeless travesty of the true spirit of Christendom. We have learnt that

Christianity may be a principle of ordinary life, and may hallow its ordinary joys and sorrows. But still it remains that by the very fact that it has only one aim and one test, which it applies to all things, it must involve sacrifice to the point of asceticism. It need not aim at increasing the pain of the world by voluntary and purposeless self-torment; but still there must be no shadow in any Christian life of the pagan horror of sickness and pain and deformity, no attempt to avoid their claim for help and sympathy. We may admire the Greek delight in the sound and healthy state of body and mind, but we must not allow our minds to be charmed away from realities. We may be sound and healthy ourselves, physically and morally, but that is only a challenge to us to help in bearing the burdens of others. Those who are neither sound nor healthy, physically or morally, have their place in the kingdom and their rights within its liberties. We must voluntarily enter into their pain, bear with their follies and ill-regulated passions, hope the best of them, and fight off the temptation to despair of them. And this is laid upon us by our Christian profession, not because there is any harm in happiness and joy, but because these are not universal; because we dare not in Christ's name give ourselves over to the free enjoyment of ease and leisure, so long as expenditure of labour on our part can in any way modify the harder conditions of some for whom Christ died: and what we dare not do in Christ's name we dare not do at all.

Nor is this the limit of our ascetic self-renunciation. We must enter with sympathy not only into the troubles of those whom the blind operation of circumstances, as it seems, has brought to grief which they could not help; but also with the troubles of those who are merely paying the penalty of their own misdeeds. Apart from the mere repulsion which the sight of trouble causes in some minds, it is easy to sympathize with inevitable misfortune. But when men's own stupidity has brought them to ruin, it then becomes a great strain upon the will to avoid standing aloof and lecturing where we ought to try to console. And so much of the evil of the world is of this unnecessary kind. People are well-meaning but ill-balanced in their enthusiasms: they have right on their side but they appeal to the wrong arguments: they use force, perhaps, instead of persuasion, and refuse to wait. The history of recent labour agitations will offer plenty of instances in point. But in all such cases, without in any way justifying the wrong done, the wrong-doers have a right to our sympathy and interest. For there is hope of them, as there is, from the Christian point of view, of every one whose heart is stirred with a desire for better things and a hatred of injustice. Those for whom it is hardest to find solid grounds for hope are those who are complacent with themselves, and content with the existing order which secures their comfort, and who strive to hide from their own eyes the mass of evil which exists and is a perpetual challenge to all Christian men.

That the Christian ideal is ascetic in this sense—in the sense that it involves a voluntary withdrawal from individual separateness, and a voluntary entering into the whole condition of the world—would, I suppose, hardly be denied by any one. It does not seek for pain as such, but it is contented to accept it—more than contented to endure it sacrificially, for the sake of others. And it is not joyless, inhumanly indifferent and insensate. But the joy to which it gives rise is not the violent emotional disturbance against which Plato warned men—the pleasure which is without measure or reason and can only be distinguished as greater or less—but the quiet, restrained and intense joy of men who are certain of themselves, and have hold of a certain clue to the problems of life. Such asceticism is really only the practical expression of that which all Christian men profess.

And this is why it is a source of the effectiveness of the Christian ideal. It emphatically displays in action our confidence in the truth of that which we profess, and it adds to the vigour of all that we do the strength of self-surrender, without which nothing serious has ever been achieved.

We need not fear, then, that the discipline of the Church, acting as it does indirectly upon the questions of the day, will fail to produce a perceptible effect. We need only imagine to ourselves the result, if all who love Christ's name gave themselves wholly to the fulfilment of His work on the lines which He laid down: if there were no self-seeking, no insincerity, no shrinking from the full demands of the Christian faith upon the whole of life: if the various deflections from the highest path, in which men indulge themselves and think no harm, were seen in their true light, as breaches of Christian order, wounds dealt anew upon the very Body of Christ. The presence in the world of a body of men consciously pursuing this end in common, using to the full all the aids of external organization and division of labour and sacramental help to strengthen their own individual wills to the accomplishment of their purposes, would surely soon change the face of the earth. So far as this has been actually achieved, it has been achieved by these methods.

It is, perhaps, a bold or even a foolhardy effort to attempt to set out the influence of Christianity upon moral ideas. The whole region is crossed by endless controversial matters, of which the discussion must be left on one side. And a person who makes the effort is always open to the charge of inconsistency in practice with the principles he professes—a charge which he has probably been the first to bring against himself. It is strange, perhaps, that after all these centuries there should still be any room for doubt or discussion as to the exact function of Christianity in the world; indeed, the fact that there is may seem to be a proof of its failure. But as a matter of fact the area of controversy is smaller than appears at first sight. The impression of its vastness of extent depends much more on the fact that each successive age has its own controversies and its own way of raising the questions suggested by Christianity, than upon any really wide uncertainty as to the bearing and the claims of the Christian faith. That which seemed axiomatic in one age is matter for discussion in the next; and again, questions which were once hotly controverted pass in the movement of the ages into the calm atmosphere of history. But in all ages the same question presses upon every reasonable man, how he shall best order his life and adjust himself to the conditions in which he lives. I have endeavoured to show, by reasoning from the character and history of the Christian faith in this regard, that the revelation of God Incarnate offers an answer to this question which is at once final and progressive: final, because it places the present life of man in an assured relation to the world beyond the grave; and progressive, because its principles, changeless though they are, continually require expression in terms of the changing thoughts of man.

Through all time a single issue has been placed before men, an issue which the Christian faith expresses as an alternative between Christ and the world.

The challenge and the appeal of the world comes in various forms, but it always means ultimately the same thing. It is an appeal to prefer the lower to the higher, the material to the spiritual, the transitory to the eternal. In ancient days the choice was difficult, for there was a haze of uncertainty over all that lay beyond the verification of the senses. But in the presence of the facts of the Incarnation, Resurrection, and Ascension this uncertainty disappears. These facts, because they are facts and not merely aspirations or hopes, give its special colour to the Christian view of life. Without them we fall back in reality into the dim light of paganism, though the effect of the long presence of Christianity in the world may partially conceal from us the greatness of our fall. With them present with us, not as theories or dogmas, but as operative principles, as facts carrying definite consequences in the world, we have the power to live, even while we are here, in the spiritual fellowship of God and His saints, and the power to discern, with the Holy Spirit's perpetual help, the true solution of the moral problems that perplex us.

The world protests, charging us to return from the skies, to adopt a more elastic standard, to expect less, and thus incur less risk of disappointment. And this appeal, sympathetic and tolerant as it is, is the most dangerous form in which the world calls upon us for our allegiance to-day. For we know how much there is still to do, and how slow the march of God's purpose seems to short-lived men, how far off the coming of the kingdom. But it has never been a mark of the Spirit's leading to hope and scheme only for what human foresight sees may easily be achieved. When the Lord pours out His Spirit, young men see visions, and old men dream dreams—visions and dreams that rise like other dreams out of an experience actually attained in life, and are prophetic of a fullness of triumph yet to come.

INDEX.

Academic mind, 354.
Accidia, 231, 263, 264.
Allegory, limited value of, 153.
Almsgiving, 342.
Ambrose, treatise of *De Officiis*, 186; his method of exegesis, 186; his moral theory, 187, 188.
Anabaptists, 330.
Antinomianism, 75.
Apostolic preaching, 59; its effect in the ethical region, 62; lack of system, 77.
Aquinas, 299-301.
Aristotle, theory of virtue, 102; use of the word πίστις, 108.
Art, 366.
Asceticism, 369.
Augustine, relation to Neo-Platonism, 190; the import of the doctrine of the Incarnation, 191, 194; theory of evil and the Fall, 192; of the cardinal virtues, 193; effect of Christianity on ethical life, 193; view of sin, 245, 246; of the classification of sins, 258.
Authority, 329.

Basil the Great, 204, 261.

Cassian, 261, 262.
Casuistry, 264, 347; of Pharisees, 353; of Jesuits, 353.
Ceremonial, spiritual value of, 14, 39, 40, 45.
Chrysostom, 203.
Church, the fellowship of, 123, 125 seqq.; its use of legal penalties, 316; cosmopolitan character of, 321; corruption of, 321, 322; its supreme claim, 346, 347; mode of exercising it, 349; ground of discipline, 350.

City, idea of, in Greece, 119, 134; in the Church, 136.
Classical days, life in, 26 seqq.; difficulty of appreciating, 26-28.
Clement of Alexandria, use of πίστις by, 110; his moral theory, 166 seqq.; attitude towards pagan and secular life, 167; doctrine of sin, 238, 239.
Climates, psychological, 286.
Community of goods, 348.
Conscientiousness, excessive, 355.
Courage, 117, 137, 141.
Cowardice, 230, 253.
Cyprian, 241, 242; on varieties in sin, 257.

Didache, 342, 348.
Dionysius the Areopagite, 282, 297.
διψυχία, 221.
Discipline, basis of, 224, 225, 350; range of, 226, 364, &c.; to be resumed, 352; its value, 358; its effect on moral ideas, 358; on the casuistical temper, 359; nature of it, 360; mode of exercise, 362, 363; how far possible, 363; essential to the idea of the Church, 363.
Donatists, 227.
δύναμις, meanings of the word, 103.

Edgar, Penitential of, 343.
End of man's life: a problem for Ethics, 85; how influenced by Christianity, 86 seqq., 94; importance of Christian view of, 368.
Enthusiasm, 338.
Envy, the divine, among the Greeks, 29; its philosophical meaning, 29.
Epictetus, 30, 119 *note*, 149 *note*.
Epicureans, 30 *note*.

Ethics, Christian, its differentia, 67; its social character, 88; relation to previous ethical speculations, 115; its severe tone, 122.
Evil, origin of, 183, 192, 210; mechanical theories of, 210; their inadequacy, 211; as rebellion, 212, 219; prophetic view of it, 243; its existence denied in Dionys. Areop., 298.
Ezra, his work, 41 seqq.

Faith, 89, 90, 96; its various meanings, 107 seqq.
Fall, the, 24, 192; in Philo, 234; in Plotinus, 235; in Augustine, 247.
Fatalism, its philosophical meaning, 29.
Father, revelation of the, 63.
Freedom, 76, 217 seq.; in Philo, 234; in Plotinus, 235; in Clement of Alexandria, 238; in Origen, 240; in Tertullian, 242; Christian aspect of, 245; in Augustine, 247, 249; in relation to virtue and to sin, 250.

God, nature of, in Tertullian rational and moral, 183; holiness of, 214; Greek and Christian idea of, 280, 292-295; problems rising about, 305.
Gospels, position of ethics in, 49.
Gregory the Great, 201; his exegesis, 201.

Hermas, 236, 255.
Hope, 90-92.
Humanism, 325.
Humility, 126.

Ideals, value of, in moral philosophy, 7, 8, 11; their failure, 23; how far affected by being historical, 52; force of Christian ideal, 368.
Incarnation, ethical import of the, 62; illustrated by Clement of Alexandria, 171, 172; and the solidarity of man, 223; and the human will, 251; philosophical import of, 288-291.
Individual, use of, in Stoic ethics, 9; and in Neo-Platonist, 10, 243; position of, in the Church, 330, 349.

Intellect, moral capacity of, 220; moral danger of, 353.
Irenæus, 36.
Isidorus Hispalensis, 202.

Jerome, 199, 200.
Jerusalem Letter of Council, 229.
Jew and Gentile, 269.
Judaism, ruling ideas of, 13; failure of Jewish moral ideas, 19; after captivity, 41; importance of Jewish conception of God, 45, 213.
Judgement, 218.
Justice, 118, 137, 138, 140, 141.

Knowledge and virtue, 209, 212.

Law, the Jewish, 14, 17; its importance for Jewish moral conceptions, 18, 24; its failure, 19; its place in St. Paul, 44; its sanction, 236; and the law of love, 275.
Law, the moral, its bearing upon Christians, 64; how affected by the new faith, 65.
Legal morality, 23-25; contrasted with the obedience of love, 93.
Life of Christ, its supremacy in the Gospels, 51; as the moral ideal, 51; compared with Greek ideals, 52; the secret of its power, 52 seqq.; compared with the Jewish preconceptions, 54; its ethical effect, 55-58; as an example, 65.
Literature and the Church, 366.
Love, 92, 93, 274; in Clem. Alex. 168.
Luxury, in Clement of Alexandria, 167.

Man, his emotional nature, 31, 98; morality and the nature of man, 114; solidarity, 222; as fallen, 247; constitution of, in Augustine, 248.
Middle Age, 311, 312.
Monasticism, 200, 204, 312, 340, 341.
Montanists, 227.
Morality, based on reason, 285, 286; and doctrine, 319; and religion, 334.
Mystical interpretation, 259.

Index. 379

Mysticism, in Plotinus, 86; its failure, 87.

Nationality, sense of, 326.
Nature, life according to, 119.
Nominalism, 298, 299.
Novatianists, 227.

Omnipotence, 301.
Origen, his explanation of πίστις, 112; his moral theory, 172 seqq.; the range of the appeal of the Church, 173; the possibility of moral reformation, 174; its ground, 175, 176; the two lives in Origen, 176; his view of evil, 239.

Passion, position of, in Greek thought, 31, 98.
Penitence, in Philo, 234; in Hermas, 255.
Penitential rules, 229, 342, 343.
Penitentials, 313, &c., 341-343.
Personality, value in Greek and Christian ethics, 128-132.
Philo Judaeus, use of Pentateuch and O.T. books by, 43, 151, 152; view of cardinal virtues, 117; his contribution to ethical history, 144; the difficulty of Philo, 145; doctrine of God, 146; God and the world, 147, 148; the world as a πολιτεία, 149, 150; his ethical theory, 154-161; politics, 161; value and historical relations of his theory, 162; his view of penitence, 234.
Philosophy, its character and purpose, 2; causes of its failure in ethics, 4 seqq., 12; its historic position, 196, 197; modern moral philosophy, 337.
Plato, use of πίστις by, 107; cardinal virtues in, 116; and Moses, 190; and the Incarnation, 194; idea of God in, 281.
Politics and the Church, 366.
Poverty, vows of, 348.
Predestination, in Augustine, 246 seqq.; in relation to Christianity, 267; the position of Jews and Greeks, 269; and the wisdom of God in St. Paul, 270.
Property, 365.
Prophets, their attitude towards formalism, 15, 37; their view of God, 38; and religion, 39.
Proverbial morality among the Jews, 17.
Providence, doctrine of, 205.
Prudence, 117, 137, 138, 140, 141.
Psalms, the, and the Law, 17, 40.
Psalms of Solomon, 40.

Realism, 298.
Reason and will, 307-309.
Reformation, 318, 320; political causes of, 320-325: its meaning, 327; elements of revolution in, 329.
Religion, Jewish and Pagan, 35; functions of, 292; social character of, 332, 333; how related to life, 334.
Repentance, 223.
Reserve, Greek principle of, 32.
Resurrection, ethical import of the, 62.
Ritual, antiquity of Jewish, 42.

Sacerdotalism, 356; its sources, 357.
Sacrifice, 35 seqq., 224; patristic explanation of Jewish sacrifices, 36 *notes*; of Christ, 222.
Scholasticism, 202, 296.
Scotus, 301-303.
Sectarianism, 337.
Self-sacrifice, in Greek thought, 120; in Christian ethics, 121.
Seneca, 33.
Sermon on the Mount, 20; its relation to the old and new order, 21; its legal character, 22, 46, 273, 348.
Sin, its importance in Christian ethics, 60, 121; in the Church, 71; in ethical systems, 207; in O. T., 214-216; in N. T., 216, 235; and freedom, 219; its range, 221; its connexion with Church order, 225; mortal and venial, 228; in Clem. Alex. 237; Origen, 239; Tert. 241; Augustine, 245 seqq.
Sin, classification of, in N. T., 252; in Hermas, 253; in Tertullian, 255; in Cyprian, 257; in Augustine, 258; in Origen, 259; the list of seven, 229, 259-266; ecclesiastical and legal views of, 316;

Index.

Christian sympathy in regard to, 370, 371.
Solidarity, 222.
Specialism in morality, 368.
Spirit, dispensation of the, 56; moral activity of, 64, 65; effect on social relations of man, 66.
Spiritual order, man's relations with, 88 seqq., 121.
State, relations of Church with the, 316, &c., 331; in England, 335.
Stoicism, 9, 30, 32, 33; cardinal virtues in, 117; life according to nature in, 119; criticized by Cyprian, 257.
Superbia, 262-264.

Temperance, 117, 137, 139, 140, 141, 338.
Tertullian, 180; the separateness of the Church, 181; its inward unity and continuity, 182; its relation to the Old Testament revelation, 183-185; evil, 185; his view of sin, 241; of unpardonable sin, 255.
Theodoret, his use of πίστις, 112.
Tolerance, 338.
Transcendence of God, 282.
Trent, Council of, 328.

Unity, sense of, in the Church, 350.
Unpardonable sin, 257, 258.

Virtues, theological: in St. Paul, 79; St. Peter, 80; Hebrews, 80; their meaning, 81 seqq.; their philosophical significance, 85 seqq.; their inter-relation and practical bearing, 90; in Augustine, 195.
Virtues, cardinal: in Greek philosophy, 116, 117; their moral value, 118; in Origen, 138; Ambrose, 139; Augustine 139; Gregory, 140; Aquinas, 141.

Will, problems of, 236; final decision by the Church, 251.
Wisdom of God, 18, 269, &c.; meaning of it, 270; its difficulty, 273; relation to the life of man, 276; to various conceptions of morality, 278; in Plato, 281; wisdom and freedom, 283; speculative and practical conceptions of, 284; and love, 287.
World, the, in Christian thought: hostility to it, 122; the conversion of it, 124.

THE END.

www.ingramcontent.com/pod-product-compliance
Lightning Source LLC
Chambersburg PA
CBHW022119290426
44112CB00008B/737